Educators Praise the Work

"Thank you for developing an engaging, flexible, and authentic approach to teaching history! My students can connect important themes across time, and they love portraying a historical persona in our Summits!"

—Mike B., Columbia, MO

"Using *Teaching U.S. History Thematically* has shifted the role of the teacher from a deliverer of content to a facilitator of learning, centering class around students with the goal of creating a relevant curriculum that focuses on application and historical thinking skills. Because *Teaching U.S. History Thematically* creatively organizes documents and sources from all eras by theme, it allows you to connect the past to more recent history so students find relevance while seeing the root of the issue at the same time."

—Anthony G., La Grange Park, IL

"Thank you for your work and dedication to making social studies more relevant to our students."

—Emily K., Des Moines, IA

"I want to say thank you as I have used your thematic units this year and it has transformed my teaching."

—Nicole P., Las Vegas, NV

"At first, changing our curriculum to the thematic approach felt quite daunting. Thankfully *Teaching U.S. History Thematically* has not only made this attainable, but also made the curriculum far more engaging and enriching for my students."

—Victoria S., La Grange Park, IL

Teaching
World History
Thematically

Essential Questions and Document-Based Lessons to Connect Past and Present

Rosalie Metro

TEACHERS COLLEGE PRESS

TEACHERS COLLEGE | COLUMBIA UNIVERSITY

NEW YORK AND LONDON

Published by Teachers College Press, 1234 Amsterdam Avenue, New York, NY 10027

Cover art via Wikimedia Commons except where noted otherwise. Top row: Mary Wollstonecraft, Igbo woman, Julius Caesar. Second row: Emperor Meiji, Jean-Jacques Dessalines, Emiliano Zapata. Third row: Qiu Jin, Mahatma Gandhi, Inuit woman. Fourth row: Henry the Navigator, Leonardo da Vinci drawing via Alamy. Bottom row: Greta Thunberg courtesy of Rebecca Lessard via Flickr creative commons, Muawiyah I.

Library of Congress Cataloging-in-Publication Data

Names: Metro, Rosalie, author.
Title: Teaching world history thematically : essential questions and
    document-based lessons to connect past and present / Rosalie Metro.
Description: New York, NY : Teachers College Press, 2020. |
    Includes bibliographical references and index.
Identifiers: LCCN 2020024732 (print) | LCCN 2020024733 (ebook) |
    ISBN 9780807764466 (paperback) | ISBN 9780807764473 (hardcover) |
    ISBN 9780807779132 (ebook)
Subjects: LCSH: History—Study and teaching (Secondary) | History—Sources.
Classification: LCC D16.2 .M478 2020 (print) | LCC D16.2 (ebook) |
    DDC 907.1/273—dc23
LC record available at https://lccn.loc.gov/2020024732
LC ebook record available at https://lccn.loc.gov/2020024733

ISBN 978-0-8077-6446-6 (paper)
ISBN 978-0-8077-6447-3 (hardcover)
ISBN 978-0-8077-7913-2 (ebook)

Printed on acid-free paper
Manufactured in the United States of America

We are capable of bearing a great burden,
once we discover that the burden is reality.
~ James Baldwin

I dedicate this book to my parents,
Alexander Metro and Judith Metro,
who have helped me understand these words.

Contents

8. Resistance, Revolution, and Reform: How Should People Bring About Political and Social Change?   **223**

9. Continuity and Change: What Are the Long-Term Changes and Recurring Patterns in World History?   **257**

Acknowledgments

My first appreciation goes to my own high school and college teachers who encouraged me to question what I had been taught and how education should look, including Greg Coleman, John Farley, and Douglas Fix.

Thank you to Jean Ward, my editor at Teachers College Press, for encouraging me to write this "sequel" to *Teaching U.S. History Thematically*, as well as to other TCP staff including Christina Brianik, Emily Freyer, Michael McGann, Joy Mizan, Karl Nyberg, Nancy Power, and Jamie Rasmussen, who helped me through the publication process. I would also like to thank Jitendra Kumar and Gary Morris of Westchester Publishing Services, who assisted in editing my manuscript.

I am grateful to Jason Bricker, Diane Bruckerhoff, Mike Burden, and other colleagues at Columbia Independent School who supported me in developing, implementing, and revising this curriculum. Thank you as well to Amy Alvarez, Prince Johnson, Jason Wagner, and other colleagues at Millennium Art Academy who helped me think through my approach to teaching history. I am indebted to the students who helped me test and refine these materials— to every kid who told me honestly, "This is boring," or "This is great!" or "It would be better this way." I am also grateful to my colleagues in the College of Education at the University of Missouri-Columbia, who provide such stellar examples of scholarship and advocacy.

Thanks to my family, who supported me in writing this book: my husband, Sean Franzel; my father, Alexander Metro; my children, Mae and Louis Franzel; and especially my mother, Judy Metro, for reading every word of this book and correcting countless errors. Thanks to my sister Zoe Metro for providing a model of hard work and determination. Rebecca Tuhus-Dubrow, you're family, too—thanks for the tireless encouragement. To Jane Levey, in memoriam, thank you for inspiring me to study history.

I am also indebted to the teachers and scholars who gave me feedback and advised me on what to include in this book: Sheri-Marie Harrison, Chris Hitchcock, Martha Kelly, Sharif Randhawa, Matthew Reeder, and Sravya Tadepalli. Of course, they bear no responsibility for my omissions or oversights.

Finally, I would like to thank to the thinkers who have shaped my view of history, including Michelle Alexander, Benedict Anderson, Karen Armstrong,

Partha Chatterjee, Dipesh Chakrabarty, Roxanne Dunbar-Ortiz, Frantz Fanon, Michel Foucault, Eric Hobsbawm, Ibram X. Kendi, Jill Lepore, James Loewen, Edward Said, James C. Scott, Gayatri Spivak, Michel-Rolph Trouillot, Thongchai Winichakul, and Howard Zinn.

Teaching
World History
Thematically

Why Use a Thematic, Document-Based Approach for Teaching World History?

When I published *Teaching U.S. History Thematically: Document-Based Lessons for the Secondary Classroom*, I didn't know how teachers and students would respond. I knew that my own 8th- and 9th-grade students had loved working with primary source documents, and that the thematic structure of my curriculum had helped them make amazing connections between history and current issues. I was confident that the research I had encountered in my doctoral studies supported my method of teaching to promote critical thinking, literacy, and active citizenship for secondary students. I was certain that as an educator, I much preferred teaching this way to plodding through sequential events in a textbook. And I knew that when I had looked for resources on how to teach history thematically, I was disappointed by how little I found, and therefore ended up creating my own curriculum from scratch. But I wasn't sure how well this method would work in other classrooms.

Now I know that it does work, in a variety of settings, for diverse student populations. Teachers from across the country have reached out to me to share their positive experiences with using *Teaching U.S. History Thematically*, and they have also given me wonderful suggestions for how to improve this world history book you currently hold in your hands.

I hope that the testimonials at the front of book inspire you as you begin or continue your journey with teaching history thematically. It can be difficult to change long-held practices; to challenge the expectations of students, parents, and administrators; and to adjust to a new way of teaching. Yet it can also be extremely rewarding.

Teaching history thematically is more sustainable and more fun if you have a community of educators to support you. I encourage you to try to create such a community at your school or in your area, but there is also the possibility to make connections with teachers across the country and even the world who are using this book or this method. My Facebook page, Teaching History Thematically <www.facebook.com/teachinghistorythematically>, is one place to share resources and ideas. I also invite you to check out my blog "Big Questions Many Answers," which covers various topics related to teaching social studies, at <www.rosaliemetro.com/bigquestionsmanyanswers>. And if you have comments or suggestions for me, please do share them with me through my website at <www.rosaliemetro.com>.

Whether you are a veteran teacher or starting your first year, this book contains the tools you need to get started with an innovative approach to teaching history, one that develops literacy and higher-order thinking skills, connects the past to students' lives, and meets Common Core and other high-quality state standards, National World History Content Standards, and National Council for the Social Studies Standards as well. This approach is the product of both research and practice, and I am eager to share it with teachers who are tired of hearing students say that history is boring.

WHY THEMATIC?

The standard way to teach history is to start with the earliest event to be covered and proceed forward in time toward the present. This approach has certain advantages: moving chronologically helps students sequence events; it allows them to understand what was happening around the world during a given period of time. But I think the main reason history is taught chronologically is out of habit. We do it because that is the way we learned; that is the way textbooks are organized; that is what students and parents expect.

However, teaching history chronologically has several drawbacks. First, it is difficult to forge the past-present connections that make history relevant to students' daily lives. Often, the school year ends before teachers make it to the present (or even the past 30 years) (Loewen, 2008). Second, teaching chronologically makes history feel like a barrage of events, connected to each other only insofar as they happened around the same time. So much happens in a day, a year, a century. How do teachers decide what is important and what is not? Without some organizing principles, criteria for what is included in the curriculum and what is left out can feel random.

Organizing a history curriculum by theme, on the other hand, allows students to gain an understanding of how an issue develops over time. Take the theme of Unit 8: resistance, revolution, and reform. How should people bring about social and political change? Across place and time, people have answered this question differently, but those answers build on each other. It is easier to understand Algerian people's conviction, in the 1950s, that they had to use violence to win independence from French colonization in light of French people's own 18th-century revolution, as well as Haiti's successful revolt against French rule at the turn of the 19th century. Comparing Martin Luther's 95 Theses with Egyptian activist Asmaa Mahfouz's vlog protesting her government's abuses some 500 years later helps us see both continuity and change in how people share information and work for change. If we want students to make these connections, let us structure our curriculum in a way that facilitates comparison, rather than burying these relationships under a landslide of facts.

Teaching history thematically doesn't mean that we let go of chronology. Having students create their own timelines of the events they study, and keeping a timeline on the classroom wall, solidifies the sequence of events in their minds. Apps such as Timeline Eons, which students can use to construct and annotate illustrated timelines, can also be helpful. Revisiting each era multiple times over the course of the school year allows students to gradually build an understanding of historical periodization. Each theme is a new journey through the past, another opportunity to see continuity and change.

There is a dearth of research comparing outcomes of thematic versus chronological approaches to teaching history, although there is increasing interest in thematic teaching (Brown & Schnell, 2016). Moving chronologically is likely preferable if the goal is for students to memorize dates. Yet most teachers have broader purposes: inspiring intellectual curiosity, promoting deep engagement with the past, empowering students to find their own answers to the questions that have recurred across time and space. In that sense, teaching thematically provides exciting opportunities. As someone who taught chronologically early in my career and thematically later, I can say that it would be hard for me to go back. Teachers who use this approach may find the same is true for them.

WHY DOCUMENT BASED?

Ask any student who dislikes history why, and you will hear, "The textbook. It's boring." Textbooks can be useful for reference, but they don't make history come alive. History curricula that use textbooks as the main or only source of information not only risk deadening students' curiosity, but may also mislead them about the nature of historical inquiry.

Why do we use textbooks? Because they simplify decisions about what to teach. We may believe that in most cases they contain a reasonably accurate representation of events. The idea that there is one correct interpretation of world history may be comforting.

But I am inspired by Harvard historian Jill Lepore's (2018) insight that history is not a subject, but a method—as she explains it, to "let the dead speak for themselves" (p. xix) (and, I would add, the living). Yet traditional textbooks speak with a monolithic voice of authority, concealing the debates historians have with each other about the meaning of sources and about theories of cause and effect. While many textbooks have made strides toward including primary documents interspersed through the text or in an appendix, these documents are treated as supplements to the main narrative, rather than as constitutive of its meaning.

In these respects, textbooks alone cannot build the students' habit of engaging critically with every source, a disposition that is essential to historical inquiry (Wineburg, 2001). Scholars who study historical thinking with the Stanford History Education Group (SHEG, n.d.) have come up with a set of questions students should bring to every source, including: "Who wrote this?" "What is the author's perspective?" and "What do other documents say?"

It is certainly possible to ask these questions of a textbook. Some teachers do engage their students in critical analysis of their textbook as a document that illustrates the biases of its authors. Yet most of the time, the textbook is taken to be a neutral collection of facts, an objective truth. Students are expected to accept their textbooks wholesale, rather than treat them as products of specific historical circumstances (Loewen, 2008). In this sense, textbooks are not the best resource for helping students develop the literacy and higher-order thinking skills that they will need in order to be critical consumers of information.

Finally, most world history textbooks available in the U.S. market are centered on White European men. In the 1990s, my own high school "world" history class began with the Middle Ages and ended with World War II. I remember wondering why we spent so long on the Hapsburgs, and whether anything happened in the Americas before Columbus sailed the ocean blue. In my world history textbook, nothing transpired in Africa until Rommel's invasion in 1941.

Certainly, world history textbooks have improved since then. The textbooks I used to teach world history before I developed this approach included information on river valley civilizations in Asia, ancient South American cultures, and empires in Africa. Yet even today, world history textbooks written in the United States devote the most space to Classical Greece and Rome, and Europe (Sewall, 2004). This "Western" tradition is not only privileged, but also treated separately from the rest of the world, as the roots of "our" culture. White European men remain the main protagonists of history, and "other" people and places are treated as fodder for their discoveries and conquests—a paradigm that is damaging to all students (Gopal, 2019). The very discipline of "world history" is entwined with histories of racism and colonization, and with the effort of White European men to gain totalizing knowledge of and effective domination over the whole world. As curriculum theorist Tadashi Dozono (2020) points out, "[B]y presenting White European ways of knowing and being as universal and superior, educators conduct epistemic violence" (p. 4). If we want to counter this dynamic as teachers, we need to move beyond the textbook.

I want to distinguish my project from this traditional understanding of world history in several ways. First, I am not attempting to cover every important topic, event, or person. That would be hopeless within the page limit I have been allotted, and I don't even believe it is possible. Instead, I want to offer students a starting point for their own inquiries, which exposes them to key themes and questions as a springboard for in-depth studies aligned with their interests. And I want to offer alternatives to the exclusionary metanarratives in most textbooks.

A document-based* approach is the perfect match for these goals. It is easier to place civilizations all over the world on par with each other, while also questioning the definitions of civilization created by White European men. That said, this book, despite my best efforts, overrepresents the views of those men. Because of racism, sexism, and class hierarchy, that demographic has dominated positions of power, and thus their writings have been preserved (and are often available without copyright protection). However, I do hope that the juxtaposition of their words with strategically chosen documents by women, people of many ethnicities, races, and nations, as well as those with less socioeconomic power, will bring to the surface the very dynamics that have led to this discrepancy in historical representation. I would also like to note that because this book is primarily for the U.S. market, and secondary students are usually required to take at least one course in U.S. history, I avoid centering lessons on U.S. historical figures or events—not because the United States is somehow separate from the rest of the world, but because the opportunity to learn about other places is so valuable. However, I have included opportunities for students to compare their own communities, countries, and cultures with those discussed in the documents.

Basing the curriculum on documents also addresses a related issue of bias. Any world history curriculum is open to accusations of partiality. In document-based approaches, the biases of the curriculum designer influence the selection of documents and the questions asked about them (as do mine in this book). However, a document-based approach allows students significant freedom to interpret the material according to their own values and emerging political orientations. Some students may be inspired by Karl Marx's vision of a classless society; other students may prefer Adam Smith's account of a capitalist market. The important thing is that students have direct access to Marx's and Smith's words and an understanding of their historical contexts, rather than being limited to the interpretations of a textbook author whose own opinions invariably creep in. Moreover, as students examine historical documents—firsthand accounts, speeches by politicians and activists, works of art—they come to understand multiple perspectives on history and develop a healthy skepticism about the claims they encounter.

---

*I prefer the term *documents* to *primary sources* because even a secondary source such as a textbook can be analyzed in the same manner that "primary" sources can.

Nonetheless, I think it is important to be explicit about the principles that have guided my selection and editing process. First, I reject artificial distinctions between "East" and "West" in favor of showing historical interconnections among regions and multiple centers of agency (Chakrabarty, 2007; Said, 1994). For the same reasons, I include documents that illustrate how racial, ethnic, and national categories have been socially constructed and historically conditioned (Anderson, 2016; Chatterjee, 1994; Winichakul, 1997). In that vein, I present documents about the colonial encounter that illustrate racism as prior to and the source of the construction of racial categories, rather than vice versa (Fanon, 2004; Kendi, 2016). Because this racism has so often influenced the portrayal of Africa, Asia, and South America (Mann, 2006), I have resisted presenting these continents as "underdeveloped," "uncivilized," or somehow lacking, but instead tried to give students opportunities to unpack the assumptions of the European thinkers who held such views, and to help them question who and what has been defined as "civilized" (Scott, 2018). Additionally, my intention is to present Indigenous peoples as distinct and living cultures rather than as homogenous or extinct groups (Dunbar-Ortiz, 2015; Shear et al., 2015). In order to avoid obscuring the violence of the colonial encounter, I have used the active voice when discussing colonizers' deeds (Dozono, 2020). I have taken all the opportunities I could find to represent women as a vital part of history, the present, and the future, especially through the 21st-Century Issues that begin each unit. While acknowledging the powerful forces that have shaped history, I have also tried to let students discover how people have struggled to change their worlds and resist injustice—with varied results (Hobsbawm, 1996). Finally, because representations of religion are often deeply politicized (Armstrong, 2011), I have placed foundational scriptures in a unit apart, separately from the way those teachings have been applied. All of these choices are based on the assumptions that the construction of knowledge and narratives of history are inextricably entwined with power (Foucault, 1982; Spivak, 2006; Trouillot, 2015), and that curriculum—including this textbook—is inherently political (Apple, 1990). All that said, my perspective is limited by my experience and positionality (Metro, 2019); if my blind spots cause errors or misrepresentations of individuals or groups, I apologize, and I invite readers to reach out to me to broaden my understanding.

Nonetheless, I stand firm with the positions above because I agree with Howard Zinn that "in . . . a world of conflict, it is the job of thinking people, as Albert Camus suggested, not to be on the side of the executioners," but also to remember that "the lines are not always clear," and that "in the long run, the oppressor is also a victim" (p. 10). May all of us find inspiration to teach in ways that express our values, while remaining open to differing perspectives.

MEETING COMMON CORE AND OTHER STATE AND NATIONAL STANDARDS

Meeting state and national standards has become a primary responsibility of teachers and schools. This curriculum aligns with Common Core and other high-quality state standards, as well as national standards for world history and the National Council for the Social Studies C3 Framework.

More than 40 states have adopted the Common Core State Standards (CCSS) (or very similar ones), which aim to "provide teachers, parents, and students with a set of clear expectations to ensure that all students have the skills and knowledge necessary to succeed in college, career, and life upon graduation from high school, regardless of where they live" (Common Core State Standards Initiative, 2016). Specific standards for history/social studies outline the disciplinary skills that students are supposed to gain. While many states have since decided to develop their own standards, most have written them with an eye toward the same objectives seen in the CCSS, including interrogating documents and thinking critically.

Meanwhile, UCLA History (2019) has developed a set of content standards for world history that cover the specific events, people, and groups that students should learn about. These guide teachers and states nationwide as they develop their curricula. Finally, the National Council for the Social Studies has developed the C3 Framework for College, Career, and Civic Life readiness. These standards illustrate why studying history and other social studies subjects is so vital to our democracy and to helping students meet their goals.

It would be difficult to meet all of these standards while teaching in the traditional manner, chronologically and solely from a textbook. Moreover, the standards focus on skills rather than content, which gives teachers more freedom about which topics to teach and in what order. Therefore, I hope this book can be useful as a main text, or as a resource for teachers who are trying to incorporate document analysis into their curriculum. It is also possible to use the documents in this book selectively as one of many supplemental texts. Below, I've highlighted a few of the ways in which this book encourages students to develop the skills described in the standards.

The National Council for the Social Studies' College, Career, and Civic Life (C3) Readiness Framework

Change, Continuity, and Context, D2.His.3.9–12

Use questions generated about individuals and groups to assess how the significance of their actions changes over time and is shaped by the historical context.

In Lesson 7.5, Queen Elizabeth I tries to justify her rightful place as a ruler, despite her gender, in her speech to the troops at Tilbury. Students consider how female politicians today do or don't discuss their gender; in this way, they explore how context shaped Queen Elizabeth I's words.

Perspectives, D2.His.6.9–12

Analyze the ways in which the perspectives of those writing history shaped the history that they produced.

In Lesson 5.4, students read Giovanni da Pian del Carpini's account of the Mongol court and analyze how his biases shaped his views.

Causation and Argumentation, D2.His.16.9–12

Integrate evidence from multiple relevant historical sources and interpretations into a reasoned argument about the past.

In Unit 3, students compare the writing of Roman, Austrian, Spanish, and Chinese authors to make an argument about how definitions of civilization have evolved across place and time.

Common Core State Standards

CCSS.ELA-LITERACY.RH.9–10.1

Cite specific textual evidence to support analysis of primary and secondary sources, attending to such features as the date and origin of the information.

Throughout the units, students answer questions such as "Who created this document?" and "Choose a quotation that shows how different the author's perspective is from yours today," which draw their attention to sourcing and historical context.

CCSS.ELA-LITERACY.RH.9–10.6

Compare the point of view of two or more authors for how they treat the same or similar topics, including which details they include and emphasize in their respective accounts.

In Unit 7, students compare the writings of Roman orator Hortensia, English writer Mary Wollstonecraft, and Egyptian nationalist Huda Sha'arawi for the details they emphasize on women's rights.

CCSS.ELA-LITERACY.RH.11–12.7

Integrate and evaluate multiple sources of information presented in diverse formats and media (e.g., visually, quantitatively, as well as in words) in order to address a question or solve a problem.

Students examine visual sources such as a print by Käthe Kollwitz and a painting of Catherine the Great alongside text sources to understand how women have asserted their power.

National Standards in World History for Grades 5–12 (UCLA History, 2019)

These standards for secondary world history divide the past into 10 eras, each of which contains specific content to be conveyed. In Unit 9, students examine a selection of sources from each of these eras in turn, which helps them to develop a sense of periodization and chronology to complement the in-depth understanding of themes that they have already gained.

WHAT ARE THE LONG-TERM CHANGES AND RECURRING PATTERNS IN WORLD HISTORY?

This question, one of the nine "essential questions" around which this book is constructed, serves as a touchstone for students' inquiry into world history. Essential questions are not intended to yield final or correct answers, but rather to promote critical thinking (McTighe & Wiggins, 2013). They are questions that have preoccupied people for centuries and will engage students both because they remain relevant today and because the stakes in answering them are high.

I took this question about continuity and change from the National Content Standards for World History (UCLA, 2019) because it allows students to consider the breadth of world history and how they fit into it. One potential weakness of a thematic approach to teaching history is that students don't get as strong a sense of historical periodization as they might from a chronologically arranged course. Explicitly considering continuity and change helps students reflect on how what they have learned fits together.

Teachers can introduce this essential question at the beginning of the school year, alongside activities designed to elicit students' backgrounds and prior knowledge. A Course Entry Survey (Appendix B) prompts students to reflect on their own experiences of these patterns and changes. Students can discuss their responses to this survey, and even create collages or multimedia projects describing the changes and continuities they have observed in their own and their family members' lifetimes. Those projects could serve as visual reminders of their initial understandings, which inform how they interpret the many changes and patterns that will emerge from the documents. A Course Exit Survey (Appendix C) allows students to reflect on how their own views of continuity and change have evolved over the course of the year.

STRUCTURE OF A UNIT

Each of the nine units is structured around an essential question that highlights one theme in world history. For example, Unit 4, on the theme of conflict, asks, "What is worth fighting for?" This unit, like each of the others, begins with a 21st-Century Issue that highlights the topic's importance to the present; in this case: "What are the effects of the war in Yemen on civilians?" Teachers introduce these questions, and students complete a Unit Entry Survey (Appendix D) in which they report their personal views. Beginning with a 21st-Century Issue enables students to see immediately what is at stake in the unit. Students' first concern when studying history is often "Why does this matter?" or "How does this affect me today?" and starting with a recent issue addresses those questions.*

Students then rewind history to the earliest point covered in the unit and proceed to analyze about a dozen documents, chronologically arranged, that address the essential question in some way.** Each document is linked with a historical event and with a historical figure (often, but not always, the document's author). (See Quick Reference Guide in Appendix A for a list of documents, events, and historical figures associated with each theme.) These linkages provide context for the documents and focus any background reading that students might do.

At the beginning of the unit, each student (or pairs or trios, depending on class size) should choose a historical figure represented in the documents to research. They become experts on these historical figures and represent them in a "summit" at the end of the unit. Students' task is to understand how their historical figure would have answered the Unit Question, and how they would respond to the 21st-Century Issue if they were alive today. The documents students read in class provide the basis for their answers, but students may also conduct independent research and/or supplementary assignments such as a Biographical Research Paper (see Appendix E for Biographical Research Paper Instructions and Appendix F for the Summit Research Worksheet).

Once students have discussed the 21st-Century Issue and chosen their historical figures, they start with the earliest document in the unit and continue toward the present day, analyzing each source. The structure of individual lessons is explained in detail below, but briefly, teachers introduce the topic, place the document in context, highlight key vocabulary, and then guide students in analyzing the document, applying the knowledge students have gained, and reflecting on what students have learned.

Every unit*** culminates in a "summit," in which each student (or team of students) represents the historical figure they've chosen (see instructions below). Students imagine that all the historical figures discussed in the unit

---

*I have selected a 21st-Century Issue for each unit, but times change quickly, and teachers may find that other topics are more salient in their contexts.

**In some cases, lessons are ordered based on event instead of document date, when the dates are very different or when there is some intuitive reason for the lesson order, as in the case of keeping the lessons on the creation of Israel and the Palestinian resistance together, or grouping the Abrahamic religions together in Unit 2.

***Except Unit 2, Religion and Society. Please see my notes in Unit 2 about why a summit is not appropriate in this case.

could travel through time to be in the same place—their classroom. Each historical figure makes an opening statement, providing brief biographical details and presenting their answers to the Unit Question and response to the 21st-Century Issue. Students must stay in character, while also citing evidence from the documents they've read to support their positions. Then there is time for questions and answers, during which the historical figures interact spontaneously. Students must consider what these historical figures would have to say to each other. What would Pericles and Indira Gandhi say to each other about democracy? How would the Qianlong Emperor and King Ferdinand of Spain explain their respective criteria for separating civilized people from barbarians? Finally, in the last section of the summit, students drop their characters and discuss how their personal views on the Unit Question and 21st-Century Issue have evolved or been confirmed by their studies and interactions.

Summit Instructions for Students

You will participate in a summit representing a historical figure. During this summit, you have three tasks:

1. Make an "opening statement" in which you:
   - introduce yourself and provide relevant biographical information in order to explain your importance in world history.
   - present your answer to the Unit Question and give an example of something you did or said that proves you would answer that way.
   - present your view on the 21st-Century Issue for this unit and explain why you have this view.

2. Listen attentively to other students' presentations.

3. Participate in a question-and-answer session in which you address your classmates as the historical figures they represent, challenging or agreeing with their ideas.
   - Prepare at least two questions for other historical figures.
   - Anticipate two questions you are likely to be asked and provide answers.
   - Cite the document we read in class and at least one other source.

4. Drop your character and discuss your personal views on the Unit Question and 21st-Century Issue.

In order to provide plenty of material for discussion, the historical figures in each unit represent a range of views. For instance, Unit 3, Us vs. Them, in which students examine concepts of civilization and barbarism, includes both Charles Malik, an author of the Universal Declaration of Human Rights, and Adolf Hitler, whose views on the supremacy of the Aryan race run directly counter to the concept of universal human rights. Discussions are more thought-provoking when there are stark contrasts between historical figures' positions.

Summits fit into a tradition of applied theater, in which people use drama for social purposes. In particular, I've been inspired by Augusto Boal's (1993) practice of "theater of the oppressed," in which people return to unresolved scenes of oppression in order to create change in the present and imagine different futures. I share a belief with Boal (1993) and his fellow Brazilian educator Paulo Freire (2000) that students are not empty vessels waiting to be filled with knowledge by their teachers; instead, they can be active in creating meaning and changing society.

That said, a summit can be as low-key or as formal as students and teachers want it to be. Teachers might require students to write out in advance or even memorize their speeches, or to deliver them from notes. I do not recommend that students try to reproduce the way their historical figure would have spoken, acted, or dressed; this would have too much potential to devolve into caricature or cause offense. Students can delve deeply into the content of historical figures' thought without dramatizing their behavior. In any case, the students' critical thinking skills are engaged as they separate their own viewpoint from that of their historical figure, provide evidence to support their views, and predict how their historical figure would respond to spontaneous questions.

In my experience, the first summit of the year is challenging for students. They tend to ask questions not relevant to the theme, or questions that reflect their own experience rather than that of their historical figure. For instance, Hammurabi might ask Louis XIV what it was like to be a king. Yet over the course of the year, students become increasingly adept at setting aside their own views in order to represent historical figures from a very different time and place from their own.

The summit ends with students dropping their characters and discussing the Unit Question and 21st-Century Issue as themselves. This was always the most rewarding part of the unit for me as a teacher—I got to see how much students had learned from history. It was wonderful to hear them considering a range of perspectives and articulating their own emerging views, informed by the documents we had read.

Students can consolidate these reflections in a Unit Exit Survey (Appendix G), in which they consider how their answers to the Unit Question and 21st-Century Issue have either changed or been confirmed by their studies. This metacognition solidifies their learning. They identify the event, historical figure, or document that most affected their own view, and they can also bring their learning into the present by writing a letter to a world leader or organization regarding the 21st-Century Issue (see Appendix H). Thus, students end each unit by finding their own answers to the big questions that have occupied people's minds through history.

Each unit might take three to four weeks to complete, allowing class time for background reading, drafting Biographical Research Papers, and preparing for the summit. This schedule allows adequate time in a school year for students to complete each of the nine units included in this book.

STRUCTURE OF A LESSON

Within the previously described architecture of a unit, individual lessons also have a dependable structure, making it easier for teachers and students to become comfortable with each element. Each document is incorporated into a lesson that sets it in context and connects it to the other documents in the unit. Every lesson within each unit includes:

- A Guiding Question for Interrogation of the Lesson's Document
- Historical Figure and Event
- Introduction
- Mini-Lecture
- Vocabulary
- Document and Source
- Comprehension Check
- Activities
- Reflection Questions
- Resources for Extension

These lessons are planned to take from 45 to 90 minutes, depending on whether teachers assign some or all of the questions and activities. Teachers may wish to spread one lesson out over two days, depending on the length of their class periods and their students' needs.

Teachers may vary the order or content of the activities in order to keep students' energy up and their minds fresh. For instance, they might start a lesson with a video from the Resources section at the end of the lesson instead of with the introduction question. Confident teachers rarely teach directly from any textbook or curriculum, and I encourage you to modify and remix this content in any way that excites you and your students.

Setting Up the Lesson

Before the lesson, teachers can build background knowledge on events, concepts, or historical figures related to the document. For instance, before examining the bas-relief of Suryavarman II, teachers may assign a reading on the Angkor Empire. Such readings are widely available in traditional textbooks, and teachers will have their own preferred or required secondary sources. This background information could be conveyed in a prior lesson or assigned as homework the day before. It is also possible to pre-teach the vocabulary related to each document in a prior class period or through homework exercises.

Lesson Question

Each lesson is titled with a question that students should be able to answer by the lesson's conclusion; for example, "How did Confucius envision the ideal society?"* These questions are different from the essential questions that title each unit in that they have specific (although not always straightforward) answers. By the end of the lesson, students should be able to answer the question by citing specific passages in the document. Students may come to different conclusions, but they should be able to support their interpretations.

It is important to differentiate the kind of questions asked here from those in comparable approaches to teaching history. For example, the Stanford History Education Group has designed a fantastic collection of document-based lessons for their Reading Like a Historian program (SHEG, n.d.). Their approach is to provide students with multiple documents pertaining to the same event, and to ask them to compare these documents in order to arrive at a conclusion about history. For example, their "central historical question" for one lesson is "Was ancient Athens truly democratic?" SHEG provides students with several documents related to this question. In contrast, my lesson on Athenian democracy asks, "How did Pericles describe direct democracy in Athens?" I provide only one document, *Pericles' Funeral Oration*. In other words, I focus on what students can learn from one document, instead of asking them to arrive at a broader conclusion about cause and effect in history based on multiple sources.

Asking the kind of questions that SHEG does is certainly valuable, and teachers could use SHEG's lessons to complement mine (or vice versa). Although I don't provide multiple documents about each event, in the Resources section of each lesson I do suggest other accounts teachers could use to deepen students' perspective. Indeed, outside research will be essential for students to begin questioning and contextualizing the claims that historical figures make in these documents.

Historical Figure and Event

Following the Lesson Question, teachers will find a historical figure and an event connected to the document. The event is described in or related to the document. Students should keep a personal and/or class timeline on which these events are added before, during, or after each lesson.

---

*Lesson Questions can be transformed into objectives: "Students will analyze how Confucius envisioned the ideal society."

Introduction

Each lesson begins with an introductory question or activity designed to capture students' attention, connect with their prior knowledge, and/or relate the topic to their lives. These questions do not have right or wrong answers, but are intended to spark thought and discussion and connect each student's current understandings with the knowledge they will gain.

Mini-Lecture

Following the introduction, the teacher can deliver a mini-lecture that puts the document in context. These mini-lectures are intended to review information students have gained from background readings and provide specific information about the document itself. In other words, they are not intended to convey a breadth and depth of historical understanding but rather to refresh students' memories and prepare them to analyze the document. These mini-lectures can be delivered orally and/or in digital format (e.g., PowerPoint). Teachers may wish to have students take notes on these lectures, or they might create fill-in notes for students to complete as they listen. These lectures take 5 to 10 minutes, unless students have many questions or teachers want to take time to delve into certain topics in more detail.

Vocabulary

A list of vocabulary words pulled from each document accompanies the lesson. I provide simple definitions addressing how the words are used in context. Some teachers may find that their students don't need these lists; others may find that some students require more assistance with reading comprehension. Teachers might pre-teach vocabulary through homework or class activities, present it during the course of the lesson, and/or review it afterward.

Document

The next step is for students to read the document. Each document is prefaced with its title, its author, and the year in which it was created or published. Most documents are excerpts of approximately 500 words that were originally part of a longer text. I have abridged them to omit details unrelated to the unit's theme and to make them manageable for students and teachers to analyze within a class period or two. Teachers may want to read the document aloud as students follow along; have students read it aloud, as a class or in pairs; or have students read it silently. Active reading strategies, such as predicting, visualizing, and asking questions, may be helpful.

Several documents are in the form of images. In those cases, teachers can use Visual Thinking Strategies (VTS), including speculating, questioning, and analyzing (Visual Thinking Strategies, 2016), to have students examine the photo or political cartoon. Printable versions of all documents, along with the instructions and handouts included in the appendices, are available for download at www.tcpress.com/MetroWorld (see Appendix J for a list of materials available there). The printable versions are arranged in chronological order by the date of the document, not in the order they are presented in this book.

Source

Following the document itself, I include a citation indicating where teachers can find the full document from which I took the excerpt. Whenever possible, I include an online source for ease of access.

Comprehension Check

Comprehension checks follow each document. These tasks are aimed at the lower levels of Revised Bloom's Taxonomy (Iowa State University of Science and Technology, 2016), and they allow teachers to assess whether students have understood the document thoroughly enough to proceed to analysis, synthesis, and evaluation. Students might answer these in writing and/or orally, individually or in groups. While the answers to some of these questions might be debatable, it shouldn't be difficult for teachers to determine correct answers and pinpoint misunderstandings.

Activities

Once teachers are confident that students have comprehended the document's main points, students complete activities that allow them to apply, analyze, and evaluate what they have learned from the document. Students can complete these activities individually or through group and partner activities. There are no "correct" responses to these questions; students could arrive at various conclusions, depending on their interpretation of the documents and their own views. The activities I suggest include writing letters from one historical figure to another, role-playing or creating cartoons illustrating conversations between historical figures, sketching Venn diagrams to compare historical figures' views, finding evidence to support arguments, conducting research and making presentations, and participating in small-group discussions or class debates.

These activities scaffold students' learning to build toward the summit at the end of the unit. Teachers may want to adapt these activities (e.g., turning a group assignment into an individual one or asking for a written dialogue instead of having students act it out), or they may want to generate additional activities, depending on their own preferences, on student needs, on district or school guidelines, or on constraints of time, space, or resources. For more activity ideas, books on group work (Cohen & Lotan, 2014) and active learning strategies (Casale-Giannola & Green, 2013) are helpful.

The questions I ask require students to use "historical thinking skills" identified by SHEG and others: sourcing, contextualization, corroboration, and close reading of documents. For students who need support in developing these skills prior to engaging with documents in this book, I suggest SHEG's introductory materials for the Reading Like a Historian program (SHEG, n.d.), which break down each skill into easy-to-follow steps.

Reflection

Each lesson ends with a question for students to reflect on as they synthesize what they've learned and make connections to the rest of the unit. Teachers might have students complete these questions on exit tickets or have them discuss answers in pairs, in small groups, or with the whole class. These questions, as well as the introduction questions, sometimes ask about students' personal experiences—but it is important to establish from the start that no one is obligated to share unless they feel comfortable doing so.

Resources

Rounding out each lesson are one or two resources that teachers can use to build their own knowledge or create extension activities for students. These resources may contain different or broader perspectives than the documents do, so they can be helpful for corroboration or contextualization.

ASSESSMENT

This approach to teaching history provides rich opportunities for both formative and summative assessment. Comprehension checks allow for confirmation that students have understood the documents at a basic level. Observations of and artifacts from activities show whether students are engaging with the material at a higher level by applying, analyzing, and evaluating what they've learned. Reflections show teachers whether students are connecting new information to what they've already learned in the unit. Teachers may also wish to conduct weekly or bimonthly quizzes covering historical figures and events. This material is also compatible with Standards-Based Grading

(Marzano, 2009), in that units and/or lessons can be aligned with learning outcomes based on content standards.

The summit that ends each unit is a great opportunity for summative assessment, as it enables students to use the analysis and evaluation they've done to create something new: an interpretation of a historical figure's perspective. Students might also write a Biographical Research Paper on the historical figures they've chosen (Appendix E). The Unit Exit Survey (Appendix G) shows how much students have gained from the unit. Students can also write letters about the 21st-Century Issue to local, state, federal, or school leaders. For instance, at the conclusion of the unit on conflict, they might write to the United Nations to express their views on how to address the conflict in Yemen. After the unit on forms of government, they might write to their country's ambassador to Saudi Arabia to express their opinions on the killing of Jamal Khashoggi (see Appendix H). These letters not only allow teachers to assess students' synthesis of the material covered but also encourage students to become active citizens. Teachers may also wish to create tests covering the historical figures and events in the unit, and/or to test students' comprehension of the documents. An end-of-the-year project could be a presentation on one of the historical eras covered in Unit 9.

ACCOUNTING FOR GRADE LEVEL AND DIFFERENTIATING INSTRUCTION

I recommend this approach to teaching history in grades 7 to 12. I know it can be done in 8th grade from my own experience; as Levstik and Barton (2005) show, the capacity of young students for historical inquiry is often underestimated. It would be possible to adapt this method to younger grades, or even college-level courses, but this book is intended for secondary students.

The design of this book makes it easy for teachers to adapt this material to various grade levels or to differentiate instruction within a class. Most documents are abridged, both to focus on the parts that refer to the Unit Question and to remove details that may require additional explanations that aren't directly related to the topic at hand. For instance, in Lesson 1.4, I take out Xenophon's explanation of the Spartan term "pythii." Students already have to learn about ephors and oligarchs, and another classification of nobles would not add much to their understanding. This type of allusion to events or people outside the main topic is one reason, I find, that teachers hesitate to use primary source documents—it takes too much time to explain every detail, and students' curiosity often takes the conversation in directions tangential to the lesson's objectives.

However, for higher grade levels or more advanced students, teachers might assign original documents in their entirety alongside the excerpts in this book. Links to the full documents can be found following the excerpts and at www.tcpress.com/MetroWorld. On the other hand, some teachers may wish to abridge the documents further or amplify their meaning for multilingual learners (MLLs) or students who struggle with comprehension. There is no scientific process to abridging documents, so teachers should feel free either to restore parts of the document that I have cut or excerpt them further. The important thing is that students have direct access to the ideas. Suggestions for accommodations and modifications for MLLs or those with special needs can be found respectively in Gibbons (2009) and Gore (2012).

It is also possible to differentiate instruction by choosing which and how many exercises students will do. Students who complete the comprehension checks quickly and easily can move on to the activities, perhaps completing two of them, while students who needed more time and support with the comprehension check might complete only one of the activities. As a teacher, you know your students best, and you will be able to adapt and sequence the activities for individuals and groups of students in ways that I as a curriculum designer cannot predetermine.

CLASSROOM CLIMATE

In order for this approach to teaching history to work well, teachers need to create a classroom climate in which students respect each other's differing opinions and discuss facts and values openly. This climate can be difficult to establish in a world as politically divided as ours. However, political polarization makes it all the more important that kids learn to listen to each other, consider evidence, and disagree productively. Some teachers try to sidestep potential problems by avoiding current events altogether. But although conversations about racial, economic, social, and gender inequality can be difficult, avoiding them makes us more likely to reproduce these hierarchies (Milner, 2010). I agree with Diana E. Hess and Paula McAvoy that history is most meaningful to students when it is connected to the debates that animate our world today. I would go further and say that to analyze history without relating it to the present is to rob the past of its meaning.

Nonetheless, some teachers may not find it prudent to reference current events as much as this book does. Their administrations or school communities may not be supportive. Teachers may not feel confident about managing the difficult conversations that could arise. Or the dynamics of their classrooms and communities might make discussing sensitive issues too risky.

I would advise teachers who use the approach I describe in this book to reflect on how their own political, socioeconomic, religious, and ethnic or racial backgrounds may affect how they teach this material. For example, I am the child of Polish and Syrian immigrants who grew up in a left-leaning

White family in an urban Democratic stronghold. Many of the students in my first classroom, in New York City, were from outside the United States (e.g., the Dominican Republic, Jamaica, and Trinidad), and often identified with their families' countries of origin. I had to think carefully about how these Black, Latinx, and West Indian students would respond, for instance, to the history of colonization of the Americas and the racial hierarchies that continue today; their interpretation would certainly be different from the one I had been taught. When I moved to a "red state," on the other hand, my students were almost all White, and from more conservative and rural backgrounds than I had previously experienced. I had to design a curriculum that welcomed these students while helping them learn about places they might consider foreign. Teachers will have to decide for themselves how much of their own background and views are appropriate to share with their students, but reflecting on these topics personally is indispensable.

I have consciously included documents in this book that reflect perspectives across political and social spectrums. That does not mean we need to see these perspectives as of equal value, just that they are all important in helping us understand our world today. Seeking to understand historical figures is distinct from accepting their arguments, and leaving disturbing or controversial elements out of world history curricula impedes students' ability to understand the past and the present.

Nevertheless, teachers should carefully evaluate the identity dynamics of their classes when covering sensitive topics. LaGarrett King (2016), a specialist in social studies education and Black history, has pointed out that simulations (such as the summits) run the risk of retraumatizing Black students by exposing them to documents that disparage members of their race or force them into the role of victims. Students of any race might feel uncomfortable representing the views of White supremacists like Hitler; and unfortunately, some students may consciously or unconsciously embrace these views. From another angle, some White students might feel awkward representing the views of non-White people. Some students might be upset by Yasser Arafat's justification of the Palestinian Liberation Organization, others by Theodor Herzl's endorsement of Zionism.

I encourage teachers to have conversations with students and their families, and with colleagues and administrators, about how best to navigate these challenges. Creating an atmosphere of trust and respect is key when discussing issues such as such as racism, LGBTQ+ (lesbian, gay, bisexual, transgender, and queer or questioning) rights, and civil liberties. Teachers can give students the right to "pass" when answering questions during class discussions, and follow up with them later about their discomfort. Teachers can also provide explicit examples of how to disagree respectfully.

Yet it is important that "politeness" or "civility" does not become an excuse to silence passionate voices. Jasmine D. Williams, Ashley N. Woodson, and Tanner LeBaron Wallace (2016) explain that creating psychological safety when discussing race (and, I would argue, other identity-related topics) in the classroom means that students "[feel] supported to take intellectual and social risks" (p. 16)—not that teachers try to eliminate risk altogether. They urge teachers to develop their capacities to show attunement to their students' situations, to demonstrate authenticity, and to share power with students during these important discussions (Williams, Woodson, & Wallace, 2016).

For those reasons, I offer the discussion guidelines below as an example of what teachers might work to develop with their students. I think it is crucial to involve students in the process of setting parameters around what is acceptable or encouraged in their learning community.

Guidelines for Respectful Discussion

GUIDELINES	NO	YES
1. Assume positive intentions and give classmates the benefit of the doubt—disagree with ideas, don't attack people.	"If you don't believe in human-caused climate change, you're stupid!" "If you believe humans cause climate change, you're brainwashed by the liberal media!"	"Let's talk about the evidence for human-caused climate change."
2. Speak to your classmates as you would to a role model you respect.	"You idiot!"	"I strongly disagree with you."
3. Don't blame your classmates for what members of a group they belong to have done, and don't ask classmates to speak for all members of a group they belong to.	"Why do you Black people always think violence is necessary?" "Why do you White people always colonize other people's land?"	"I have questions about Frantz Fanon's idea of using violence to end colonization." "As a Vietnamese person, I feel upset when I learn that French people colonized my ancestors' land."
4. Reflect on how your own experiences and biases affect your views—avoid blame and shame.	"I don't see why we need to study women in history; men did most of the important stuff." "All men should feel guilty about how they have treated women."	"As a male, I realize that I've been seeing history through the eyes of men." "I'm angry about sexism I've experienced, and how women have been oppressed throughout history."
5. If you feel upset, angry, or confused during a discussion, take a break. Take care of yourself and take care of each other.	"No one leaves this room until we can all agree!" "I don't care how you feel!"	"I'm confused, and I need some time to think about this. Can we come back to this discussion tomorrow?"

It is also helpful for teachers to consider their goals in teaching history. Some teach to promote social justice, others to promote patriotism; some teach to prepare students to create change, others to help students succeed in the society that exists. The purposes served by this text are as follows: to expose students to a wide range of viewpoints on history, which provides context for contemporary life; to teach them to consider evidence carefully; to enable them to listen to other points of view; and to encourage them to decide for themselves what resonates with their values, experiences, and logic.

DESIGNING YOUR OWN THEMATIC UNITS

The units in this book are examples of what teachers could do with a thematic, document-based approach for world history. Many other thematic units are possible, for instance:

- *Generational Divides:* How have different age groups interacted?
- *Geography:* How have geographical features influenced the development of human societies?
- *Art History:* How has the art people created reflected and shaped their worlds?

For more ideas, see the blog "Big Questions, Many Answers" on my website at rosaliemetro.com. Here you will find lists of documents that could be included in thematic units like these, as well as blog posts about developing your own units.

Adding additional topics or units can be helpful, because the content included here is by no means exhaustive. The units in this book touch on key themes in world history, and I've tried to cover major events and important historical figures while also drawing attention to lesser known people and ideas. Teachers may wish to replace or supplement units with additional material that reflects their students' communities.

I hope that this book will inspire teachers to create their own thematic units for world history—or for other courses, such as U.S. history, women's history, or Black history. Doing so is fairly straightforward and quite rewarding, although planning takes time (see Appendix I). Regardless of how teachers choose to use this book, I hope that they and their students find the reading and critical interrogation of these documents and themes a rich and stimulating way to study history together.

Forms of Government

Unit Question: What Should Be the Rights and Responsibilities of the Rulers and the Ruled?

In this unit, students will learn about a range of ways in which societies have been governed, from repressive one-party states to democracies. The 21st-Century Issue, on the murder of Jamal Khashoggi, draws attention to how the right to a free press may be restricted in absolute monarchies like Saudi Arabia. Students then revisit some of the first laws recorded, in Hammurabi's Code. The rivalry between Athenian democracy and Spartan oligarchy sets the stage for forms of government, like the Roman Republic, in which power was shared among the people, the military leaders, and elected representatives. Asian models of imperial monarchy, as embodied in the Han Dynasty's Emperor Wu and Angkor's Suryavarman II, make an interesting comparison with European absolute monarchies exemplified by Louis XIV. The Igbo people's stateless society provides an important counterpoint to the more structured forms of government in this unit. Indira Gandhi's defense of democracy—a system that she was accused of undermining—recalls Greek and Roman models while also highlighting how much has changed in the past several thousand years. The Finnish Constitution presents a government that guarantees the social welfare of its citizens and opens a discussion about the left-center-right political spectrum. Finally, documents from the Inuit territory of Nunavut show that egalitarianism can be a basis for government.

One recurring pattern in this unit is the gap between leaders' words and leaders' actions, between the ideal form and the often messy reality of their systems of government. Students may want to hold up some of the people profiled in this unit as heroes, while tearing down others as tyrants. It can be helpful for teachers to encourage a critical examination of all the historical figures under study.

Several major religions are also introduced in this unit—Islam, Christianity, Buddhism, and Confucianism—and teachers will want to be aware of their students' religious background before broaching these possibly sensitive topics. Students will study these belief systems in depth in Unit 2.

As this is the first unit, teachers may need to spend some time introducing students to activities that will be repeated frequently in this book—for instance, creating political cartoons, imagining dialogues between historical figures, and creating graphic organizers including Venn diagrams and T-charts to synthesize information. Finally, as teachers may be still establishing the classroom climate required to discuss these potentially controversial issues of rights and responsibilities, they may wish to spend extra time solidifying norms for discussion and creating a culture of respect.

LESSON 1.1

WHAT ARE ACTIVISTS ASKING THE UNITED NATIONS TO DO ABOUT THE MURDER OF JOURNALIST JAMAL KHASHOGGI?

Historical Figure: Jamal Khashoggi

Event: Murder of Jamal Khashoggi, 2018

Introduction: Do you think that journalists criticize governments too much, too little, or the right amount? Give an example to support your view.

Mini-Lecture:

- Jamal Khashoggi was a journalist from Saudi Arabia who wrote for many newspapers, including *The Washington Post*.
- Saudi Arabia is an absolute monarchy, which means that the king controls all aspects of the government; the government supports a strict interpretation of Islam called Wahhabism, and there is little religious or social freedom.
- Mohammad bin Salman has been Crown Prince and heir to the throne since 2017.
- Khashoggi criticized the royal family's decisions, and after facing pressure from the government, he went to live in the United States.
- In 2018, Jamal Khashoggi went to a Saudi embassy in Turkey, where he was murdered by Saudi officials.
- This document is an open letter to United Nations Secretary General António Guterres regarding Khashoggi's death that was signed by more than one hundred writers, including J. K. Rowling, John Green, and Rita Dove, organized by press freedom organization PEN America.

Vocabulary:

grave: serious
apparent: seems to be true
diplomatic: relating to international relations
state terror: terrorism committed by a government

dissident: person who criticizes their government
impunity: when people are not punished for their crimes
authorize: give approval for
dismember: cut a body into pieces

detain: prevent someone from leaving
admission: something that someone admits to doing
premeditated: planned in advance
culpability: guilt

prominent: famous
escalation: worsening
perpetrators: people who committed a crime
grievous: terrible

Document: PEN America calls for independent investigation into Jamal Khashoggi's disappearance and apparent murder, 2018

As writers, journalists, artists, and Members of PEN America and the Authors Guild, we write to express our grave concern about the apparent horrific murder of Jamal Khashoggi, the Saudi journalist, *Washington Post* contributor, and U.S. resident who disappeared in Istanbul on October 2 after entering the Saudi Arabian consulate. If true, the murder of a journalist inside a diplomatic facility would constitute nothing less than an act of state terror intended to intimidate journalists, dissidents, and exiled critics the world over. The United Nations has rightly recognized the importance of ensuring the safety of journalists and fighting impunity for those who attack them with the publication of the UN Plan of Action on the Safety of Journalists and the Issue of Impunity endorsed in 2012. In the spirit of that initiative, we respectfully call on you to immediately authorize an independent, international investigation into Jamal Khashoggi's disappearance and apparent murder.

Since his disappearance, Turkish authorities have claimed to have evidence suggesting that Jamal Khashoggi was brutally murdered and dismembered inside the consulate, and that the operation was likely carried out by a team including individuals very close to Saudi Crown Prince Mohammed bin Salman, making it look extremely likely that the Crown Prince was behind Khashoggi's assassination. After weeks of denying any involvement in his disappearance, on October 19 Saudi Arabia admitted that Khashoggi was killed inside the consulate, claiming his death was the result of a "fight" during attempts to detain him. Global leaders have responded to the details of this admission with significant skepticism. More recently, Saudi authorities have said the murder was "premeditated," though the details and culpability remain unclear.

The violent murder of a prominent journalist and commentator on foreign soil is a grave violation of human rights and a disturbing escalation of the crackdown on dissent in Saudi Arabia, whose government in recent years has jailed numerous writers, journalists, human rights advocates, and lawyers in a sweeping assault on free expression and association. It is also yet another data point in a global trend that has seen an increasing number of journalists imprisoned and murdered for their work. As writers and journalists ourselves, we fear the potential chilling effect of this trend, at a moment when the work of all those who would speak and expose the truth has never been more important. . . .

We therefore respectfully call on you to immediately authorize an independent, international investigation into the murder of Jamal Khashoggi that would lay the groundwork for identifying and holding accountable the perpetrators of this grievous crime.

Source: PEN America. (2018). PEN America calls for independent investigation into Jamal Khashoggi's disappearance and murder. https://pen.org/investigate -jamal-khashoggi-disappearance-murder/

Comprehension Check:

1. What do the writers who signed the letter think was the reason that the Saudi Arabian authorities killed Khashoggi?
2. What does the letter ask Sec. Gen. Guterres to do, and why?

Activities:

1. With a partner, make a list of the actions people can take in a democracy if they do not support the government. Then cross off the list those that would be difficult or impossible in an absolute monarchy, and explain why.
2. Read the article by Jamal Khashoggi from the Resources section. Underline the parts that corroborate PEN America's claims about the Saudi Arabian government, and circle any parts that contradict those claims. Share your findings with the class.

Reflection: Do you think the open letter will be effective? Why or why not? What other actions could people take to pursue justice in the murder of Jamal Khashoggi?

Resources:

Khashoggi, J. (2017). Saudi Arabia wasn't always this repressive. Now it's unbearable. *The Washington Post.* https://www.washingtonpost.com/news/global-opinions/wp/2017/09/18 /saudi-arabia-wasnt-always-this-repressive-now-its-unbearable/?noredirect=on&utm _term=.078a8cc63540

United Nations. (2016). UN plan of action on the safety of journalists and the issue of impunity. https://unesdoc.unesco.org/ark:/48223/pf0000246014

WorldAtlas. (2019). What type of government does Saudi Arabia have? https://www .worldatlas.com/articles/what-type-of-government-does-saudi-arabia-have.html

LESSON 1.2

WHAT KIND OF LAWS DID KING HAMMURABI MAKE FOR HIS SUBJECTS?

Historical Figure: Hammurabi

Event: Hammurabi publishes code of law, 1750 BCE

Introduction: If you were a ruler, what kinds of laws would you make to protect weaker people from stronger people?

Mini-Lecture:

- Hammurabi was a king of Babylon, which is in modern-day Iraq.
- Babylon was part of a region called Mesopotamia, the land between the Tigris and Euphrates Rivers where some of the earliest cities existed.
- Hammurabi had 282 laws carved into a stone pillar and placed in a temple where they could be read; these are some of the first laws that were recorded.
- In Hammurabi's kingdom, there were many classes of people whose status varied, including free-born people with different levels of wealth, freed slaves, and slaves.
- The women in each class had less status than the men.
- These laws were among the first to give rights to people accused of crimes, and to set limits on what punishments could be given.

Vocabulary:

exalted: wonderful
righteousness: fairness
charge: claim
capital offense: crime punished with death
mina: Babylonian unit of money
shekel: Babylonian money; fifty shekels made one mina

render: deliver
congenial: pleasant
dowry: money or property that a man gets from a woman's family when he marries her
hewn: sawed

Document: Hammurabi's Code of Law, Hammurabi, 1750 BCE

Anu [Babylonian creator god] and Bel [the lord of Heaven and earth] called by name me, Hammurabi, the exalted prince, who feared God, to bring about the rule of righteousness in the land, to destroy the wicked and the evil-doers; so that the strong should not harm the weak; . . . to further the well-being of mankind. . . .

2. If any one bring an accusation against a man, and the accused go to the river and leap into the river, if he sink in the river his accuser shall take possession of his house. But if the river prove that the accused is not guilty, and he escape unhurt, then he who had brought the accusation shall be put to death, while he who leaped into the river shall take possession of the house that had belonged to his accuser.

3. If any one bring an accusation of any crime before the elders, and does not prove what he has charged, he shall, if it be a capital offense charged, be put to death. . . .

5. If a judge try a case, reach a decision, and present his judgment in writing; if later error shall appear in his decision, and it be through his own fault, then he shall pay twelve times the fine set by him in the case, and he shall be publicly removed from the judge's bench, and never again shall he sit there to render judgement. . . .

142. If a woman quarrel with her husband, and say: "You are not congenial to me," the reasons for her prejudice must be presented. If she is guiltless, and there is no fault on her part, but he leaves and neglects her, then no guilt attaches to this woman, she shall take her dowry and go back to her father's house.

143. If she is not innocent, but leaves her husband, and ruins her house, neglecting her husband, this woman shall be cast into the water. . . .

195. If a son strike his father, his hands shall be hewn off.

196. If a man put out the eye of another man, his eye shall be put out.

197. If he break another man's bone, his bone shall be broken.

198. If he put out the eye of a freed man, or break the bone of a freed man, he shall pay one gold mina.

199. If he put out the eye of a man's slave, or break the bone of a man's slave, he shall pay one-half of its value. . . .

202. If any one strike the body of a man higher in rank than he, he shall receive sixty blows with an ox-whip in public.

203. If a free-born man strike the body of another free-born man or equal rank, he shall pay one gold mina.

204. If a freed man strike the body of another freed man, he shall pay ten shekels in money.

205. If the slave of a freed man strike the body of a freed man, his ear shall be cut off.

206. If during a quarrel one man strike another and wound him, then he shall swear, "I did not injure him wittingly," and pay the physicians.

Source: Lillian Goldman Law Library. (2008). The code of Hammurabi. http://avalon.law.yale.edu/ancient/hamframe.asp

Comprehension Check:

1. What did ancient Babylonians believe would happen to a person falsely accused of a crime who jumped into a river? What about someone who had indeed committed a crime?
2. What would happen to a freed man (former slave) who hit another freed man? What if the person who hit the freed man was a slave?

Activities:

1. Hammurabi states that the purpose of his Code of Laws is that "the strong should not harm the weak." Create a poster on one side of the room with a list of his laws that seem to serve that purpose, and a poster on the other side with a list of his laws that seem to go against that purpose. Small groups can be responsible for adding several laws to the proper list, being ready to explain their reasoning.

2. Compare one of Hammurabi's laws with a law we have today. What are the similarities and differences?

Reflection: Do you think these laws made Hammurabi's job as king harder or easier? Why?

Resources:

Mark, J. J. (2011). Babylon. *Ancient history encyclopedia.* https://www.ancient.eu/babylon/
Rattini, K. B. (2019). Who was Hammurabi? https://www.nationalgeographic.com/culture
    /people/reference/hammurabi/#close

LESSON 1.3
HOW DID PERICLES DESCRIBE DIRECT DEMOCRACY IN ATHENS?

Historical Figure: Pericles

Event: Peloponnesian War, 431–404 BCE

Introduction: In the United States today, only 40% to 60% of eligible voters actually vote in elections. What reasons might people have for not voting?

Mini-Lecture:

• Pericles was a Greek politician and military general from Athens, Greece.
• While he was leader, the Athenians were involved in the Peloponnesian War, against Sparta and its allies.
• In the 5th century BCE, a system of "direct democracy" was developed in Athens, in which each citizen could cast a vote on important decisions.
• Only adult men who had completed military service—a minority of the population—were considered citizens; the citizenry excluded women, slaves, and foreigners.
• This document is from a speech Pericles gave honoring the Athenians who had died in the war; it was written down by the historian Thucydides.

Vocabulary:

afford: provide
private: individual
advancement: getting ahead in life
capacity: skills
hinder: hold back
obscurity: lack of fame
surveillance: monitoring others' behavior
injurious: hurtful
inflict: cause

positive: actual
magistrate: judge
statute: law
public men: men holding office in government
industry: producing goods or making a living
stumbling-block: obstacle
indispensable: necessary
preliminary: beginning

Document: Pericles' Funeral Oration, Pericles, 431 BCE

Our constitution does not copy the laws of neighboring states; we are rather a pattern to others than imitators ourselves. Its administration favors the many instead of the few; this is why it is called a democracy. If we look to the laws, they afford equal justice to all in their private differences; if no social standing, advancement in public life falls to reputation for capacity, class considerations not being allowed to interfere with merit; nor again does poverty bar the way, if a man is able to serve the state, he is not hindered by the obscurity of his condition. The freedom which we enjoy in our government extends also to our ordinary life. There, far from exercising a jealous surveillance over each other, we do not feel called upon to be angry with our neighbor for doing what he likes, or even to indulge in those injurious looks which cannot fail to be offensive, although they inflict no positive penalty. But all this ease in our private relations does not make us lawless as citizens. Against this fear is our chief safeguard, teaching us to obey the magistrates and the laws, particularly such as regard the protection of the injured, whether they are actually on the statute book, or belong to that code which, although unwritten, yet cannot be broken without acknowledged disgrace. . . .

Nor are these the only points in which our city is worthy of admiration. . . . Our public men have, besides politics, their private affairs to attend to, and our ordinary citizens, though occupied with the pursuits of industry, are still fair judges of public matters; for, unlike any other nation, regarding him who takes no part in these duties not as unambitious but as useless, we Athenians . . . instead of looking on discussion as a stumbling-block in the way of action, we think it an indispensable preliminary to any wise action at all.

Source: Hallsall, P. (2000). Thucydides (c. 460/c. 399 BCE): Pericles' funeral oration from the Peloponnesian war (Book 2.34–46). https://sourcebooks.fordham.edu/ancient/pericles-funeralspeech.asp

Comprehension Check:

1. According to Pericles, who can be involved in government in Athens?
2. According to Pericles, how are decisions made in Athens?

Activities:

1. Work with a partner to make a Venn diagram comparing and contrasting democracy in ancient Athens with the government in your country today.
2. How might a female slave have responded to Pericles's claims about Athenian democracy? Imagine and write down what she would say.

Reflection: Do you think societies are better off if more people participate in making decisions? Why or why not?

Resources:

Cartwright, M. (2018). Athenian democracy. *Ancient history encyclopedia*. https://www.ancient
.eu/Athenian_Democracy/

LESSON 1.4

How Did Sparta's Oligarchy Work?

Historical Figure: Lycurgus

Event: Lycurgus rules Sparta, 9th century BCE

Introduction: If you were a ruler, how would you make sure that people followed the laws that you made?

Mini-Lecture:

- Sparta was a city-state (small country) located in what is now Greece that was most powerful between the 9th and 3rd centuries BCE.
- Sparta was an oligarchy; it was ruled by a small group of wealthy and powerful people called an aristocracy.
- Sparta always had two kings, who were believed to be related to gods; five "ephors," or judges elected by citizens, who helped the king rule; and a group of about 30 older men who had been appointed to a citizen's assembly.
- Only land-owning adult males could vote for ephors and participate in politics, although Spartan women could own property, unlike Athenian women.
- The king who is credited with inventing the Spartan system of government was named Lycurgus.
- Spartans expressed pride in their strong military, athletic training, and discipline.
- The Spartans, like the Athenians, believed that a priestess called Pythia, also known as the Oracle of Delphi, could communicate with their many gods and predict the future.
- Our document was written by historian Xenophon, who though Athenian-born, spent time in Sparta and was friendly with Spartan kings.

Vocabulary:

conjecture: guess

demeaning: insulting

submissive: doing what someone else says

cow: pressure someone to do something

tyrant: powerful person who rules unfairly

device: method

populace: people living in a certain place

prescription: law

impious: going against the wishes of god or religion

ordain: make an official announcement

sacrifice: killing an animal to please the gods

dispatch (despatch): send

oath: promise

abide: follow

prerogative: choice or right

Document: Spartan society, Xenophon, c. 378 BCE

Now we all know that at Sparta there is the strictest obedience to both the authorities and the laws. I think, however, that Lycurgus did not even attempt to establish this discipline until he had won the agreement of the most influential men in the state. I make this conjecture because in other states the more powerful people do not even want to give the impression of fearing the authorities, but instead consider that to be demeaning to free men. But at Sparta the most influential figures are in fact particularly submissive towards the authorities: they take pride in being humble as well as in responding at a run rather than by walking whenever they are summoned. For they believe that if they should take the lead in showing exceptional obedience, the rest also will follow—as has indeed been the case. It is also likely that these same figures collaborated in establishing the power of the ephorate too, since they recognized that obedience is of the greatest benefit in a state, as in an army and a house-hold. For the more power the office had, the more they thought it would also cow the citizens into submission. So the ephors have the power to fine anyone they wish, the right to secure payment on the spot, the right also to dismiss office-holders, and actually to imprison and put them on trial for their lives. With power of this degree they do not, as in other cities, always permit elected officials to exercise their authority just as they please for a full year; but in the style of tyrants and umpires at athletic competitions, if ever they detect any irregular behaviour on anyone's part, they at once punish it on the spot.

In order to make the citizens willing to obey the laws Lycurgus was responsible for many other admirable devices. One of the most admirable in my view is this: he issued his laws to the populace only after going to Delphi with the most powerful figures and asking the god if it would be preferable and better for Sparta to obey the laws he personally had drawn up. Once the god responded that it would be better in every way, only then did he issue them, with the prescription that it would be not only unlawful but also impious to disobey laws ordained by the Pythian god. . . .

Lycurgus laid it down that a king, by virtue of his divine descent, should perform all the public sacrifices on the city's behalf and should lead the army wherever the city despatches it. . . .

[T]here is a monthly exchange of oaths, ephors acting for the city, a king on his own behalf. The king's oath is to rule according to the city's established laws, while that of the city is to keep the king's position unshaken so long as he abides by his oath. These, then, are the prerogatives granted to a king at home during his lifetime—nothing much above the level of private citizens. For it was not Lycurgus' intention either that kings should acquire a tyrannical attitude or that citizens should come to envy their power.

Source: Erenow. (2019). Xenophon, Spartan society.
https://erenow.net/ancient/on-sparta/9.php

Comprehension Check:

1. According to Xenophon, why do Spartan citizens follow laws? List as many reasons as you can.

Activities:

1. Make a Venn diagram comparing and contrasting Athenian democracy (Lesson 1.3) with Spartan oligarchy.
2. Use the chart as the basis for a debate in which half the class argues on behalf of Lycurgus that Spartan oligarchy was superior to Athenian democracy, and half the class argues the opposite on behalf of Pericles (Lesson 1.3).

Reflection: Is it better to have a society where the laws are always fair but people don't always follow them, or a society where people always follow the laws but the laws aren't always fair? Why?

Resources:

Cartwright, M. (2013). Sparta. *Ancient history encyclopedia*. https://www.ancient.eu/sparta/

LESSON 1.5

WHAT WAS THE ROLE OF THE IMPERIAL MONARCH IN HAN DYNASTY CHINA?

Historical Figure: Wu of Han

Event: Han Dynasty, 202 BCE–9 CE

Introduction: What happens when rulers do not fulfill their duties? Why?

Mini-Lecture:

- The Han Dynasty was an imperial monarchy, or a kingdom ruled by an emperor who inherited absolute power, in what is now southeastern China.
- The dynasty was influenced by two belief systems: Confucianism (the teachings of the philosopher Confucius, who believed that social harmony resulted when each person fulfilled their duty to others); and Daoism (a philosophy of living peacefully by following the flow of nature).
- One of the strongest leaders of the Han Dynasty was Emperor Wu of Han, who expanded the empire's territory and supported trade throughout Central Asia along the Silk Road.
- It was believed that the emperor or empress had the "Mandate of Heaven"; they were chosen by the gods to rule, and if they ruled well, their empire would be peaceful; if they ruled poorly, they could lose the Mandate of Heaven and there would be natural disasters and war.
- Our document describing the proper role of the emperor was written by a scholar and government official named Dong Zhongshu.

Vocabulary:

foundation: base
state: government
reverence: respect
institute: create
filial: describing the respect of children
   for their parents
rite: ceremony
engender: give life to

clod: lump
barricade: protect
pass: valley
usurp: take away power
wilds: wilderness
befall: happen to
relinquish: give up

Document: Luxuriant Gems of the Spring and Autumn Annals, Dong Zhongshu, 2nd century BCE

He who rules the people is the foundation of the state. Now in administering the state, nothing is more important for transforming [the people] than reverence for the foundation. If the foundation is revered, the ruler will transform [the people] as if a spirit. If the foundation is not revered, the ruler will lack the means to unite the people. If he lacks the means to unite the people, even if he institutes strict punishments and heavy penalties, the people will not submit. . . .

Heaven, Earth, and humankind are the foundation of all living things. Heaven engenders all living things, Earth nourishes them, and humankind completes them. With filial and brotherly love, Heaven engenders them; with food and clothing, Earth nourishes them; and with rites and music, humankind completes them. These three assist one another just as the hands and feet join to complete the body. None can be dispensed with because without filial and brotherly love, people lack the means to live; without food and clothing, people lack the means to be nourished; and without rites and music, people lack the means to become complete. If all three are lost, people become like deer, each person following his own desires and each family practicing its own customs. Fathers will not be able to order their sons, and rulers will not be able to order their ministers. Although possessing inner and outer walls, [the ruler's city] will become known as "an empty settlement." Under such circumstances, the ruler will lie down with a clod of earth for his pillow. Although no one endangers him, he will naturally be endangered; although no one destroys him, he will naturally be destroyed. This is called "spontaneous punishment." When it arrives, even if he is hidden in a stone vault or barricaded in a narrow pass, the ruler will not be able to avoid "spontaneous punishment." . . .

If these three foundations are all served, the people will resemble sons and brothers who do not dare usurp authority, while the ruler will resemble fathers and mothers. He will not rely on favors to demonstrate his love for his people nor severe measures to prompt them to act. Even if he lives in the wilds without a roof over head, he will consider that this surpasses living in a palace. Under such circumstances, the ruler will lie down upon a peaceful pillow. Although no one assists him, he will naturally be powerful; although no one pacifies his state, peace will naturally come. This is called "spontaneous reward." When "spontaneous reward" befalls him, although he might relinquish the throne and leave the state, the people will take up their children on their backs and follow him as the ruler, so that he too will be unable to leave them.

Source: Asia for Educators (n.d.). From luxuriant gems of the spring and autumn annals: "The responsibilities of leadership."
http://afe.easia.columbia.edu/ps/cup/dongzhongshu_rulership.pdf

Comprehension Check:

1. According to Dong Zhongshu, what are the three parts or elements that a ruler represents as the foundation of the country?
2. What does Dong Zhongshu claim will happen if the ruler does not strengthen those three elements?

Activities:

1. Work with a group to create a poster illustrating either the "spontaneous reward" or the "spontaneous punishment" that Dong Zhongshu describes. What would society look like in each case?
2. Write a letter from Emperor Wu to Lycurgus (Lesson 1.4) complimenting him on some aspects of his country and offering constructive criticism on others.

Reflection: Do you believe the prosperity and peace of a society depends on its ruler? Why or why not?

Resources:

Asia for Educators. (2009). The early Chinese empire: The Qin and the Han. http://afe.easia
.columbia.edu/main_pop/kpct/kp_qinhan.htm

Dull, J. L. (2016). Wudi. https://www.britannica.com/biography/Wudi-emperor-of-Han-dynasty

---

LESSON 1.6

HOW DID THE ROMAN REPUBLIC RESEMBLE A MONARCHY, AN ARISTOCRACY, AND A DEMOCRACY?

Historical Figure: Polybius

Event: Roman Republic, 509 BCE–27 BCE

Introduction: If you were a government official, which power would you choose to have: to wage war, to decide whether people are guilty of crimes, or to determine what the punishment for crimes will be? Why?

Mini-Lecture:

- The Roman Republic lasted several centuries, and its form of government evolved over that time period.

- This document was written by Polybius, a Greek historian who lived in Rome for about 15 years during the 2nd century BCE.
- In this period, Rome was a republic—it was ruled by the citizens and their representatives, and the government was divided into several parts.
- The Senate consisted of several hundred men, mostly from the patrician (aristocratic) class of noble families who inherited wealth and power.
- The consuls were two noblemen who led the Senate for periods of one year only, and who led the army.
- Ordinary citizens, called plebeians, gathered to make decisions by voting; there were several classes of citizens, some of whom (including women) could not vote.
- Slaves could not be citizens.
- The balance of power between the three groups Polybius describes broke down over time, as the ordinary citizens grew more powerful. Finally, in 27 BCE, the Roman Republic became a dictatorship ruled by one emperor.

Vocabulary:

commonwealth: country
monarchy: government by a king, queen, or royal family
aristocracy: government by a ruling class that inherits their power from their family
democracy: government by the people
assurance: certainty
denominated: be called
popular: ruled by the people
subject: have to obey someone
decree: law
office: job

transact: do
ratify: approve
expend: spend
sole: only
cognizance: knowing about
adjust: judge
censure: punish
allot: be given to
distinction: carefulness
estimation: status
deliberation: discussion
annul: cancel a law

Document: *The Histories*, Polybius, 2nd century BCE

The three kinds of government—monarchy, aristocracy and democracy—were all found united in the commonwealth of Rome. And so even was the balance between them all, and so regular the administration that resulted from their union, that it was no easy thing to determine with assurance, whether the entire state was to be estimated an aristocracy, a democracy, or a monarchy. For if they turned their view upon the power of the consuls, the government appeared to be purely monarchical and regal. If, again, the authority of the senate was considered, it then seemed to wear the form of aristocracy. And, lastly, if regard was to be had to the share which the people possessed in the administration of affairs, it could then scarcely fail to be denominated a popular state. . . .

The consuls, when they remain in Rome, before they lead out the armies into the field, are the masters of all public affairs. For all other magistrates . . .

are subject to them, and bound to obey their commands. . . . They propose also to the senate the subjects of debates; and direct all forms that are observed in making the decrees. Nor is it less a part of their office likewise, to attend to those affairs that are transacted by the people; to call together general assemblies; to report to them the resolutions of the senate; and to ratify whatever is determined by the greater number. . . . Add to this, that they have the power likewise to expend whatever sums of money they may think convenient from the public treasury. . . .

To the senate belongs, in the first place, the sole care and management of the public money. For all returns that are brought into the treasury, as well as all the payments that are issued from it, are directed by their orders. . . . To the senate also is referred the cognizance of all the crimes, committed in any part of Italy, that demand a public examination and inquiry: such as treasons, conspiracies, poisonings, and assassinations. Add to this, that when any controversies arise, either between private men, or any of the cities of Italy, it is the part of the senate to adjust all disputes; to censure those that are deserving of blame: and to yield assistance to those who stand in need of protection and defense. . . .

There is, however, a part still allotted to the people; and, indeed, the most important part. For, first, the people are the sole dispensers of rewards and punishments; which are the only bands by which states and kingdoms, and, in a word, all human societies, are held together. For when the difference between these is overlooked, or when they are distributed without due distinction, nothing but disorder can ensue. Nor is it possible, indeed, that the government should be maintained if the wicked stand in equal estimation with the good. The people, then, when any such offences demand such punishment, frequently condemn citizens to the payment of a fine. . . . To the people alone belongs the right to sentence any one to die. . . . To the people belongs the power of approving or rejecting laws and, which is still of greater importance, peace and war are likewise fixed by their deliberations. When any alliance is concluded, any war ended, or treaty made; to them the conditions are referred, and by them either annulled or ratified.

Source: Hallsall, P. (1998). Ancient history sourcebook: Polybius (c. 200–after 118 BCE):
Rome at the end of the Punic Wars.
https://sourcebooks.fordham.edu/ancient/polybius6.asp

Comprehension Check:

1. Create a poster listing the powers held by each group: the consuls, the Senate, and the people.

Activities:

1. Using your poster as a basis, illustrate or describe the possible conflicts that could come up among the three groups.

2.   Does Polybius seem biased for the Roman form of government, biased against it, or neutral toward it? Circle words and phrases in the document that support your claim.

Reflection: What improvements would you suggest to the Roman model of government, and why?

Resources:

Livius.org. (2018). Senate. https://www.livius.org/articles/concept/senate/
Livius.org. (2018). Plebs. https://www.livius.org/articles/concept/plebs/

LESSON 1.7
HOW DID SURYAVARMAN II RULE AS *DEVARAJA*?

Historical Figure: Suryavarman II

Event: Angkor Wat built, 12th century

Introduction: Do you think it is possible to respect a ruler too much? Why or why not?

Mini-Lecture:

•   Suryavarman II was king of the Khmer, or Angkor, Empire, which ruled what is now Cambodia as well as parts of Thailand and Laos, from the 9th to 14th centuries.
•   The Khmer culture blended Hinduism and Buddhism, honoring Hindu gods including Shiva and Vishnu while also following Buddhist principles.
•   Suryavarman II was an absolute monarch who declared himself *devaraja*, which means "king of the gods" or "god-king"; he was also called a "universal monarch."
•   Rulers including Suryavarman II had temples such as Angkor Wat constructed (see Figure 1.1), which featured carvings in stone called bas-reliefs.
•   A bas-relief from the Angkor Wat temple (Figure 1.2) that shows Suryavarman II sitting on a platform whose legs are carved to look like mythical "naga" dragon-snakes, surrounded by his servants and advisors.

Documents: See Figures 1.1 and 1.2

Comprehension Check:

1.   Look at what Suryavarman II is wearing in the bas-relief, and the people who surround him. List all the signs you can find that he is respected as a god.

Activities:

1.   Do you think it would have been possible for Suryavarman II and other rulers of Angkor to oversee the construction of elaborate temples filled with bas-relief carvings if they had *not* been seen as gods? Why or why not? Research other examples from history to prove your point.

Figure 1.1. Angkor Wat Temple

Source: Tørrissen, B. C. (2005). Angkor Wat, the front side of the main complex, photographed in the late afternoon. https://commons.wikimedia.org/wiki/File:Angkor_Wat.jpg

Figure 1.2. Bas-Relief of Suryavarman II, unknown artisan, 12th century

Source: Gunther, M. (2014). Suryavarman II Angkor Wat. https://commons.wikimedia.org/wiki/File:Suryavarman_II_Angkor_Wat_0869.jpg

2. Imagine a discussion between Suryavarman II and Pericles (Lesson 1.3). What advice would they have for each other on how to rule their countries? Put your answers in the form of a comic strip.

Reflection:

1. The 15th-century Italian philosopher and politician Niccolò Machiavelli said that it was better for rulers to be feared than loved. What do you think? Do you think Suryavarman II was more feared or loved by his people?

Resources:

State of Victoria. (n.d.). Angkor and the mighty Khmer empire. https://fuse.education.vic.gov .au/ResourcePackage/LandingPage?ObjectId=9864a43b-1465-4b16-b410 -4cd5e61fe1b4&SearchScope=All

---

LESSON 1.8

How Did Muawiyah I Govern His Caliphate?

Historical Figure: Muawiyah I

Event: Umayyad Caliphate, 661–750

Introduction: Do threats to a country or empire usually come from inside of it or outside of it? Give an example to support your argument.

Mini-Lecture:

- The Umayyad Caliphate was a 7th–8th-century Muslim dynasty that extended through Andalus (now Spain), and much of Mesopotamia (now Turkey, Syria, and Iraq).
- Muslims worship one god, Allah, and follow the teachings of the Quran, which was transcribed by the Prophet Muhammad in the 7th century in what is now Saudi Arabia.
- Muawiyah I founded the Umayyad Caliphate and was one of its most respected rulers.
- Córdoba was the capital of the Umayyad Caliphate; it also had a power center in Damascus, in what is now Syria.
- Our document was written by Ibn Said, a historian who wrote about Muslim history in the 12th and 13th centuries.

Vocabulary:

allegiance: loyalty
successor: ruler who comes after another ruler
person: body
retinue: group of followers

functionary: official
reverential: extremely respectful
inexorable: consistent
rigor: strictness
chastise: punish

impartiality: fairness
anxious: concerned
solicitude: caring
observance: following
learned: wise
incur: to receive
salutary: healthy
province: area within a country

contrive: try
prodigal: wasteful
extravagant: unnecessarily expensive
pomp: fanciness
ostentation: showiness
extemporize: speak or perform
petitioner: someone asking a ruler for
    something

Document: *The Book of the Maghrib,* Ibn Said, 13th century, Andalus

It was not until the arrival of the [Umayyad Caliphate] in Andalus that the fabric of Islam may be said to have rested on a solid foundation. When [Muawiyah I] had conquered the country, when every rebel had submitted to him, when all his opponents had sworn allegiance to him, and his authority had been universally acknowledged, then his importance increased, his ambition spread wider, and both he and his successors displayed the greatest magnificence in their court, and about their persons and retinue, as likewise in the number of officers and great functionaries of the state. . . . It is generally known that the strength and solidity of their empire consisted principally in the policy pursued by these princes, the magnificence and splendor with which they surrounded their court, the reverential awe with which they inspired their subjects, the inexorable rigor with which they chastised every aggression on their rights, the impartiality of their judgments, their anxious solicitude in the observance of the civil law, their regard and attention to the learned, whose opinions they respected and followed, calling them to their sittings and admitting them to their councils, and many other brilliant qualities; . . . for instance, that whenever a judge summoned the [Caliph], his son, or any of his most beloved favorites, to appear in his presence as a witness in a judicial case, whoever was the individual summoned would attend in person—if the [Caliph], out of respect for the law—and if a subject, for fear of incurring his master's displeasure.

But when this salutary awe and impartial justice had vanished, the decay of their empire began, and it was followed by a complete ruin. . . . This continued until the disastrous times of the civil war, when the surviving members of the royal family hated each other, and when those who had neither the nobility nor the qualities required to honor the [Caliphate] pretended to it and wished for it; when the governors of provinces and the generals of armies declared themselves independent and rose everywhere in their governments. . . .

As long as the dynasty of [Umayyad] occupied the throne of [Córdoba], the successors of [Muawiyah I] contrived to inspire their subjects with love of their persons, mixed with reverential awe; this they accomplished by surrounding their courts with splendor, by displaying the greatest magnificence whenever they appeared in public . . . : they continued thus until the times of the civil war, when, having lost the affections of the people, their subjects began to look with an evil eye at their prodigal expense, and the extravagant pomp with which they surrounded their persons. . . . These princes showed also great ostentation . . . ; for instance, whenever a [poet] wanted to extemporize some verses in praise of his sovereign, or any subject wished to address him on particular business, the poet or the petitioner was introduced to the presence of the [Caliph], who sat behind a curtain and spoke without showing himself, the . . . curtain drawer standing all the time by his side to communicate to the party the words or intentions of the [Caliph].

Source: Hallsall, P. (1996). Ibn Said, *Book of the Maghrib*, 13th Century. https://sourcebooks.fordham.edu/source/maghrib.asp

Comprehension Check:

1. Create a T-chart. On one side, put into your own words the good qualities Ibn Said identifies in Muawiyah; on the other side, put into your own words the bad qualities he identifies in Muawiyah's successors.

Activities:

1. Create a Venn diagram comparing Ibn Said's description of the Umayyad Caliphate under Muawiyah I with Dong Zhongshu's description of the Han Dynasty under Emperor Wu (Lesson 1.5).
2. Ibn Said wrote his history of the Umayyad Caliphate hundreds of years after it ruled. Do you find his explanation of the caliphate's fall convincing? Why or why not? What other factors could have caused the caliphate to lose power?

Reflection: Which actions that leaders take today might be criticized for being "extravagant" or "ostentatious"?

Resources:

Gardner, R. (2007). *Cities of light: The rise and fall of Islamic Spain*. [Film.] Unity Productions Foundation.

LESSON 1.9

How Did Louis XIV Create an Absolute Monarchy in France?

Historical Figure: Louis XIV

Event: Reign of Louis XIV, 1643–1715

Introduction: Is it positive or negative for all people in a country to practice the same religion? Why?

Mini-Lecture:

*   In the 17th century, France was ruled by an absolute monarchy in which kings had "divine right"; supposedly, they were chosen by God to rule and should have total power.

- King Louis XIV was Roman Catholic and felt strongly that only his religion should be practiced in France.
- Catholicism and Protestantism are both sects, or kinds, of Christianity; while they share belief in Jesus Christ as the savior of people, they differ in some ways.
- Louis XIV's grandfather, Henry IV, had created the Edict of Nantes (a city in France), a law that allowed French Protestants, known as Huguenots, to practice their religion.
- Our document is an excerpt from a law that Louis XIV passed revoking, or overturning, the Edict of Nantes.
- As a result of Louis XIV's edict, hundreds of thousands of Huguenots left France.

Vocabulary:

perpetual: forever
irrevocable: unchangeable
edict: law
revoke: overturn
null and void: not valid
exercise: practice
pretext: reason
soever: any kind
fief: piece of land given to a noble family by a king
inflict: punish
confiscation: taking away property
enjoin: force
apostolic: related to the 12 disciples of Jesus Christ
fortnight: two weeks

reside: live
exhortation: convincing people of one's opinion
on pain: with punishment
galley: prison
concession: privilege
baptize: be brought into a Christian sect in a ceremony involving water
livre: coin
express: specific
prohibition: forbidding
effect: property
enlighten: make someone understand the truth
on condition: as long as

Document: Revocation of the Edict of Nantes, Louis XIV, 1685

Be it known that . . . we have, by this present perpetual and irrevocable edict, suppressed and revoked . . . the edict of our said grandfather, given at Nantes in April, 1598, in its whole extent . . . ; we declare them null and void, . . . ; and in consequence we desire, and it is our pleasure, that all the temples of those of the said [Protestant Church] situated in our kingdom, countries, territories, and the lordships under our crown, shall be demolished without delay. . . .

   II. We forbid our subjects of the [Protestant Church] to meet any more for the exercise of the said religion in any place or private house, under any pretext whatever, . . .

   III. We likewise forbid all noblemen, of what condition soever, to hold such religious exercises in their houses or fiefs, under penalty to be inflicted upon all our said subjects who shall engage in the said exercises, of imprisonment and confiscation.

IV. We enjoin all ministers of the said [Protestant Church], who do not choose to become converts and to embrace the Catholic, apostolic, and Roman religion, to leave our kingdom and the territories subject to us within a fortnight of the publication of our present edict, without leave to reside therein beyond that period, or, during the said fortnight, to engage in any preaching, exhortation, or any other function, on pain of being sent to the galleys. . . .

VII. We forbid private schools for the instruction of children of the said [Protestant Church], and in general all things what ever which can be regarded as a concession of any kind in favor of the said religion.

VIII. As for children who may be born of persons of the said [Protestant Church], we desire that from henceforth they be baptized by the parish priests. We enjoin parents to send them to the churches for that purpose, under penalty of five hundred livres fine, to be increased as circumstances may demand; and thereafter the children shall be brought up in the Catholic, apostolic, and Roman religion, which we expressly enjoin the local magistrates to see done. . . .

X. We repeat our most express prohibition to all our subjects of the said [Protestant Church], together with their wives and children, against leaving our kingdom, lands, and territories subject to us, or transporting their goods and effects therefrom under penalty, as respects the men, of being sent to the galleys, and as respects the women, of imprisonment and confiscation. . . .

XII. . . . liberty is granted to the . . . persons of the [Protestant Church], pending the time when it shall please God to enlighten them as well as others, to remain in the cities and places of our kingdom, lands, and territories subject to us, and there to continue their commerce, and to enjoy their possessions, without being subjected to molestation or hindrance on account of the [Protestant Church], on condition of not engaging in the exercise of the said religion, or of meeting under pretext of prayers or religious services, of whatever nature these may be, under the penalties above mentioned of imprisonment and confiscation.

Source: Hallsall, P. (1998). Revocation of the Edict of Nantes, October 22, 1685.
https://sourcebooks.fordham.edu/mod/1685revocation.asp

Comprehension Check:

1. List the rights that French Protestants lost when Louis XIV revoked the Edict of Nantes.

Activities:

1. Write a response to PEN America's open letter about Jamal Khashoggi (Lesson 1.1) from Louis XIV.

2. Divide the class in half and debate this proposition: People should follow the teachings of their religion more than the laws of their country.

Reflection: What do you think you would have done if you had been a Huguenot in France when Louis XIV had revoked the Edict of Nantes? Why?

Resources:

Chateau de Versailles. (n.d.). History. http://en.chateauversailles.fr/discover/history#the-reign -of-louis%C2%A0xiv1638%C2%A0–1715

LESSON 1.10

How Did Igbo Women Command Respect in a Stateless Society?

Historical Figure: (legendary) Eze Nwanyi, Queen of Women

Event: Eze Nwanyi mask, created late 19th century

Introduction: If there were no central government, how would people decide what is acceptable and not acceptable in their society?

Mini-Lecture:

- The Igbo people have lived in what is now Nigeria for thousands of years; there are currently about 32 million Igbo people there.
- Although Nigeria is currently a democracy, many historians believe that traditional Igbo society was stateless, meaning that there was no central government.
- Instead, Igbo people relied on the wisest and most respected members of their society to negotiate about what was best for the group.
- As Igbo people get older and gain the respect of their communities, they earn titles with meanings such as "one who helps the poor," "the powerful wind," or "lady who enjoys wealth"; these titles are used to address them.
- Our document is a photo of a mask created in the late 19th century of a character whose title is Eze Nwanyi, or "Queen of Women," which is used in Igbo performances and festivals.
- The Eze Nwanyi mask was used in a festival called Otutara, which Igbo people believed united them with their ancestors.
- The Birmingham Museum of Art, which owns this mask, explains that Igbo scholar Chike Aniakor has noted that the Queen of Women's "wealth and title remind us that all are not equal, for her achievements are outside the reach of most."

Document: See Figure 1.3

Comprehension Check:

1. Look at the mask. How does it convey the power and strength of Eze Nwanyi?

Figure 1.3. Eze Nwanyi, Queen of Women Mask

Source: Birmingham Museum of Art. (2014). Queen of women mask.
https://artsbma.org/collection/queen-of-women-mask-eze-nwanyi/
Museum purchase with funds given in memory of Mrs. Dorothy Steiner

Activities:

1. If respected women earned titles in your society today, what might some of these titles be? Illustrate the titles you choose and do a gallery walk to view other students' work.
2. Create a T-chart to show what praise and criticism Eze Nwanyi might have for Sparta's form of government (Lesson 1.4).

Reflection: Would you rather live in a society where there are laws enforced by the government, or one in which the wisest and most respected people make decisions on a case-by-case basis? Why?

Resources:

Achebe, C. (1994). *Things fall apart.* Penguin Books.

Nwora, U. (2012). On Igbo titles. ChickenBones: A journal for literary and artistic African-American themes.

Udeze, C. (2018). Igbo people language, culture, tribe, religion, women, food, masks. Buzz Nigeria. https://buzznigeria.com/igbo-people/

LESSON 1.11
HOW IS INDIA'S DEMOCRACY STRUCTURED?

Historical Figure: Indira Gandhi

Event: India becomes a democracy, 1949

Introduction: Do you think it is easier to have a democracy with a large population or a small population? Why?

Mini-Lecture:

- India gained independence from British colonization in 1947 and established a democratic government in 1950.
- India was then and remains now the largest democracy in the world, with more than 1.3 billion people.
- Indira Gandhi was a politician (not related to Mahatma Gandhi, Lesson 8.8), who served as the first female Prime Minister of India from 1966 to 1977, and from 1980 to 1984.
- Gandhi was criticized for restricting democracy. After she was convicted of cheating in an election, she declared a state of emergency during which Indians' constitutional rights were suspended and she imprisoned many of her critics.
- Gandhi was assassinated by her bodyguards, who were of the Sikh religion and believed she had treated their group unfairly.
- Our document is from a speech Gandhi made in London in 1971.

Vocabulary:

encompass: include
indices: ways of measuring
futile: pointless
mere: simple
Westminster system: democracy as practiced in the United Kingdom, with a parliament of elected representatives and party leaders
literacy: knowing how to read and write
illiterate: not knowing how to read or write

vicissitudes: ups and downs
propaganda: one-sided information designed to convince people of a certain political view
divert: distract
irrelevant: not important in the current situation
sophistication: wisdom and awareness of the world
soundness: good judgment

Document: Democracy in India, 1971, Indira Gandhi

During our struggle for independence, it seemed that freedom itself would be fulfillment. But, when we achieved it we knew that every completion was a beginning. For us, this was a start of a great experiment in the creation of democracy in an ancient, complex and vast country.

The story of Indian development is not without significance for the rest of the world. How could it be otherwise when it encompasses the aspirations and struggles of over 550,000,000 human beings? Political theorists with their neatly labelled indices have sometimes spoken of democracy in India as a futile quest. To them, democracy could only be a two-party system worked by those who were educated in a particular way. Perhaps as advanced people of the West a generation ago protested that the colonial countries were not ready for freedom, so it was said that the under-developed societies of Asia and Africa were not ready for democracy, and could achieve order only under dictatorship of some kind or, at most, a controlled or guided democracy. Can democracy be guided any more than freedom? Is not a guided democracy a contradiction? . . . To us it conveyed the equality of all people to participate in every level in the development of their country and the functioning of government. . . .

Our democracy is dedicated to planned economic development, the peaceful transformation of an old social order and the uplifting of millions of people from conditions of social, economic and technological under-development. Thus, what we are attempting in India is not mere imitation of the Westminster system but a creative application of a meaningful democracy to the vastly different economic and social problems of India. . . .

Education has expanded tremendously. Today there are 2.5 million students in colleges. The number of children in schools has gone up from 23.4 million in 1951 to 83,000,000 this year. But I am sorry to say that we have not done as well as we should in our program for adult literacy. Without being able to read, a person's world is a limited one for he cannot share the knowledge and companionship that comes with books. We must do and we are doing more for primary education, for strengthening secondary education and for adult literacy programs. At the same time, I cannot agree with the common belief in the West that literacy by itself gives greater wisdom or understanding. Our people, illiterate though they may sometimes be, are the inheritors of an ancient culture of philosophy which has sustained them through the vicissitudes of their long history.

Indian voters have shown extraordinary insight and understanding of what goes on around them. If some are misled by false propaganda or diverted by irrelevant factors, their number is not larger than those of their literate—even educated—counterparts in other countries. The Indian voter knows where his interests lie and has exercised his right to vote with great political sophistication in spite of the competitive political platforms of numerous parties, even in the face of threat and violence. It is because of this basic soundness of our people that democracy has taken root in India.

Source: California State University Long Beach. (n.d.). Indira Gandhi, "Democracy in India." http://web.csulb.edu/~ssayeghc/nationalism/indiragandhi.htm

Comprehension Check:

1. According to Gandhi, how did people in the West misjudge Indian people?
2. List the strengths and weaknesses of democracy in India, according to Gandhi.

Activities:

1. Work with a partner to write out a dialogue between Gandhi and Muawiyah (Lesson 1.8) about the best way to rule a large country or empire.
2. Create a political cartoon that illustrates the contradiction between what Gandhi says here and what happened when she was ruling India.

Reflection: How do you think the people's education level affects the form of government in your country today?

Resources:

Auerbach, S. (1984). "Indira is India." *The Washington Post.* https://www.washingtonpost.com /archive/politics/1984/11/01/indira-is-india/3a5a4ea5-53d9-47e7-8a30-4f6b39b2e6f6/ ?utm_term=.86d2cc1fd639

LESSON 1.12

HOW DOES FINLAND GUARANTEE SOCIAL WELFARE TO ITS CITIZENS?

Historical Figure: Sanna Marin

Event: Finnish Constitution ratified, 2000

Introduction: As an adult, would you be willing to pay more in taxes if the government guaranteed everyone enough resources to survive, a free college education, and free health care? Why or why not?

Mini-Lecture:

- Finland is a parliamentary democracy, which means that voters choose members of Parliament, and those who are elected choose a prime minister from among themselves.
- Along with Sweden, Denmark, Iceland, and Norway, Finland uses the "Nordic Model" of economic policy, in which people pay some of the world's highest tax rates and the government provides a social welfare system in which education, health care, child care, and other benefits are provided free or at a very low cost.
- Sanna Marin became prime minister in 2019; at 34, she was the youngest PM serving at that time.
- Marin is from the Social Democratic Party, which is "center-left"; see the chart below.
- Although each country has a unique political situation, governments around the world today can be placed on a left-center-right scale; in some places, such as the United States, "left" is also known as "progressive" or "liberal"; "right" is also known as "conservative"; and "center" is also known as "moderate."

Figure 1.4. Basic 21st-Century Political Spectrum

Issues	Left	Center	Right
Leadership	Power shared among people	Balance of power between leaders and people	One powerful leader or small group of powerful leaders
Taxes	High tax rates	Medium tax rates	Low tax rates
Social welfare	Larger government with many social welfare guarantees	Medium-sized government with some social welfare guarantees	Smaller government with few social welfare guarantees
Business	Many regulations on businesses to protect workers and environment	Some regulations on businesses	Few regulations; businesses free to maximize profits
National identity	Less nationalistic and more open to immigrants	Moderately nationalistic, moderately open to immigrants	More nationalistic and less open to immigrants
Social issues	Tolerance of changing ways of life	Balance between preserving and changing ways of life	Wanting to preserve ways of life based on tradition or religion

Vocabulary:

regulations: rules or laws that governments put in place to control businesses or individuals

nationalistic: supporting one's own country or ethnic group more than others

provisions: rules

act: law

social security: having enough resources to survive

means: resources or money

indispensable: necessary

subsistence: the minimum level of food, shelter, and other survival needs

provider: someone who earns money for a household

biodiversity: variety of plant and animal life in a healthy environment

endeavor: try

Document: Constitution of Finland, 1999

16. Educational rights: Everyone has the right to basic education free of charge. Provisions on the duty to receive education are laid down by an Act. The public authorities shall, as provided in more detail by an Act, guarantee for everyone equal opportunity to receive other educational services in accordance with their ability and special needs, as well as the opportunity to develop themselves without being prevented by economic hardship. The freedom of science, the arts and higher education is guaranteed. . . .

18. The right to work and the freedom to engage in commercial activity: Everyone has the right, as provided by an Act, to earn his or her livelihood by

the employment, occupation or commercial activity of his or her choice. The public authorities shall take responsibility for the protection of the labor force. The public authorities shall promote employment and work towards guaranteeing for everyone the right to work. Provisions on the right to receive training that promotes employability are laid down by an Act. No one shall be dismissed from employment without a lawful reason.

19. The right to social security: Those who cannot obtain the means necessary for a life of dignity have the right to receive indispensable subsistence and care. Everyone shall be guaranteed by an Act the right to basic subsistence in the event of unemployment, illness, and disability and during old age as well as at the birth of a child or the loss of a provider. The public authorities shall guarantee for everyone, as provided in more detail by an Act, adequate social, health and medical services and promote the health of the population. Moreover, the public authorities shall support families and others responsible for providing for children so that they have the ability to ensure the wellbeing and personal development of the children. The public authorities shall promote the right of everyone to housing and the opportunity to arrange their own housing.

20. Responsibility for the environment: Nature and its biodiversity, the environment and the national heritage are the responsibility of everyone. The public authorities shall endeavor to guarantee for everyone the right to a healthy environment and for everyone the possibility to influence the decisions that concern their own living environment.

Source: Finlex. (n.d.). The Constitution of Finland.
https://www.finlex.fi/en/laki/kaannokset/1999/en19990731.pdf

Comprehension Check:

1. In which situations does the Finnish government promise to help people with subsistence?
2. What choices does the Finnish government promise that people can make for themselves?

Activities:

1. Work in small groups to research current challenges that "Nordic Model" countries such as Finland are currently experiencing, and how they are responding to those challenges. Report your findings to the class.
2. Where does the government of your country fall on the left-center-right political spectrum? Choose one of the issues in Figure 1.4 and work with a partner to research it; as a class, highlight the sections of the chart according to your findings.

Reflection: Where do your personal views about government fall on the political spectrum, and why?

Resources:

BBC. (2019). Finnish minister Sanna Marin, 34, to become world's youngest PM. https://
    www.bbc.com/news/world-europe-50709422
Investopedia. (2019). Nordic model. https://www.investopedia.com/terms/n/nordic-model.asp

LESSON 1.13
How Have Inuit People Practiced Egalitarianism?

Historical Figure: Sheila Watt-Cloutier

Event: Nunavut territory created, 1999

Introduction: Can you imagine a peaceful society in which each person had equal rights? What would it be like?

Mini-Lecture:

- Inuit people, sometimes called Eskimos by outsiders, are an Indigenous or First Nations people who have lived in the Arctic regions of Canada, Russia, Greenland, and the United States for thousands of years.
- Inuit culture can be called egalitarian, in that there is little social hierarchy; elders and people with special skills are respected, but all adults play a role in making decisions for the community.
- British settler-colonialists conquered Inuit territories in 1880 and declared them part of Canada.
- During the late 19th and 20th centuries, Canadian officials subjected Inuit people to various forms of oppression: they forced children to attend residential schools away from their families, forbade them to speak their native language of Inuktitut; exploited their land for natural resources; and relocated them from their homes.
- In 1999, due to the activism of Inuit leaders, an area in northwestern Canada was declared the Inuit homeland of Nunavut.
- Our document comes from a plan written by the government of Nunavut in 2018 called the Turaaqtavut.
- Sheila Watt-Cloutier is an Inuit activist who was born in Canada in 1953 and currently lives in Nunavut; she has worked as a political representative for Inuit people, and authored a book on the effects of climate change on Inuit communities.

Vocabulary:

mandate: rule
Nunavummiut: people who live in
    Nunavut

consensus: model of decisionmaking in
    which people discuss an issue until
    they can agree
Qaujimajatuqangit: traditional knowledge

Document: Turaaqtavut, 2018

Nunavut will turn 20 years old during the Fifth Assembly's mandate. . . . As we look ahead to the next 20 years, we envision Nunavummiut living with a sense of personal well-being, and in harmony with one another and our land. We respect one another and express pride in the accomplishments of our people. We respect our Elders and call upon them to help us remember the past and use it to shape our future. Twenty years from now, we envision that families, communities, government, and other organizations work in partnership to provide care and support to Nunavummiut as they age. Our youth are positive-minded and take advantage of opportunities for education, travel, and employment. There are more Inuit professionals in our communities and our public service. We function as an inclusive and balanced society in which people and communities contribute to a positive future for all. Government supports communities to build on their strengths, and enables their self-reliance.

As with other governments before us, we will be guided by eight Inuit societal values:

Inuuqatigiitsiarniq: Respecting others, relationships and caring for people.
Tunnganarniq: Fostering good spirits by being open, welcoming and inclusive.
Pijitsirniq: Serving and providing for family and/or community.
Aajiiqatigiinniq: Decision making through discussion and consensus.
Pilimmaksarniq/Pijariuqsarniq: Development of skills through observation, mentoring, practice, and effort.
Piliriqatigiinniq/Ikajuqtigiinniq: Working together for a common cause.
Qanuqtuurniq: Being innovative and resourceful.
Avatittinnik Kamatsiarniq: Respect and care for the land, animals and the environment.

We will also make government more effective and relevant through Inuit Qaujimajatuqangit and Inuit Societal Values within legislation and policy.

Nunavut is a vast territory, comprising 20 per cent of Canada's land mass. Our population is approximately 38,000, and continues to grow rapidly. More than 30 per cent of our population is under age 15 and the number of seniors has doubled since 2004. Our people and communities are widely dispersed across our land, which presents great challenges in the delivery of health and social programs and services. Food and housing are costly, and our housing stock is insufficient to meet the needs of our population. Self-reliance is the foundation of our way of life, enabled by traditional knowledge and contemporary knowledge and tools. Individuals, families, communities, and government share a responsibility to encourage and support self-reliance. We will work towards the well-being and self-reliance of our people and our communities.

Our priorities are: Valuing our Elders by listening to them, paying attention to their traditional knowledge, and meeting their needs for care in the territory; Responding to the needs of Nunavummiut for safe and affordable housing and food security; Enhancing the health care services that are available in the territory; Increasing support for community-based justice and healing programs to address family violence and sexual abuse; and Improving the outcomes of mental health, addictions, and family counselling through existing and traditional counselling systems.

Source: Nunavut Legislative Assembly. (1999). Turaaqtavut. https://gov.nu.ca/sites/default/files/eia_mandate2018_content_en_web_0.pdf

Comprehension Check:

1. How are decisions made in Inuit communities, and how is this different from a democratic "majority rules" model?
2. What special roles do elders and young people have in the Turaaqtavut?

Activities:

1. Choose one of the eight Inuit social values, and work with a small group to create a poster illustrating how you could apply this principle in your classroom.
2. In her book *The Right to Be Cold*, Sheila Watt-Cloutier wrote about how problems originating outside Inuit communities, such an environmental contamination and climate change, had affected those communities. Have one half of the class brainstorm the ways that an egalitarian community would respond to these problems, and the other class brainstorm the way communities with strong social hierarchies would respond. Then discuss which ways would be most effective, and why.

Reflection: Indigenous people who use consensus-based decisionmaking tend to have egalitarian societies. Why do you think that is?

Resources:

Pauktuutit. (2006). The Inuit way: A guide to Inuit culture. https://www.relations-inuit .chaire.ulaval.ca/sites/relations-inuit.chaire.ulaval.ca/files/InuitWay_e.pdf
Robinson, A. (2017). Sheila Watt-Cloutier. https://www.thecanadianencyclopedia.ca/en /article/sheila-watt-cloutier

Religion and Society

Unit Question: How Should Belief Systems Influence Our Lives?

In this unit, students will gain an introduction to seven of the world's major religions and belief systems: Hinduism, Confucianism, Daoism, Buddhism, Judaism, Christianity, and Islam. A sacred text from each of these traditions is excerpted, and activities encourage students to compare these beliefs. The unit begins with some quotations from scientist Albert Einstein, explaining his spiritual beliefs and agnosticism.

This unit is an important foundation for the rest of the book, because these belief systems shape so many of the social and political themes that will be covered later. I made a conscious choice to focus here on the core beliefs of each religion, rather than highlighting more controversial aspects—for instance, the caste system entwined with Hinduism, or the idea of jihad in Islam. However, such topics are covered in other units; Lesson 5.9 addresses resistance to the caste system, Lesson 4.6 covers the Crusades, and Lesson 4.11 introduces Zionism. This unit is an important way of preparing for later units and putting into context the unit of forms of government that students have already completed. Please note that demographic information in the mini-lectures comes from the Pew Research Center.

Teaching about religions evenhandedly is a challenge, because all teachers have their own beliefs, and because students and parents are likely to be sensitive to the way their own and other faiths are represented. I recommend that teachers reflect on their own biases, and also inform students, parents, and administrators in advance that the unit will be starting, so that they can anticipate any issues that might arise.

This is the only unit for which I do not recommend holding a summit. Having students represent figures such as Jesus Christ or the Prophet Muhammad is too great of a responsibility, and there is too much potential for offense. Instead, teachers might consider having students work in groups to create posters summarizing key facts and beliefs of each system, which could be displayed on the classroom walls for reference throughout the year.

This unit is also different in that the "21st-Century Issue" is actually from the 20th century—but the sense of scale is different in a unit where all the belief systems emerged more than a thousand years ago.

LESSON 2.1

WHAT WERE ALBERT EINSTEIN'S ARGUMENTS FOR AGNOSTICISM?

Historical Figure: Albert Einstein

Event: Albert Einstein develops the theory of special relativity, 1905

Introduction: Would you describe yourself as a religious person? Why or why not?

Mini-Lecture:

- Albert Einstein was a theoretical physicist who made many discoveries, including the law of special relativity ($E = mc^2$).
- He was born in Germany to a Jewish family, did academic work in Switzerland, and came to the United States as a refugee before World War II.
- Einstein's views on religion were complicated, and both religious and nonreligious people claimed that he agreed with them.
- Einstein described himself as agnostic, or someone who believes that no one can be sure about the existence or nature of God.
- Worldwide today, there are about 1.1 billion people, or 16% of the population, who, like Einstein, are not part of any organized religion; they may be atheists (not believing in God), agnostic, or may not feel that any religion represents their beliefs.
- These quotations come from an archive of Einstein's papers that was published after his death, and from a letter he wrote to Rabbi Solomon Goldman of Chicago's Anshe Emet congregation.

Vocabulary:

impute: give credit to; attribute
anthropomorphic: like a human
mysticism: belief in the supernatural
personal: like a person
alien: strange
naïve: lacking experience or wisdom
endeavor: project or effort
morality: doing the right thing
foremost: most important

myth: story that is not true but has symbolic meaning
lest: in case
legitimacy: correctness
imperil: endanger
sound: reasonable
tolerant: accepting
adherent: person who follows a religion
might: power

Document: Quotations on religion, Albert Einstein

I am a deeply religious nonbeliever. This is a somewhat new kind of religion. I have never imputed to Nature a purpose or a goal, or anything that could be understood as anthropomorphic. What I see in Nature is a magnificent structure that we can comprehend only very imperfectly, and that must fill a thinking person with a feeling of humility. This is a genuinely religious feeling that has nothing to do with mysticism. The idea of a personal God is quite alien to me and seems even naive. . . .

The most important human endeavor is the striving for morality in our actions. Our inner balance and even our very existence depend on it. Only morality in our actions can give beauty and dignity to life. To make this a living force and bring it to clear consciousness is perhaps the foremost task of education. The foundation of morality should not be made dependent on myth nor tied to any authority lest doubt about the myth or about the legitimacy of the authority imperil the foundation of sound judgment and action.

Source: Dukas, H., & Hoffman, B. (Eds.). (1981). *Albert Einstein, the human side: Glimpses from his archive.* Princeton University Press, p. 49.

Document: Letter to Rabbi Solomon Goldman

A man who is convinced of the truth of his religion is indeed never tolerant. At the least, he is to feel pity for the adherent of another religion but usually it does not stop there. The faithful adherent of a religion will try first of all to convince those that believe in another religion and usually he goes on to hatred if he is not successful. However, hatred then leads to persecution when the might of the majority is behind it.

Source: Goldman, R. N. (1996). *Einstein's god—Albert Einstein's quest as a scientist and as a Jew to replace a forsaken god.* Jason Aronson, p. 51.

Comprehension Check:

1. Did Einstein believe, like other Jewish people, that God created humans in his own image? Find a quote that supports your view.
2. According to Einstein, how do people who believe strongly in their religion treat people from different religions?

Activities:

1. As a scientist, Einstein studied the universal laws that applied to matter and energy. Highlight parts of his quotations that show how science may have influenced his religious beliefs; then compare your answers with a partner.
2. Summarize in your own words how Einstein defined being "religious." Then, with a partner, come up with several other possible definitions of being religious.

Reflection: Einstein says that teaching morality should be one of the most important jobs of education. What has your education, inside or outside of school, taught you about morality?

Resources:

Cline, A. (2019). What is agnosticism? https://www.learnreligions.com/what-is-agnosticism
   -248049

Nobel Prize Organization. (n.d.). Albert Einstein: Other resources. https://www.nobelprize
   .org/prizes/physics/1921/einstein/other-resources/

LESSON 2.2

How Is Brahman Described in the Hindu Upanishads?

Historical Figure: Maitreyi

Event: Vedic Period, c. 1500–500 BCE

Introduction: What do you know about Hinduism? Where did you learn it?

Mini-Lecture:

- Hinduism is a collection of religions and beliefs that originated in what is now India and spread throughout South and Southeast Asia.
- Currently, over 1 billion people, or 15% of the world's population, practice Hinduism.
- Hindus worship Brahman, a divine creative force that represents oneness and includes all of reality; they also believe in various gods and goddesses that are part of Brahman, including Brahma (the creator), Shiva (the destroyer), and Vishnu (the preserver).
- Hindu philosophy teaches about reincarnation (samsara), the idea that living beings have an eternal soul (atman) that is born again and again in different bodies.
- Many Hindus also believe in karma, a universal law of cause and effect in which good actions (dharma) produce good results while bad actions produce bad results.
- Many Hindus try to do dharma and gain good karma in order to be reborn in good conditions and eventually reach moksha, or enlightenment, which would free them from the cycle of rebirth and unite them with Brahman.
- Our document consists of quotations from the Upanishads, which are among the Vedas (scriptures or holy texts of Hinduism).
- The Vedas were written during the Vedic Period (c. 1500–500 BCE), in what is now India.
- Many Hindus believe that the Upanishads were inspired by gods and goddesses and written down by many different philosophers; one who participated in this process was Maitreyi, a woman who lived in what is now India in the 8th century BCE and whose ideas are recorded in other Upanishads.

Vocabulary:

arose: lived
impart: teach
sage: wise person
ungraspable: not able to be understood
origin: beginning
attribute: qualities or characteristics
eternal: existing forever
all-pervading: everywhere
subtle: difficult to understand, special
imperishable: cannot die
immutable: unchangeable
meditation: focus the mind

matter: something physical that takes up space
self-realization: understanding what the self really is
supreme: greatest
radiantly: brightly
discourse: reading and talking
intellectual: thinking
attain: get or achieve
austerities: giving up luxuries
abode: home

Document: Mundaka Upanishad, chapters 1 and 3, c. 800 BCE–500 BCE

Brahma, the creator of the universe, the protector of the world, arose before all the gods. He taught the knowledge of Brahman, which is the foundation of all knowledge, to his son Atharvan. That knowledge Atharvan imparted in ancient times to Angir. He in turn taught it to Satyawaha, son of Bharadvaja, and the son of Bharadvaja passed it on to Angiras, the science thus descending from the greater to the lesser sages. . . .

That which is invisible, ungraspable, without origin or attributes, which has neither eyes nor ears, hands nor feet; which is eternal and many-splendored, all-pervading and exceedingly subtle; that Imperishable Being is what the wise perceive everywhere as the source of creation.

As the spider sets forth and gathers in (its web), as herbs sprout upon the face of the earth, as hair grows upon the head and body of man, so, from the Immutable, springs forth the universe.

By concentrated meditation Brahman expands; from Him matter is born, from matter life, mind, truth, and immortality through works. From Brahman, the all-seeing, the all-knowing, whose energy consists of infinite wisdom, from Him is born Brahma, matter, name and form. . . .

The man of self-realization knows the supreme Brahman upon which the universe is based and shines radiantly. The wise who, free from desire, worship Brahman pass beyond the seed of rebirth. Whoever in his mind longs for the objects of desire is born again and again for their fulfillment; but one whose desire for Brahman is fully satisfied, for such a perfected soul all his desires vanish even here in this life.

Not by discourse, nor by intellectual analysis, nor through much learning can the Atman be attained. He is attained only by one whom he chooses; to such a one the Atman reveals its own form. This self cannot be attained by one without strength, nor by the careless, nor through improper austerities. But the wise who strive by all these means enter into the abode of Brahman.

Source: Singh, K. (1987). *Mundaka Upanishad: The bridge to immortality.* Bharatiya Vidya Bhavan. https://www.holybooks.com/wp-content/uploads/Mundaka-Upanishad.pdf

Comprehension Check:

1. Describe Brahman in your own words, or create a visual representation.
2. According to this text, who will attain enlightenment (moksha, also described as realization of atman or unity with Brahman), and who will not?

Activities:

1. Draw a diagram that connects the main ideas of Hinduism, including Brahman, atman, karma, dharma, samsara, and moksha.
2. Hinduism is known as a belief system that is pluralistic, or accepting of many beliefs; Hindus believe that there are many paths to enlightenment. Try to find and underline evidence or counter-evidence for this idea in the Mundaka Upanishad.

Reflection: How did what you learned about Hinduism from the Upanishads compare to what you stated in the introduction?

Resources:

Hindu American Foundation. (n.d.). Resources. https://hafsite.org/resources

Tadepalli, S. (2018). Hinduism: Misunderstood and mistaught in the classroom. Teaching Tolerance. https://www.tolerance.org/magazine/hinduism-misunderstood-and-mistaught-religion-in-the-classroom

LESSON 2.3

How Did Confucius Envision the Ideal Society?

Historical Figure: Confucius

Event: Life of Confucius, 551 BCE–479 BCE

Introduction: Do you think you should treat everyone as equal, or should you show more respect to some people than to others? Why?

Mini-Lecture:

- Confucianism is a belief system that originated in what is now China, and it has influenced many Asian societies.
- It is difficult to say how many people practice Confucianism, because it has so deeply influenced societies in China and other Asian countries.
- Confucius was a Chinese philosopher who lived in the 6th century BCE in what is now China.

- Our document is from *The Analects,* which is a collection of Confucius's sayings and conversations with others that was written down by his followers after he died; in this document, Master You and Master Zheng are two followers, and "the Master" refers to Confucius himself.
- Confucius believed that people should live in accordance with the Way, or the Dao, which is the truth and natural order of the universe.
- Filial piety is an important concept in Confucius's writing, and it describes the respect and obedience that children should have toward their parents, and that people should have toward their rulers; these relationships had clear superiors and inferiors, with older men having more status than younger people or women.
- Confucius believed that there would be harmony and stability in society if each person followed traditional rituals (*li*), carried out the duties appropriate to their role in life, and acted in a good and compassionate (*ren*) way in relation to others.
- Confucius's teachings influenced how Chinese rulers or noble people (*junzi*) understood their relationship to their subjects, and how people understood their relationships to their family members, friends, and business associates.

Vocabulary:

filial: showing respect to parents by obeying them and taking care of them

offend: do something wrong

superior: people with higher status

state: country

regulate: be careful with

expenditures: money that is spent

cleave: stay near

refinements: detailed knowledge

awe: respect

crude: uneducated

pivot: guide

err: make a mistake

align: rule

evade: escape or avoid

shame: being embarrassed to do bad things

mean: low

rank: status

merit: deserve

position: job or status

recognize: praise

urge: try to convince

incline: want to do something

bear no complaint: do not complain

Document: *Analects of Confucius,* c. 200 BCE

Master You said: It is rare to find a person who is filial to his parents and respectful of his elders, yet who likes to oppose his ruling superior. . . .

Master Zheng said: Each day I examine myself upon three points. In planning for others, have I been loyal? In company with friends, have I been trustworthy? And have I practiced what has been passed on to me?

The Master said: To guide a state great enough to possess a thousand war chariots: be attentive to affairs and trustworthy; regulate expenditures and treat persons as valuable; employ the people according to the proper season.

The Master said: A young man should be filial within his home and respectful of elders when outside, should be careful and trustworthy, broadly caring of people at large, and should cleave to those who are ren (good). If he has energy left over, he may study the refinements of culture. . . .

The Master said, "If a junzi (ruler) is not serious he will not be held in awe. If you study you will not be crude. Take loyalty and trustworthiness as the pivot and have no friends who are not like yourself in this. If you err, do not be afraid to correct yourself." . . .

The Master said, "Guide them with policies and align them with punishments and the people will evade them and have no shame. Guide them with virtue and align them with li (traditional rituals) and people will have a sense of shame and fulfill their roles." . . .

The Master said, Wealth and high rank are what people desire; if they are attained by not following the dao (the Way), do not dwell in them. Poverty and mean rank are what people hate; if they are attained by not following the dao, do not depart from them. . . .

The Master said, Do not be concerned that you have no position, be concerned that you have what it takes to merit a position. Do not be concerned that no one recognizes you, seek that which is worthy of recognition. . . .

The Master said, When one has several times urged one's parents, observe their intentions; if they are not inclined to follow your urgings, maintain respectfulness and do not disobey; labor on their behalf and bear no complaint.

Source: Eno, R. (2015). *The Analects of Confucius: An online teaching translation.* https://scholarworks.iu.edu/dspace/bitstream/handle/2022/23420/Analects_of_Confucius_%28Eno-2015%29-updated.pdf?sequence=2&isAllowed=y

Comprehension Check:

1. Describe in your own words how Confucius believes that children and parents, and rulers and subjects, should treat each other.
2. According to Confucius, what will happen if rulers punish people?

Activities:

1. Underline the parts of Dong Zhongshu's (Lesson 1.5) description of an emperor's duties that show the influence of Confucianism, compare results with a small group, and present your answers to the class.
2. Work with a partner to create a chart listing some of the advantages and disadvantages of living in Confucius's ideal society.

Reflection: How do Confucius's teachings apply to how teachers and students should treat each other in the classroom?

Resources:

Asia for Educators. (2009). Introduction to Confucian thought. http://afe.easia.columbia.edu/special/china_1000bce_confucius_intro.htm

Livaccari, C. (2010). Just who was Confucius, anyway? https://asiasociety.org/china-learning-initiatives/just-who-was-confucius-anyway

LESSON 2.4

What Did the Dao De Jing Advise People to Do?

Historical Figure: Laozi

Event: Laozi writes the Dao De Jing, c. 500 BCE

Introduction: Have you ever found that the harder you try to achieve something, the less able you are to do it, whereas when you relax your effort, you are able to do it easily? Give examples from your own life—for instance, sports or hobbies.

Mini-Lecture:

- Daoism (also spelled Taoism) is a philosophical and religious belief system that emerged in what is now China in the 4th century BCE.
- Because Daoist traditions have influenced Chinese culture so deeply, it is difficult to estimate the number of people who actively practice Daoism versus those who identify with some of its traditions.
- The Dao means the Way, or the natural order of things; Daoists try to live in harmony with this natural order.
- Laozi was a legendary Chinese philosopher who is worshipped by some followers of Daoism; historians are not sure when he lived, but it was probably between the 6th and 4th centuries BCE.
- Laozi is credited with writing the Dao De Jing (or Tao Te Ching), a sacred text of Daoism, from which our document is taken.
- Daoist "Masters" are those who are experts in living in harmony with the Dao and can teach others to do so.
- One important concept in Daoism is wu wei, "not-doing," also described as "action without action" or "action without intention"; Daoists believe that trying too hard will leave you frustrated, but acting spontaneously in accordance with the Dao is better.

Vocabulary:

overesteem: give too much respect to
turmoil: confusion
contemplate: think about
source: beginning

constant: stable and continuous
disinterested: fair, not preferring one
   outcome to another
industry: business

Document: Dao De Jing, Laozi, c. 500 BCE

> The dao that can be told is not the eternal Dao. The name that can be named is not the eternal Name. The unnamable is the eternally real. Naming is the origin of all particular things. Free from desire, you realize the mystery. Caught in desire, you see only the manifestations. Yet mystery and manifestations arise from the same source. This source is called darkness. Darkness within darkness. The gateway to all understanding.

When people see some things as beautiful, other things become ugly. When people see some things as good, other things become bad. Being and non-being create each other. Difficult and easy support each other. Long and short define each other. High and low depend on each other. Before and after follow each other. Therefore the Master acts without doing anything and teaches without saying anything. Things arise and she lets them come; things disappear and she lets them go. She has but doesn't possess, acts but doesn't expect. When her work is done, she forgets it. That is why it lasts forever.

If you overesteem great men, people become powerless. If you overvalue possessions, people begin to steal. The Master leads by emptying people's minds and filling their cores, by weakening their ambition and toughening their resolve. He helps people lose everything they know, everything they desire, and creates confusion in those who think that they know. Practice not-doing (wu-wei), and everything will fall into place. . . .

Empty your mind of all thoughts. Let your heart be at peace. Watch the turmoil of beings, but contemplate their return. Each separate being in the universe returns to the common source. Returning to the source is serenity. If you don't realize the source, you stumble in confusion and sorrow. When you realize where you come from, you naturally become tolerant, disinterested, amused, kindhearted as a grandmother, dignified as a king. Immersed in the wonder of the Dao, you can deal with whatever life brings you, and when death comes, you are ready. . . .

Throw away holiness and wisdom, and people will be a hundred times happier. Throw away morality and justice, and people will do the right thing. Throw away industry and profit, and there won't be any thieves.

Source: Mitchell, S. (Trans.). (1988). Tao te ching.
https://terebess.hu/english/tao/mitchell.html

Comprehension Check:

1. Go through the text and highlight the parts that are most difficult for you to understand. Then switch with a partner. They may be able to explain some parts you don't understand, and vice versa.

Activities:

1. Create a Daoist advice column. Write a letter about a problem or difficulty you or a friend are having. Switch with a partner, and then write the advice that you think Laozi would give on how to deal with that problem. Quote the Dao De Jing to support your answer.
2. Laozi and Confucius (Lesson 2.3) both use the term "the Way," or the Dao, but do they mean the same thing? Write down a dialogue between them about how to live in harmony with the Dao.

Reflection: The yin yang symbol ☯ is often used to represent Daoism. Based on the document you read, why do you think that is?

Resources:

Littlejohn, R. (n.d.). Daoist philosophy. https://www.iep.utm.edu/daoism/

Duignan, B. (n.d.). What is the difference between Daoism and Confucianism? Encyclopedia Britannica. https://www.britannica.com/story/what-is-the-difference-between-daoism -and-confucianism

---

LESSON 2.5

WHAT DID THE BUDDHA TEACH WAS THE PATH TO ENLIGHTENMENT?

Historical Figure: Siddhartha Gautama

Event: Siddhartha Gautama reaches enlightenment, 5th century BCE

Introduction: Do you think life includes more pain and suffering, or more pleasure and happiness? Give examples.

Mini-Lecture:

- Buddhism is a spiritual tradition that originated in what is now South Asia in the 6th century BCE, and currently there are about 488 million Buddhists worldwide, making up 7% of the world's population.
- Siddhartha Gautama was a prince who was born in what is now Nepal in the 6th century BCE; he is often referred to as "the Buddha," the "Blessed One," or the "Tathagata," meaning one who has truly gone (to enlightenment).
- Buddhists share many beliefs with Hindus, including in reincarnation and karma; they call enlightenment Nibbana (or Nirvana), and they use the dharma to refer both to the way the world works and to the Buddha's teachings.
- Our document is from a *sutta*, or holy text, in which the Buddha's followers passed on his teachings; it is called "Setting in Motion the Wheel of the Dharma," because the Buddha shared these teachings so that people could become enlightened themselves.
- In the document, the Buddha is talking to a group of bhikkus, or monks, who have "gone forth into homelessness," giving up their possessions and surviving off "alms," or food that people donate to them.
- Before becoming enlightened, the Buddha lived first as a prince who had a luxurious life and then as an ascetic, or a person who gives up pleasures (tasty food, nice clothing, and comfortable houses) for spiritual reasons.
- In this document, the Buddha explains the Four Noble Truths, which cover the causes of suffering and how to end it, and then describes the Noble Eightfold Path (the way to achieve enlightenment).

Vocabulary:

dwelling: living

sensual: physical, having to do with the five senses

vulgar: gross

ignoble: not a good way to live

unbeneficial: not good

self-mortification: punishing or not taking care of the body

craving: wanting something very much

disbecoming: death

cessation: end

remainderless: with nothing left over

relinquishing: giving up

eightfold: having eight parts

Document: Setting in motion the wheel of the dharma, 1st century BCE

Thus have I heard. On one occasion the Blessed One [the Buddha] was dwelling at Baranasi in the Deer Park at Isipatana. There the Blessed One addressed the bhikkhus of the group of five thus:

"Bhikkhus, these two extremes should not be followed by one who has gone forth into homelessness. What two? The pursuit of sensual happiness in sensual pleasures, which is low, vulgar, the way of worldlings, ignoble, unbeneficial; and the pursuit of self-mortification, which is painful, ignoble, unbeneficial. Without veering towards either of these extremes, the Tathagata [Buddha] has awakened to the middle way, which gives rise to vision, which gives rise to knowledge, which leads to peace, to direct knowledge, to enlightenment, to Nibbana.

"And what, bhikkhus, is that middle way awakened to by the Tathagata, which gives rise to vision . . . which leads to Nibbana? It is this noble eightfold path; that is, right view, right intention, right speech, right action, right livelihood, right effort, right mindfulness, right concentration. This, bhikkhus, is that middle way awakened to by the Tathagata, which gives rise to vision, which gives rise to knowledge, which leads to peace, to direct knowledge, to enlightenment, to Nibbana.

"Now this, bhikkhus, is the noble truth of suffering: birth is suffering, aging is suffering, illness is suffering, death is suffering; union with what is displeasing is suffering; separation from what is pleasing is suffering; not to get what one wants is suffering. . . .

"Now this, bhikkhus, is the noble truth of the origin of suffering: it is this craving which leads to re-becoming [reincarnation], accompanied by delight and lust, seeking delight here and there; that is, craving for sensual pleasures, craving for becoming, craving for disbecoming.

"Now this, bhikkhus, is the noble truth of the cessation of suffering: it is the remainderless fading away and cessation of that same craving, the giving up and relinquishing of it, freedom from it, non-reliance on it.

"Now this, bhikkhus, is the noble truth of the way leading to the cessation of suffering: it is this noble eightfold path . . ."

Source: Bodhi, B. (Trans.). (n.d.). Setting in motion the wheel of the dhamma. BuddhaSasana. https://www.budsas.org/ebud/ebsut001.htm

Comprehension Check:

1. The Buddha describes a "middle way" between what two extremes?
2. Match the parts of the Noble Eightfold Path with the descriptions that seem to make the most sense (the answers are not in the document).

Right View	Not telling lies, using harsh words, gossiping, or chatting pointlessly
Right Intention	Focused concentration during meditation
Right Speech	Making an effort to do what makes you have positive emotions, and not do what makes you have negative emotions
Right Action	Being mindful of the body, feelings, the mind, and what is happening in the mind
Right Livelihood	Avoiding jobs that require that you hurt or kill any living being
Right Effort	Understanding that the Four Noble Truths are correct and the Eightfold Path is the way to Nibbana
Right Mindfulness	Having the intention not to hate or harm any living being
Right Concentration	Not harming any living beings, stealing, or engaging in sexual misconduct

Activities:

1. Make a T-chart of things that you want and don't want. Now imagine a "middle way" in which you felt okay whether you got or didn't get these things. Do you think you would be happier on this "middle way" or happier if you got all the things you wanted and avoided all the things you didn't want? Discuss with a partner.
2. Create a Venn diagram that shows the similarities and differences between Buddhism and Hinduism (Lesson 2.2).

Reflection: Which part of the Eightfold Noble Path do you think would be most difficult to follow, and why?

Resources:

Rahula, W. S. (n.d.). The noble eightfold path. *Tricycle*. https://tricycle.org/magazine/noble-eightfold-path/

Vail, L. F. (n.d.). The origins of Buddhism. https://asiasociety.org/education/origins-buddhism

LESSON 2.6
WHAT DID GOD COMMAND JEWISH PEOPLE TO DO IN THE TORAH?

Historical Figure: Moses

Event: The Torah says the Lord gave Ten Commandments to Moses, c. 1200 BCE

Introduction: What is the most important promise you have ever made, or that someone else has ever made to you? Why was it so important to you?

Mini-Lecture:

- Judaism is a religion that historians believe originated in what is now Israel and Palestine in the second millennium BCE.
- There are about 14 million Jewish people today, making up less than 1% of the world's population.
- Judaism is monotheistic, meaning that Jewish people believe in one God.
- Jewish people also believe that certain prophets, such as Abraham, Moses, and Miriam, communicated directly with the Lord and passed on his messages to them; they also believe they are "from the house of," or descended from, Jacob.
- Our document comes from the Jewish holy book, the Torah, or Hebrew Bible; in this section, Shemot, or Exodus, God had just guided the Jewish people out of Egypt, where they had been enslaved, and he gives them his Ten Commandments via Moses.
- Jewish people believe that the Torah is the word of God; some scholars believe that it was written down between 1200 and 165 BCE.

Vocabulary:

ascended: went up
bore: carried
covenant: promise or agreement
bondage: slavery
graven: carved
prostrate: bow down
zealous: energetic
iniquity: unethical behavior; sin
in vain: without proper respect
sanctify: make holy

sabbath: day of rest traditionally celebrated by Jewish people between sundown Friday and sundown Saturday
adultery: when a married person has a romantic relationship with someone other than their spouse
false witness: lying about what someone else did
covet: be jealous of something that belongs to someone else

Document: Shemot-Exodus chapters 19–20, The Torah, c. 1200 BCE

Moses ascended to God, and the Lord called to him from the mountain, saying, "So shall you say to the house of Jacob and tell the sons of Israel, You have seen what I did to the Egyptians, and [how] I bore you on eagles' wings, and I brought you to Me. And now, if you obey Me and keep My covenant, you shall be to Me a treasure out of all peoples, for Mine is the entire earth. And you shall be to Me a kingdom of princes and a holy nation." . . .

The Lord descended upon Mount Sinai, to the peak of the mountain, and the Lord summoned Moses to the peak of the mountain, and Moses ascended. . . .

God spoke all these words, to respond: "I am the Lord, your God, Who took you out of the land of Egypt, out of the house of bondage. You shall not have the gods of others in My presence. You shall not make for yourself a graven image or any likeness which is in the heavens above, which is on the earth below, or which is in the water beneath the earth. You shall neither prostrate yourself before them nor worship them, for I, the Lord, your God, am a zealous God, Who visits the iniquity of the fathers upon the sons, upon the third and the fourth generation of those who hate Me, and [I] perform loving kindness to thousands [of generations], to those who love Me and to those who keep My commandments. You shall not take the name of the Lord, your God, in vain, for the Lord will not hold blameless anyone who takes his name in vain. Remember the Sabbath day to sanctify it. Six days may you work and perform all your labor, but the seventh day is a Sabbath to the Lord, your God; you shall perform no labor, neither you, your son, your daughter, your manservant, your maidservant, your beast, nor your stranger who is in your cities. For [in] six days the Lord made the heaven and the earth, the sea and all that is in them, and He rested on the seventh day. Therefore, the Lord blessed the Sabbath day and sanctified it. Honor your father and your mother, in order that your days be lengthened on the land that the Lord, your God, is giving you. You shall not murder. You shall not commit adultery. You shall not steal. You shall not bear false witness against your neighbor. You shall not covet your neighbor's house. You shall not covet your neighbor's wife, his manservant, his maidservant, his ox, his donkey, or whatever belongs to your neighbor.

Source: Chabad.org. (2019). Shemot-Exodus-Chapter 19.
https://www.chabad.org/library/bible_cdo/aid/9880/jewish/Chapter-19.htm

Comprehension Check:

1. What did God promise to the Jewish people, and what are they supposed to do in return?
2. Put each of the Ten Commandments into your own words.

Activities:

1. Write down what you think Albert Einstein's (Lesson 2.1) response would be to the Ten Commandments. Cite evidence from his writings to support your points.
2. Create a Venn diagram comparing and contrasting the Eightfold Path (Lesson 2.5) with the Ten Commandments.

Reflection: How do you think the Jewish people's covenant with God might have affected their relationship with people from other religious groups? Why?

Resources:

Rabinovici, R. (n.d.). Jewish timeline: A brief history of the Jewish people on one page. http://www.odyeda.com/en/#more

WNET. (2014). The story of the Jews with Simon Schama. [Motion Picture] https://www.pbs .org/wnet/story-jews/

LESSON 2.7

WHAT DID JESUS COMMAND CHRISTIANS TO DO IN THE HOLY BIBLE?

Historical Figure: Jesus Christ

Event: Jesus's Sermon on the Mount, 1st century CE

Introduction: Do you think it is worse, better, or the same to think about doing something bad, or to actually do it? Why?

Mini-Lecture:

- Christianity is a religion that originated in what is now Israel and Palestine in the 1st century CE.
- Currently, there are more than 2 billion Christians worldwide, making up about 31% of the population; more people follow Christianity than any other religion.
- Christians, like Jewish people, are monotheistic, and they share some beliefs, such as following the Ten Commandments; both groups regard the Old Testament or Torah as a holy book.
- In Christianity, God is considered as having three unified parts, called the Holy Trinity: God the Father, Jesus (God's son), and the Holy Spirit.
- Historians believe that Jesus was born in what is now Palestine in the 1st century CE; his family was Jewish, but his teachings gave rise to Christianity.
- Christians believe that worshipping Jesus Christ is the only path to salvation, or being saved from Hell.
- Our document is from the Sermon on the Mount, a speech Jesus makes in the Gospel of Matthew in the New Testament, a part of the Bible that describes Jesus's life.

Vocabulary:

disciple: follower
abolish: get rid of
gouge: dig out
persecute: treat someone badly

hypocrite: someone who says one thing but does the opposite
synagogue: Jewish place of worship

Document: Sermon on the Mount, Matthew 5–7, The Holy Bible

Now when Jesus saw the crowds, he went up on a mountainside and sat down. His disciples came to him, and he began to teach them. . . . He said: . . .

"You are the light of the world. A town built on a hill cannot be hidden. Neither do people light a lamp and put it under a bowl. Instead they put it on its stand, and it gives light to everyone in the house. In the same way, let your light shine before others, that they may see your good deeds and glorify your Father in heaven. . . .

"Do not think that I have come to abolish the Law or the Prophets; I have not come to abolish them but to fulfill them. For truly I tell you, until heaven and earth disappear, not the smallest letter, not the least stroke of a pen, will by any means disappear from the Law until everything is accomplished. . . .

"You have heard that it was said, 'You shall not commit adultery.' But I tell you that anyone who looks at a woman lustfully has already committed adultery with her in his heart. If your right eye causes you to stumble, gouge it out and throw it away. It is better for you to lose one part of your body than for your whole body to be thrown into hell. . . .

"You have heard that it was said, 'Eye for eye, and tooth for tooth.' But I tell you, do not resist an evil person. If anyone slaps you on the right cheek, turn to them the other cheek also. And if anyone wants to sue you and take your shirt, hand over your coat as well. . . .

"You have heard that it was said, 'Love your neighbor and hate your enemy.' But I tell you, love your enemies and pray for those who persecute you, that you may be children of your Father in heaven. He causes his sun to rise on the evil and the good, and sends rain on the righteous and the unrighteous. . . .

"So when you give to the needy, do not announce it with trumpets, as the hypocrites do in the synagogues and on the streets, to be honored by others. Truly I tell you, they have received their reward in full. But when you give to the needy, do not let your left hand know what your right hand is doing, so that your giving may be in secret. Then your Father, who sees what is done in secret, will reward you.

Source: THE HOLY BIBLE, NEW INTERNATIONAL VERSION®, NIV® Copyright © 1973, 1978, 1984, 2011 by Biblica, Inc.™ Used by permission. All rights reserved worldwide.

Comprehension Check:

1. What "Law," and which "Prophets," is Jesus referring to?
2. Put in your own words how Jesus thinks people should treat: a) their enemies; b) their neighbors; c) the needy; and d) themselves.

Activities:

1. Jesus disagrees with the concept of "an eye for an eye," but what would he say about the rest of Hammurabi's laws (Lesson 1.2)? Choose three of those laws, and explain how Jesus would revise them.
2. Jesus says that Christians should "let their light shine before others" so that they will "glorify your Father in Heaven." With a small group, look back at one of the previous lessons in this unit. Find evidence for whether that religion or belief system encourages followers to spread the message or convert others, then share your findings with the class.

Reflection: You have now studied several religions and belief systems, some of which are likely more familiar to you than others. How does it feel different to study familiar and unfamiliar traditions?

Resources:

History.com. (2019). The Bible. https://www.history.com/topics/religion/bible
ReQuest. (n.d.). The Messiah. http://request.org.uk/life/the-messiah/

LESSON 2.8

WHAT DID ALLAH COMMAND MUSLIMS TO DO IN THE HOLY QURAN?

Historical Figure: The Prophet Muhammad

Event: The Quran states that Allah revealed the Holy Quran to the Prophet
Muhammad, c. 610–632 CE

Introduction: What are the similarities and differences that you know of among
Islam, Christianity, and Judaism?

Mini-Lecture:

- Islam is a religion that originated in what is now Saudi Arabia in the 7th century
  CE.
- Currently there are about 1.6 billion Muslims worldwide, making up about 23%
  of the population.
- Muslims share some beliefs with Jewish people and Christians, including belief in
  one God (whom Muslims call Allah) and in some of the events described in the
  Torah and the New Testament.
- Like Christians and Jews, Muslims believe in the Hereafter, or life after death, in
  which people go to Heaven to or Hell based on their beliefs and deeds; and in a
  Day of Resurrection, or final judgment by God.
- Muslims also believe that Allah revealed a holy book called the Quran, via the
  Archangel Gabriel, to the Prophet Muhammad in the 7th century CE; it is from
  this book that our document is taken.
- Muhammad was a merchant living in what is now Saudi Arabia before taking on
  the role of a prophet in Islam.

Vocabulary:

gracious: forgiving	*bestow:* give
torment: suffering	*scripture:* holy texts
piety: respecting god	*devout:* worshipping God
sustenance: food	*grieve:* be sad

Document: The Holy Quran, 7th century CE

> In the name of God, the Gracious, the Merciful. . . . This is the Book in which
> there is no doubt, a guide for the righteous. Those who believe in the unseen,
> and perform the prayers, and give from what We have provided for them. And
> those who believe in what was revealed to you, and in what was revealed before

you, and are certain of the Hereafter. These are upon guidance from their Lord. These are the successful. As for those who disbelieve—it is the same for them, whether you have warned them, or have not warned them—they do not believe. God has set a seal on their hearts and on their hearing, and over their vision is a veil. They will have a severe torment. . . .

O people! Worship your Lord who created you and those before you, that you may attain piety. He who made the earth a habitat for you, and the sky a structure, and sends water down from the sky, and brings out fruits thereby, as a sustenance for you. Therefore, do not assign rivals to God while you know. . . .

O Children of Israel! Remember My blessings which I bestowed upon you, and fulfill your pledge to Me, and I will fulfill My pledge to you, and fear Me. And believe in what I revealed, confirming what is with you; and do not be the first to deny it; and do not exchange My revelations for a small price; and be conscious of Me. And do not mix truth with falsehood, and do not conceal the truth while you know. And attend to your prayers, and practice regular charity, and kneel with those who kneel. Do you command people to virtuous conduct, and forget yourselves, even though you read the Scripture? Do you not understand? And seek help through patience and prayer. But it is difficult, except for the devout. Those who know that they will meet their Lord, and that to Him they will return. O Children of Israel! Remember My favor which I bestowed upon you, and that I favored you over all nations. . . .

We gave Moses the Scripture, and sent a succession of messengers after him. And We gave Jesus son of Mary the clear proofs, and We supported him with the Holy Spirit. . . .

And they say, "None will enter Heaven unless he is a Jew or a Christian." These are their wishes. Say, "Produce your proof, if you are truthful." In fact, whoever submits himself to God, and is a doer of good, will have his reward with his Lord—they have nothing to fear, nor shall they grieve. The Jews say, "The Christians are not based on anything"; and the Christians say, "The Jews are not based on anything." Yet they both read the Scripture. Similarly, the ignorant said the same thing. God will judge between them on the Day of Resurrection regarding their differences.

Source: Itani, T. (Trans.). (2012). Quran. https://www.clearquran.com/002.html

Comprehension Check:

1. According to the Quran, what is the most important thing a person has to do in order to be rewarded in the Hereafter?
2. According to the Quran, why should people worship Allah?

Activities:

1. What are the similarities and differences among Jews (Lesson 2.6), Christians (Lesson 2.7), and Muslims? Make a three-circle Venn diagram.

2. The Quran brings up the issue of how different religious groups view each other. Look back at Albert Einstein's comments (Lesson 2.1). Divide the class in half and debate Einstein's proposition, citing evidence from this unit: People who truly believe in their religions are not tolerant of those who have different beliefs.

Reflection: What new insights did you gain into the similarities and differences among Judaism, Christianity, and Islam?

Resources:

History.com. (n.d.). Islam. https://www.history.com/topics/religion/islam
Islamic Networks Group. (n.d.). Getting to know American Muslims and their faith. https://ing.org/getting-to-know-american-muslims-and-their-faith/

Us vs. Them

Unit Question: Who Is Civilized, and Who Is a Barbarian?

This unit allows students to explore ideas of civilization and barbarism by observing how these terms have been used across time and place. The unit begins with François Hollande's response to ISIS's grim vision of a civilization in which anyone who does not practice its extremist Salafi-jihadist form of Islam deserves to be killed. It is crucial to emphasize how far ISIS deviates from the vast majority of Muslims' beliefs. Nonetheless, some teachers may wish to replace this topic with a different 21st-Century Issue if their own or students' sensitivities to it are high.

The unit continues with an idea of civilization that is widely accepted in world history textbooks, which names urban centers in Mesopotamia as innovators of written language, political development, and socioeconomic stratification. We move on to classical ideas of civilization as expressed in Plutarch's praise of Alexander the Great's expansionist empire, which raises the question of what the "barbarian" Visigoths in Rome did differently. Gomes de Zurara's justification of Henry the Navigator's enslavement of African people helps students understand how ideas of race became linked to the concept of civilization. An Austrian diplomat's account of the Ottoman Empire may contradict students' expectations in its praise of Suleiman the Magnificent, while King Fernando's declaration to Indigenous peoples of South America is a sobering reminder of "civilization's" dark side. The Qianlong emperor's attempt to protect his people from European "barbarians" may broaden students' understanding of Qing Dynasty civilization. Moving into the Enlightenment, Immanuel Kant asks students in surprisingly accessible terms to question the foundations of civilization, while Jules Ferry's explanation of France's "civilizing mission" adds dimension to King Fernando's stark proclamation. The merging of modernity and tradition in the Meiji Constitution provides a fascinating example of how civilizations evolve. The last two documents, Hitler's Obersalzberg speech and the Universal Declaration of Human Rights, provide opposing views that show students how the ideas of civilization made their way into the 20th century.

Some documents in this unit, especially the Requerimiento, can be difficult to teach because of the way that religion is invoked and, many would argue, warped for political and military aims. Additionally, some students may develop a bit of intellectual vertigo as their conceptions of civilization as a "good thing" are called into question. They may want to hold on to this idea of "goodness" in Kant's Enlightenment, in the UDHR, or even in the traditional six-fold definition of civilization. Others may start to see a barbaric aspect to the very idea of separating "us" from "them." Either way, this unit can help students develop a more critical understanding of "civilized" societies.

LESSON 3.1

How Did François Hollande React to ISIS's Attack on France?

Historical Figure: François Hollande

Event: ISIS attacks in Paris, 2015

Introduction: How do you think terrorists justify killing and injuring people?

Mini-Lecture:

- The Islamic State of Iraq and Syria (ISIS), also known as the Islamic State of Iraq and the Levant (ISIL), and as Daesh, is a terrorist organization that has carried out attacks worldwide.
- ISIS views anyone who is not Muslim, as well as any Muslim who does not follow their extremist Salafi-jihadist form of Islam, as enemies; and it seeks to establish a caliphate, or state that follows its version of Islam, that covers the entire world.
- Radical terrorist groups like ISIS are a tiny minority of Muslims who do not represent the beliefs of the religion as a whole.
- On November 13, 2015, attackers representing ISIS killed 130 people in mass shootings and suicide bombings in Paris; they targeted a soccer stadium called the Stade de France, a music venue, and restaurants.
- François Hollande was the president of France from 2012 to 2017, during the attacks.
- Our document comes from a speech that President Hollande made to the French parliament shortly after the attacks.

Vocabulary:

staunch: strong
territorial base: land that is controlled
disfigure: damage

rule of law: a society where people follow rules
eradicate: destroy

Document: Speech by the President of the Republic to a Joint Session of Parliament, François Hollande, 2015

France is at war. The acts committed in Paris and near the Stade de France on Friday evening are acts of war. They left at least 129 dead and many injured.

They are an act of aggression against our country, against its values, against its young people, and against its way of life.

They were carried out by a jihadist army, by Daesh, which is fighting us because France is a country of freedom, because we are the birthplace of human rights. . . .

The French people are a staunch, tough, creative people. They do not resign themselves, and when one of their children is thrown down, they rise up.

Those who wanted to destroy them by deliberately targeting innocents are cowards who fired on an unarmed crowd. It cannot be said that we are engaged in a war of civilizations, for these assassins do not represent one. We are in a war against jihadist terrorism that threatens the entire world, not just France. . . .

On Friday, the terrorists' target was France as a whole. France, which values life, culture, sports, celebrations. France, which makes no distinction as to color, origin, background, religion. The France that the assassins wanted to kill was that of its young people in all their diversity. . . .

We are facing an organization, Daesh, which has a territorial base, financial resources, and military capabilities. Since the beginning of the year, Daesh's terrorist army has struck in Paris, Denmark, Tunisia, Egypt, Lebanon, Kuwait, Saudi Arabia, Turkey, and Libya. Every day, it massacres and oppresses populations.

That is why the need to destroy Daesh concerns the whole international community. I have therefore asked the Council of Security [of the United Nations] to meet as soon as possible to adopt a resolution expressing our common will to combat terrorism. Meanwhile, France will step up its operations in Syria. . . .

In my determination to combat terrorism, I want France to remain itself. The barbarians attacking it want to disfigure it. They will not succeed. . . . They will never succeed in destroying the French soul. They will never prevent us from living, from living the way we want to, freely and fully, and we must demonstrate that with cool heads. And I'm thinking of the young people. I am thinking of those who feel wounded through all these victims and are wondering whether they can still live in a state governed by the rule of law. . . .

We will eradicate terrorism because the French want to continue to live together without fearing anything from their neighbors. We will eradicate terrorism because we are attached to freedom and to raising France's profile around the world. We will eradicate terrorism so that the movement of people and the mixing of cultures can continue and so that human civilization is enriched. We will eradicate terrorism so that France can continue to lead the way. Terrorism will not destroy France because France will destroy it. . . .

Source: French Ministry of Foreign Affairs. (n. d.) Speech by the President of the Republic to a joint session of Parliament. https://www.diplomatie.gouv.fr/en/french-foreign-policy/security-disarmament-and-non-proliferation/news/news-about-defence-and-security/article/speech-by-the-president-of-the-republic-before-a-joint-session-of-parliament

Comprehension Check:

1. According to Hollande, why did Daesh attack France?
2. According to Hollande, why does the whole world need to be concerned about Daesh?

Activities:

1. Highlight the places in the speech where Hollande uses the terms "civilization" and "barbarian." For each one, create a mind map or visual representation of what he means.
2. Discuss the following question with a classmate; then share your answers with the whole class: How could a "civilized" society fight a "barbaric" enemy without becoming barbaric itself?

Reflection: ISIS wrote a statement explaining its reasons for carrying out the attack (see Resources). Is it valuable for students to read statements like that, or does it just give the terrorists the publicity they want? Why?

Resources:

Ray, M. (2019, November 6). Paris attacks of 2015. Encyclopedia Britannica. https://www .britannica.com/event/Paris-attacks-of-2015

Site Intelligence Group Enterprise. (2015). IS claims Paris attacks. https://ent.siteintelgroup .com/Statements/is-claims-paris-attacks-warns-operation-is-first-of-the-storm.html

Stern, J. (2019, October 27). The world is fighting more than ISIS. *The New York Times*. https://www.nytimes.com/2019/10/27/opinion/isis-al-baghdadi-dead.html

---

LESSON 3.2

How Was Sumerian Civilization Different From What Came Before It?

Historical Figure: Gilgamesh

Event: Sumerian civilization, c. 4300–1500 BCE

Introduction: How do you think people remembered and kept track of things before writing was invented?

Mini-Lecture:

• Cuneiform writing was first developed in the early fourth millennium BCE in Sumeria, in what is now Iraq.
• Cuneiform writing was created by pressing a stylus into a soft clay tablet before baking the tablets; at first, pictographs were used, but eventually an alphabet was developed.
• Cuneiform writing was often used to record economic information such as debts, taxes, and interest payments.

- Some historians define "civilization" as societies that have 1) cities, 2) art and architecture, 3) written language, 4) a system of government and laws, 5) division of labor and social hierarchy, and 6) religion. By this definition, Sumeria may have been the first civilization.
- Many historians believe that Gilgamesh was a priest-king of the Sumerian city-state of Uruk sometime between 2800 and 2500 BCE; the hero in *The Epic of Gilgamesh*, written in the second millennium BCE, seems to have been based on him.
- Historians believe that the cuneiform writing on the tablet in Figure 3.1 documents the distribution of barley by a temple, while the circles represent numbers; the seal impression underneath shows a priest-king who is using dogs to hunt wild boars.
- The cuneiform writing on the tablet in Figure 3.2 states that two men owe six minas (coins) of silver to the merchant Ashur-idi; one-third of the loan must be paid by the next harvest and the rest at a later date, after which monthly interest will accrue. Two witnesses signed the tablet.

Document: Cuneiform tablets, c. 3000 BCE; see Figures 3.1 and 3.2

Comprehension Check:

1. In Figure 3.1, what symbol could represent barley, and how many times does it appear?
2. Based on the description of Figure 3.2, what social classes of people used cuneiform writing?

Figure 3.1. Proto-Cuneiform Tablet with Seals and Impressions, c. 3100–2900 BCE

Source: Metropolitan Museum of Art. (n.d.).
Proto-Cuneiform tablet with seals and impressions.
https://www.metmuseum.org/art/collection/search/329081
Raymond and Beverly Sackler Gift, 1988

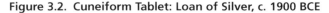

Figure 3.2. Cuneiform Tablet: Loan of Silver, c. 1900 BCE

Source: Metropolitan Museum of Art. (n.d.). Cuneiform tablet: Loan of silver.
https://www.metmuseum.org/art/collection/search/325858
Gift of Mr. and Mrs. J. J. Keljman, 1966

Activities:

1. Work with a partner to evaluate and revise the definition of "civilization" in the Mini-Lecture. What would you add or take away from the six characteristics of civilization listed above? Put your answers on a poster to present to the class.
2. Divide the class in half and debate the following proposition: The development of writing led to the formation of different social and economic classes. Use evidence from the tablets.

Reflection: In what contexts do you hear people using the word "civilized" today?

Resources:

Mark, J. J. (2018). Cuneiform. Ancient History Encyclopedia. https://www.ancient.eu /cuneiform/
National Geographic. (2018). Key components of civilization. https://www .nationalgeographic.org/article/key-components-civilization/

LESSON 3.3

HOW DID ALEXANDER THE GREAT TRY TO CIVILIZE THE WORLD?

Historical Figure: Alexander the Great

Event: Alexander the Great's reign, 336–323 BCE

Introduction: What is the opposite of civilization? How would "uncivilized" people behave?

Mini-Lecture:

- Alexander the Great was the ruler of a Greek (or Grecian) kingdom called Macedonia; in the 4th century BCE, he expanded it into one of the largest empires in the world, stretching all the way to what is now India.
- Ancient Greeks defined "barbarians" as anyone who could not speak Greek.
- Alexander took power at 20 years old, after the death of his father, King Philip.
- At that time, people in some parts of his kingdom, such as the Triballians and Thebans, were rebelling against his rule in order to get independence from his empire.
- Our document is a history of Alexander's life written by the Greek historian Plutarch in the 1st century CE.

Vocabulary:

succeeded: took the throne of, became the ruler of
beset: surrounded
rancorous: hateful
barbarous: uncivilized
impatient of: unwilling to be
sufficient: enough
sway: rule
critical: important
subjection: under the power of a ruler
allegiance: loyalty
designing: planning
indulgence: patience and understanding
arresting: stopping
counsel: advice
timorous: cowardly
prudence: wisdom

resolution: firmness
magnanimity: generosity
in correspondence with: supporting
repentance: being sorry
author: planner
retorted: responded
extremities: most violent parts
garrison: army
sallied out: advanced
hemmed in: trapped
sacked: destroyed, all valuable things stolen
razed: buildings knocked down
gratify: make happy
confederates: allies
heretofore: before
put to the sword: killed

Document: On Alexander, Plutarch, 90 CE

Alexander was but twenty years old when his father was murdered, and succeeded to a kingdom beset on all sides with great dangers, and rancorous enemies. For not only the barbarous nations that bordered on Macedonia, were impatient of being governed by any but their own native princes; but Philip likewise, though he had been victorious over the Grecians, yet, as the time had not been sufficient for him to complete his conquest and accustom them to his sway, had simply left all things in a general disorder and confusion. It seemed to the Macedonians a very critical time; and some would have persuaded Alexander to give up all thought of retaining the Grecians in subjection by force of arms, and rather to apply himself to win back by gentle means the allegiance of the tribes who were designing revolt, and try the effect of indulgence in arresting the first motions towards revolution. But he rejected this counsel as weak and timorous, and looked upon it to be more prudence to secure himself by resolution and magnanimity, than, by seeming to buckle to any, to encourage all to trample on him. In pursuit of this opinion, he reduced the barbarians to tranquility, and put an end to all fear of war from them, by a rapid expedition into their country as far as the river Danube, where he gave Syrmus, king of the Triballians, an entire overthrow. And hearing the Thebans were in revolt, and the Athenians in correspondence with them, he immediately marched through the pass of Thermopylae. . . . When he came to Thebes, to show how willing he was to accept of their repentance for what was past, he only demanded of them Phoenix and Prothytes, the authors of the rebellion, and proclaimed a general pardon to those who would come over to him. But when the Thebans merely retorted by demanding Philotas and Antipater to be delivered into their hands, and by a proclamation on their part, invited all who would assert the liberty of Greece to come over to them, he presently applied himself to make them feel the last extremities of war. The Thebans indeed defended themselves with a zeal and courage beyond their strength, being much outnumbered by their enemies. But when the Macedonian garrison sallied out upon them from the citadel, they were so hemmed in on all sides, that the greater part of them fell in the battle; the city itself being taken by storm, was sacked and razed, Alexander's hope being that so severe an example might terrify the rest of Greece into obedience, and also in order to gratify the hostility of his confederates, the Phocians and Plataeans. So that, except the priests, and some few who had heretofore been the friends and connections of the Macedonians, . . . all the rest, to the number of thirty thousand, were publicly sold for slaves; and it is computed that upwards of six thousand were put to the sword.

Source: IDPH. (n.d.). The life of Alexander the Great.
http://www.idph.net/conteudos/ebooks/AlexanderTheGreat.pdf

Comprehension Check:

1. About how long after Alexander's death did Plutarch write his history?
2. According to Plutarch, what was Alexander's solution to the rebellion of the Triballians and Thebans?

Activities:

1. With a partner, go through the text and circle the words that show Plutarch's bias as a historian. How would you describe his bias?
2. Write an account of these events from the perspective of the Triballians and Thebans.

Reflection: What biases have you noticed in the history textbooks you have used in school (including this one)?

Resources:

Mark, J. J. (2014). Alexander the Great. Ancient History Encyclopedia. https://www.ancient
.eu/Alexander_the_Great/

Walbank, F. W. (2019). Plutarch. Encyclopedia Britannica. https://www.britannica.com
/biography/Plutarch

LESSON 3.4

WHY DID ANCIENT ROMANS BLAME THE COLLAPSE OF THEIR EMPIRE ON BARBARIANS?

Historical Figure: Alaric I

Event: Decline of Western Roman Empire, 5th–6th centuries

Introduction: Can there be more or less barbaric, or more or less civilized, forms of
war? Give examples.

Mini-Lecture:

- The Roman Empire began in 27 BCE in what is now Italy, and expanded into
  what is now Northern Africa, Europe, and the Middle East.
- In the 4th century, it split into the Western Roman Empire, with its capital in
  Rome, and the Eastern Roman, or Byzantine Empire, with its capital in
  Constantinople (now Istanbul).
- The Goths (including Visigoths and Ostrogoths) were nomadic people who lived
  inside and outside Roman territory.
- In 410 BCE, a group of Goths led by Alaric I attacked the city of Rome; historians
  view this as part of the decline of the Western Roman Empire.
- Alaric I had been trained in the Roman army, and was trying to increase his people's
  territory and gain Roman citizenship for them, but the Emperor Honorius refused.
- Honorius's brother Arcadius had ruled the Byzantine Empire.
- Procopius was a Greek historian who lived in the Byzantine Empire, in what is
  now Palestine and Israel, in the 6th century CE; our document comes from his
  history of the Roman Empire.

Vocabulary:

removed: left	*wherefore:* therefore
faith: alliance	*sparsely:* not densely
sparing: allowing to live	*plunder:* steal property

Document: Alaric's sack of Rome, Procopius, c. 550 CE

But the Visigoths, separating from the others, removed from there and at first
entered into an alliance with the Emperor Arcadius, but at a later time (for faith
with the Romans cannot dwell in barbarians), under the leadership of Alaric,
they became hostile to both emperors, and, beginning with Thrace, treated all

Europe as an enemy's land. Now the emperor Honorius had before this time been sitting in Rome, with never a thought of war in his mind, but glad, I think, if men allowed him to remain quiet in his palace. But when word was brought that the barbarians with a great army were not far off, but somewhere among the Taulantii (in Illyricum), he abandoned the palace and fled in disorderly fashion to Ravenna, a strong city lying just about at the end of the Ionian Gulf, while some say that he brought in the barbarians himself, because an uprising had been started against him among his subjects; but this does not seem to me trustworthy, as far, at least, as one can judge of the character of the man. And the barbarians, finding that they had no hostile force to encounter them, became the most cruel of all men. For they destroyed all the cities which they captured, especially those south of the Ionian Gulf, so completely that nothing has been left to my time to know them by, unless, indeed, it might be one tower or one gate or some such thing which chanced to remain. And they killed all the people, as many as came in their way, both old and young alike, sparing neither women nor children. Wherefore, even up to the present time Italy is sparsely populated. They also gathered as plunder all the money out of all Europe, and, most important of all, they left in Rome nothing whatever of public or private wealth when they moved on to Gaul.

Source: Halsall, P. (1998). Procopius of Caesaria.
https://sourcebooks.fordham.edu/ancient/410alaric.asp

Comprehension Check:

1. What are the two theories about the relationship between Emperor Honorius and the barbarians? Which theory does Procopius believe, and why?
2. What is Procopius's evidence that the Visigoths were cruel?

Activities:

1. Find evidence from the text to support or oppose Procopius's theory about Emperor Honorius. Make a list of other evidence you would need to make a decision about whether you believed this theory or not.
2. Procopius says, "for faith with the Romans cannot dwell in barbarians." Do you think he classifies the Visigoths as barbarians because of their behavior, because they fought against Rome, or for some other reason? Explain your answer using quotations from the text.

Reflection: What do you think would have happened if Honorius had agreed to give Alaric I and the Goths the territory and citizenship they wanted?

Resources:

Jarus, O. (2018). Who were the barbarians? https://www.livescience.com/45297-barbarians .html
Mark, J. J. (2019). Visigoth. https://www.ancient.eu/visigoth/

LESSON 3.5

WHY DID PORTUGUESE COLONISTS PORTRAY AFRICANS AS UNCIVILIZED?

Historical Figure: Prince Henry the Navigator

Event: Portuguese colonize Guinea, 1444

Introduction: Who do you think invented racism? Why would anyone do that?

Mini-Lecture:

- In the 15th century, Portugal began sending ships to Africa, Asia, and the Americas, seeking wealth and the expansion of their empire.
- Henry the Navigator (1394–1460) was a Portuguese prince who traveled to Africa, set up colonies there, and initiated the Atlantic slave trade.
- Our document comes from a chronicle of this voyage that Henry the Navigator ordered historian Gomes de Zurara to write; Zurara refers to Henry as "the Infant," meaning Prince.
- Prince Henry's goal was to gain wealth for Portugal, and he also sought to convert to Christianity the people he captured and enslaved.
- This excerpt begins after the Portuguese had captured African people from a variety of areas and ethnic groups and were dividing them as property.

Vocabulary:

mulattoes: people with both African or Black and European or White heritage
Ethiops: Ethiopians
piteous: sympathetic
dolorously: sadly
lamentations: expressions of sadness
dirge: sad song
needful: necessary
steed: horse
retinue: people serving a leader

favors: gifts
ado: delay
dispensation: a belief system
perdition: where sinful people are in Hell forever, according to Christians
pagans: what Christians call non-Christians
lodgment: housing
bestial: like animals

Document: *Chronicle of the Discovery and Conquest of Guinea,* Gomes de Zurara, 1450

On the next day, which was the 8th of the month of August, very early in the morning, by reason of the heat, the seamen began to make ready their boats, and to take out those captives, and carry them on shore, as they were commanded. And these, placed all together in that field, were a marvelous sight; for amongst them were some white enough, fair to look upon, and well proportioned; others were less white like mulattoes; others again were as black as Ethiops, and so ugly, both in features and in body, as almost to appear (to those who saw them) the images of a lower hemisphere. But what heart could be so hard as not to be pierced with piteous feeling to see that company? For some kept their heads low and their faces bathed in tears, looking one upon another; others stood groaning very dolorously, looking up to the height of heaven, fixing their eyes upon it, crying out loudly, as if asking help of the Father of Nature; others struck their faces with the palms of their hands, throwing themselves at full length upon the ground; others made their lamentations in the manner of a dirge, after the custom of their country. . . . But to increase their sufferings still more, there now arrived those who had charge of the division of the captives, and who began to separate one from another, in order to make an equal partition of the fifths; and then was it needful to part fathers from sons, husbands from wives, brothers from brothers. . . .

The Infant was there, mounted upon a powerful steed, and accompanied by his retinue, making distribution of his favors, as a man who sought to gain but small treasure from his share; for of the forty-six souls that fell to him as his fifth, he made a very speedy partition of these; [among others] for his chief riches lay in [the accomplishment of] his purpose; for he reflected with great pleasure upon the salvation of those souls that before were lost.

And certainly his expectation was not in vain; for, as we said before, as soon as they understood our language they turned Christians with very little ado; and I who put together this history into this volume, saw in the town of Lagos boys and girls (the children and grandchildren of those first captives, born in this land) as good and true Christians as if they had directly descended, from the beginning of the dispensation of Christ, from those who were first baptized. . . .

And so their lot [those slaves taken back to Portugal] was now quite the contrary of what it had been; since before they had lived in perdition of soul and body; of their souls, in that they were yet pagans, without the clearness and the light of the holy faith; and of their bodies, in that they lived like beasts, without any custom of reasonable beings—for they had no knowledge of bread or wine, and they were without the covering of clothes, or the lodgment of houses; and worse than all, through the great ignorance that was in them, in that they had no understanding of good, but only knew how to live in a bestial sloth.

Source: Project Gutenberg. (2011). Chronicle of the discovery and conquest of Guinea vol 1. https://archive.org/stream/thechronicleofth35738gut/35738-0.txt

Comprehension Check:

1. According to Zurara, what do the people who were captured have in common with each other, and what are the differences among them?
2. What evidence does Zurara present that people enslaved by Henry the Navigator had lived "like beasts" before they were captured?

Activities:

1. Work with a partner to create a mind map of the reasons that Henry the Navigator may have had for ordering Zurara to write this history. How would this history benefit Henry's or Portugal's interests?
2. Historian Ibram X. Kendi has argued that Zurara was the first person to describe African people with various languages, cultures, and appearances as one group, and to present them as inferior to and less civilized than Europeans—in other words, Zurara was the first person to express racist ideas and use Blackness as a racial category. List evidence you could provide for or against this theory, either from this unit or from your own knowledge.

Reflection: Are you surprised that Zurara expressed sympathy with the enslaved Africans, yet also claimed they were better off as slaves? Why or why not?

Resources:

Biography.com. (2019). Henry the Navigator. https://www.biography.com/explorer/henry-the-navigator
Scene on Radio. (2017). *How race was made.* Seeing White podcast transcript. http://www.sceneonradio.org/wp-content/uploads/2017/11/SeeingWhite_Part2Transcript.pdf

LESSON 3.6

How Did Ideas of Civilization Differ in the Ottoman and Austrian Empires?

Historical Figure: Suleiman the Magnificent

Event: Ottoman Empire, 1299–1922

Introduction: Name a country or group of people different from you whom you admire. For what reasons?

Mini-Lecture:

- The Ottoman Empire was based in what is now Turkey from 1299 to 1922; at its largest extent, in the 17th century, it included parts of Southern Europe, North Africa, and the Arabian Peninsula.
- Suleiman the Magnificent was the Sultan of the Ottoman Empire from 1520 to 1566; he was known as "the Lawgiver" because he made laws apply to all people and protected religious minorities including Christians and Jews from the Muslim majority.
- The Hapsburg royal family, which ruled the Austrian Empire, based in Vienna and extending through Central and Southern Europe, held power around the same times as the Ottoman Empire and bordered it for a time.
- Ogier Ghiselin de Busbecq was the Hapsburg monarchy's ambassador to the Ottoman Empire in the 16th century.

- Our document is from *The Turkish Letters*, a book Busbecq published about his time there, in which he criticized his own society while praising the Ottoman Empire.

Vocabulary:

distinction: difference
deference: respect
precedence: rank
discharge: do
making his appointments: appointing people to positions
pretensions: pretending to be important
merits: talents
disposition: personality
contempt: hatred
undertakings: projects

birth: whether you are born into a family with high or low status
prestige: high status
thrift: not wasting anything
prevail: win
unimpaired: unlimited
exchequer: budget
insubordinate: not respecting authority
license runs riot: people do whatever they want
debauchery: unethical behavior

Document: *The Turkish Letters*, Ogier Ghiselin de Busbecq, c. 1555

No distinction is attached to birth among the Turks; the deference to be paid to a man is measured by the position he holds in the public service. There is no fighting for precedence; a man's place is marked out by the duties he discharges. In making his appointments the Sultan [Suleiman] pays no regard to any pretensions on the score of wealth or rank, nor does he take into consideration recommendations or popularity, he considers each case on its own merits, and examines carefully into the character, ability, and disposition of the man whose promotion is in question. . . . If a man be dishonest, or lazy, or careless, he remains at the bottom of the ladder, an object of contempt; for such qualities there are no honours in Turkey!

   This is the reason that they are successful in their undertakings, that they lord it over others, and are daily extending the bounds of their empire. These are not our ideas, with us there is no opening left for merit; birth is the standard for everything; the prestige of birth is the sole key to advancement in the public service. . . .

   [I]t is the patience, self-denial and thrift of the Turkish soldier that enable him to face the most trying circumstances and come safely out of' the dangers that surround him. What a contrast to our men! Christian soldiers on a campaign refuse to put up with their ordinary food. . . . It makes me shudder to think of what the result of a struggle between such different systems must be; one of us must prevail and the other be destroyed, at any rate we cannot both exist in safety. On their side is the vast wealth of their empire, unimpaired resources, experience and practice in arms, a veteran soldiery, an uninterrupted series of victories, readiness to endure hardships, union, order, discipline, thrift and watchfulness. On ours are found an empty exchequer, luxurious habits, exhausted resources, broken spirits, a raw and insubordinate soldiery, and greedy quarrels; there is no regard for discipline, license runs riot, the men indulge in drunkenness and debauchery, and worst of all, the enemy are accustomed to victory, we to defeat. Can we doubt what the result must be?

Source: Busbecq, O. G. (n.d.). Turkish letters. https://my.tlu.edu/ICS/icsfs /BusbecqTurkishLetters9pg.pdf?target=136beb42-87dc-48d9-b0ff-7d6be5167b78

Comprehension Check:

1. Create a T-chart comparing the Austrian to the Ottoman Empire, according to Busbecq.
2. Why did Busbecq write this text? Who was his audience?

Activities:

1. Imagine that a Turkish person visited the Austrian Empire. How might they criticize the aspects of their own society that Busbecq praised, and vice versa? Using your T-chart as a basis, work with a partner to write new descriptions of Ottoman and Austrian society from the opposite perspective of Busbecq's.

Reflection: Do you think that criticizing your own country or society can make it more "civilized"? Why or why not?

Resources:

Parry, V. J. (n.d.). Süleyman the Magnificent. https://www.britannica.com/biography /Suleyman-the-Magnificent

Royde-Smith, J. G. (2019). House of Habsburg. https://www.britannica.com/topic/House-of -Habsburg

---

LESSON 3.7

DID SPANISH COLONIZATION OF THE AMERICAS BRING CIVILIZATION OR BARBARISM?

Historical Figure: King Ferdinand

Event: Spanish colonization of the Americas begins, 1492

Introduction: How do you think the colonizers from Spain explained to people in the Americas who they were and why they were there?

Mini-Lecture:

- Don Fernando, also known as Ferdinand II, was king of Aragon and Castille, in what is now Spain, in the late 15th and early 16th centuries; he reigned alongside his wife, Isabella, and then his daughter Juana, or Joanna.
- During his reign, Spanish forces colonized areas in South America, beginning with Christopher Columbus's landing in what is now the island shared by Haiti and the Dominican Republic in 1492.

- The Spanish called their possessions in Central and South America Tierra-firme.
- Our document, the Requerimiento, or "the Requirement," was written by the Court of Castille to be read aloud to Indigenous people who had been conquered by Spanish forces.
- The Requerimiento was often read in Latin, without interpreting into Indigenous languages, and was sometimes read from the deck of Spanish ships to empty beaches before landing.
- Spanish colonization resulted in the genocide of millions of Indigenous people, including the Taíno and Arawak, whom the Spanish enslaved.

Vocabulary:

subduer: person who conquers
charge: power
seat: throne
tierra-firme: land

Pontiff: pope
aforesaid: previously mentioned
yoke: control
cavalier: soldier on horseback

Document: Requerimiento, Council of Castille, 1510

On the part of the King, Don Fernando, and of Doña Juana, his daughter, Queen of Castile and León, subduers of the barbarous nations, we their servants notify and make known to you, as best we can, that the Lord our God, Living and Eternal, created the Heaven and the Earth, and one man and one woman, of whom you and we, all the men of the world, were and are descendants, and all those who came after us. . . .

Of all these nations God our Lord gave charge to one man, called St. Peter, that he should be Lord and Superior of all the men in the world, that all should obey him. . . . And he commanded him to place his seat in Rome as the spot most fitting to rule the world from; but also he permitted him to have his seat in any other part of the world, and to judge and govern all Christians, Moors [Muslims], Jews, Gentiles, and all other sects.

This man was called Pope. . . . One of these Pontiffs who succeeded that St. Peter as Lord of the world, in the dignity and seat which I have before mentioned, made donation of these isles and Tierra-firme to the aforesaid King and Queen and to their successors. . . .

So their Highnesses are kings and lords of these islands and land of Tierra-firme by virtue of this donation. . . . Wherefore, as best we can, we ask and require you that you consider what we have said to you. . . .

If you do so, you will do well, and that which you are obliged to do to their Highnesses, and we in their name shall receive you in all love and charity, and shall leave you, your wives, and your children, and your lands, free without servitude, that you may do with them and with yourselves freely that which you like and think best, and they shall not compel you to turn Christians, unless you yourselves, when informed of the truth, should wish to be converted to our Holy Catholic Faith, as almost all the inhabitants of the rest of the islands have done. . . .

But, if you do not do this, and maliciously make delay in it, I certify to you that, with the help of God, we shall powerfully enter into your country, and shall make war against you in all ways and manners that we can, and shall subject you to the yoke and obedience of the Church and of their Highnesses; we shall take you and your wives and your children, and shall make slaves of them, and as such shall sell and dispose of them as their Highnesses may command; and we shall take away your goods, and shall do you all the mischief and damage that we can, as to vassals who do not obey, and refuse to receive their lord, and resist and contradict him; and we protest that the deaths and losses which shall accrue from this are your fault, and not that of their Highnesses, or ours, nor of these cavaliers who come with us.

Source: National Humanities Center. (n.d.). Requerimiento, 1510. https://nationalhumanitiescenter.org/pds/amerbegin/contact/text7/requirement.pdf

Comprehension Check:

1. According to this document, why do King Fernando and Princess Juana own the Americas?
2. What are the two choices that the people living in the Americas have?

Activities:

1. This document identifies people in the Americas as "barbarous." What evidence do King Fernando and Princess Juana try to present that they are "civilized"? Highlight the words and phrases they use to do so.
2. Write a response to King Fernando and Princess Juana from a person in the Americas.

Reflection: Is colonization something that "civilized" people do, or is it "barbaric"? Why?

Resources:

Lumen. (n.d.). Bartolomé de las Casas describes the exploitation of indigenous peoples. https://courses.lumenlearning.com/ushistory1os/chapter/primary-source-bartolome-de-las-casas-describes-the-exploitation-of-indigenous-peoples-1542/

LESSON 3.8

WHY DID QING DYNASTY CHINESE SEE PEOPLE FROM EUROPE AS BARBARIANS?

Historical Figure: Qianlong Emperor

Event: Qing Dynasty, 1644–1912

Introduction: Could a "barbarian" ever learn to be "civilized"? Why or why not?

Mini-Lecture:

- The Qing Dynasty, or, as it called itself, the "Celestial Empire," ruled territory in what is now China from 1644 to 1911 and had its capital at Peking (now Beijing).
- The Qianlong emperor reigned from 1736 to 1796 and was known for expanding the dynasty's territory and creating a multiethnic empire including not only Han Chinese but also Tibetan, Mongol, and Manchu subjects.
- In the late 17th century, the British East India Company began trading tea, porcelain, silk, and other items popular in Europe with the Qing Dynasty for silver and a drug called opium.
- The Qing Dynasty granted Britain a "mandate" or right to trade, but taxed and regulated goods, and forbade British merchants to interact with Chinese people outside the two ports it had set up for "barbarians" (non-Chinese).
- In the late 18th century, King George III of England sent a representative to ask the Qianlong emperor for better trading conditions, permission to post an ambassador in Peking, and the right of missionaries to spread Christianity.
- Our document contains the Qianlong emperor's edicts, or proclamations, in response to these requests.

Vocabulary:

impelled: inspired
partake: participate in
dispatched: sent
memorial: request
envoy: someone sent with a message
entreaty: request
nationals: citizens
be accredited to: be part of
usage: customs
entertained: considered
precincts: neighborhoods
corresponding with: communicating with
reside: live
unseemly: inappropriate

requisite: necessary
rudiments: basics
tribute: gifts given to a ruler by subjects to show loyalty
sage: wise
inculcated: taught
time immemorial: before recorded history
myriad: many
heterodox doctrine: belief contrary to one's own
intercourse: interaction
propagating: spreading
disseminate: spread

Document: Edicts from the Qianlong emperor, 1793

> You, O King, live beyond the confines of many seas, nevertheless, impelled by your humble desire to partake of the benefits of our civilization, you have dispatched a mission respectfully bearing your memorial. . . .
>
> As to your entreaty to send one of your nationals to be accredited to my Celestial Court and to be in control of your country's trade with China, this

request is contrary to all usage of my dynasty and cannot possibly be entertained. It is true that Europeans, in the service of my dynasty, have been permitted to live at Peking, but they are compelled to adopt Chinese dress, they are strictly confined to their own precincts, and they are never permitted to return home. . . . Your proposed Envoy to my Court could not be placed in a position similar to that of European officials in Peking who are forbidden to leave China, nor could he, on the other hand, be allowed liberty of movement and the privilege of corresponding with his own country; so that you would gain nothing by his residence in our midst.

Supposing that your Envoy should come to our court, his language and national dress differ from that of our people, and there would be no place in which he might reside. It may be suggested that he might adopt the dress and customs of China, but, it has never been our dynasty's wish to force people to do things unseemly and inconvenient. Besides, supposing I sent an Ambassador to reside in your country, how could you possibly make for him the requisite arrangements? . . .

If you assert that your reverence for our Celestial dynasty fills you with a desire to acquire our civilization, our ceremonies and code of laws differ so completely from your own that, even if your Envoy were able to acquire the rudiments of our civilization, you could not possibly transplant our manners and customs to your alien soil. Therefore, however adept the Envoy might become, nothing would be gained thereby.

Surveying the wide world, I have but one aim in view, namely, to maintain a perfect governance and to fulfill the duties of the State; strange and costly objects do not interest me. . . . Our dynasty's majestic virtue has penetrated unto every country under Heaven, and Kings of all nations have offered their costly tribute by land and sea.

Edict II

. . . Regarding your nation's worship of the Lord of Heaven, it is the same religion as that of other European nations. Ever since the beginning of history, sage Emperors and wise rulers have bestowed on China a moral system and inculcated a code, which from time immemorial has been religiously observed by the myriads of my subjects. There has been no hankering after heterodox doctrines. Even the European officials in my capital are forbidden to hold intercourse with Chinese subjects; they are restricted within the limits of their appointed residences, and may not go about propagating their religion. The distinction between Chinese and barbarian is most strict, and your Ambassador's request that barbarians shall be given full liberty to disseminate their religion is utterly unreasonable.

Source: Asia for Educators. (n.d.). Two edicts from the Qianlong emperor. http://afe.easia.columbia.edu/ps/china/qianlong_edicts.pdf

Comprehension Check:

1. List at least three reasons why the Qianlong emperor does not think it makes sense to have a British ambassador in Peking.
2. In your own words, how does the Qianlong emperor see his relationship to King George III and the British people?

Activities:

1. Imagine a dialogue between the Qianlong emperor and King Fernando (Lesson 3.7) about who is more civilized, and write it in the form of a comic strip.
2. "Read between the lines" to construct a "rough draft" of this letter expressing in blunter terms the Qianlong emperor's message.

Reflection: Has your experience with other cultures given you any evidence to argue against the Qianlong emperor's view that people from different cultures can't learn much from each other or shouldn't share ideas?

Resources:

Blakemore, E. (2019). How the East India Company became the world's most powerful business. https://www.nationalgeographic.com/culture/topics/reference/british-east -india-trading-company-most-powerful-business/

Encyclopedia.com. (2019). English East India Company, in China. https://www.encyclopedia .com/history/encyclopedias-almanacs-transcripts-and-maps/english-east-india-company -china

Freer Gallery of Art. (n.d.). The Kangxi and Qianlong emperors. http://projects.mcah .columbia.edu/nanxuntu/html/emperors/

LESSON 3.9

HOW DID ENLIGHTENMENT PHILOSOPHERS REDEFINE CIVILIZATION?

Historical Figure: Immanuel Kant

Event: The Enlightenment, 18th century

Introduction: Do you think it is better if people make decisions on their own, or if they take the advice of wise people in their society—for instance, rulers, teachers, and religious leaders? Why?

Mini-Lecture:

- The Enlightenment, or the "Age of Reason," was a period from the late 17th to early 19th century when philosophers and scientists encouraged questioning of religious and political authorities on the basis of rationality.
- Immanuel Kant (1724–1804) was an Enlightenment philosopher who argued for a kind of morality based on reason rather than religious tradition.

- Kant lived in Prussia, a kingdom that included parts of what is now Germany, Poland, and Baltic states, and which was ruled by Frederick the Great.
- Frederick the Great, who ruled Prussia from 1740 to 1786, supported the Enlightenment, welcoming philosophers to live in his palace, reforming the justice system, and allowing freedom of the press.
- Our document is from an essay Kant wrote explaining the Enlightenment and praising Frederick the Great.

Vocabulary:

emergence: coming out of
self-imposed: caused by one's self
minors: people who are the responsibility of someone else; children
exert: try hard
fair sex: women

docile: easy to control
second nature: something you do without thinking about it
yoke: device that controls an animal
drill: do a military exercise

Document: *What Is Enlightenment?*, Immanuel Kant, 1784

Enlightenment is man's emergence from his self-imposed nonage. Nonage is the inability to use one's own understanding without another's guidance. This nonage is self-imposed if its cause lies not in lack of understanding but in indecision and lack of courage to use one's own mind without another's guidance. Dare to know! (Sapere aude.) "Have the courage to use your own understanding," is therefore the motto of the enlightenment.

Laziness and cowardice are the reasons why such a large part of mankind gladly remain minors all their lives, long after nature has freed them from external guidance. They are the reasons why it is so easy for others to set themselves up as guardians. It is so comfortable to be a minor. If I have a book that thinks for me, a pastor who acts as my conscience, a physician who prescribes my diet, and so on—then I have no need to exert myself. I have no need to think, if only I can pay; others will take care of that disagreeable business for me. Those guardians who have kindly taken supervision upon themselves see to it that the overwhelming majority of mankind—among them the entire fair sex—should consider the step to maturity, not only as hard, but as extremely dangerous. First, these guardians make their domestic cattle stupid and carefully prevent the docile creatures from taking a single step without the leading-strings to which they have fastened them. Then they show them the danger that would threaten them if they should try to walk by themselves. . . . Thus it is very difficult for the individual to work himself out of the nonage which has become almost second nature to him. . . .

It is more nearly possible, however, for the public to enlighten itself; indeed, if it is only given freedom, enlightenment is almost inevitable. There will always be a few independent thinkers, even among the self-appointed guardians of the multitude. Once such men have thrown off the yoke of nonage, they will spread about them the spirit of a reasonable appreciation of man's value and of his duty to think for himself. . . . This enlightenment requires nothing but freedom—and the most innocent of all that may be called "freedom": freedom to make public use of one's reason in all matters. Now I hear the cry from all sides: "Do not argue!" The officer says: "Do not argue—drill!" The tax collector: "Do not argue—pay!" The pastor: "Do not argue—believe!" Only one ruler in the world says: "Argue as much as you please, but obey!" We find restrictions on freedom everywhere. But which restriction is harmful to enlightenment? Which restriction is innocent, and which advances enlightenment? I reply: the public use of one's reason must be free at all times, and this alone can bring enlightenment to mankind. . . . When one does not deliberately attempt to keep men in barbarism, they will gradually work out of that condition by themselves.

Source: Kant, I. (n.d.). What is enlightenment? (M. C. Smith, Trans.). http://www.columbia.edu/acis/ets/CCREAD/etscc/kant.html

Comprehension Check:

1. Make a T-chart comparing nonage and enlightenment.
2. Why does Kant appreciate the rule of Frederick the Great?

Activities:

1. Work with a small group to choose one of the other documents in this unit; then create a Venn diagram showing similarities and differences between the ideas of civilization expressed in it and in this document by Kant.
2. Kant mentioned that women in his society were placed in a position of "nonage," but argued that they could be making decisions for themselves. List other groups that might gain more power to make their own decisions under the Enlightenment. Why do you think Kant does not mention them?

Reflection: Do you think that people today are "enlightened" according to Kant's definition? Why or why not?

Resources:

Domínguez, M. (2017). What's so great about Frederick the Great? https://www.nationalgeographic.com/history/magazine/2017/03-04/frederick-the-great-king-prussia/
White, M. (2018). The Enlightenment. https://www.bl.uk/restoration-18th-century-literature/articles/the-enlightenment

LESSON 3.10
WHY DID FRENCH PEOPLE THINK THEY NEEDED TO CIVILIZE "INFERIOR RACES"?

Historical Figure: Jules Ferry

Event: French colonization of Indochina, 1887–1945

Introduction: Do you think countries that are more advanced in some area (e.g., technology, education, or human rights) have a duty to share their knowledge with others? Why or why not?

Mini-Lecture:

- Jules Ferry served as Prime Minister of France in the 1880s.
- In the 19th century, France began to colonize areas in Southeast Asia and Africa—what they called Indochina (today Vietnam, Cambodia, and Laos), and what are now the countries of Madagascar, Tunisia, Algeria, and Morocco.
- Ferry argued in favor of colonization and used the term "civilizing mission," or "mission civilatrice," to describe what he felt was France's duty to help the less advanced peoples in Asia and Africa.
- In the late 19th century, France's economy was struggling because other countries such as Germany and the United States did not want to import French goods.
- Our document comes from a speech made by Ferry to the Chamber of Deputies, or parliament, explaining why he supported colonization.

Vocabulary:

considerations: reasons
outlets: places to sell goods
exports: goods that a country wants to sell to other countries
irrevocably: in a way that is not possible to reverse or change
protectionist: a country that does not want to import goods but only use its own goods

market: a country or region where one can sell goods
acquit: behave
grandeur: greatness
navy: military forces that operate on the seas
provisioning: getting supplies

Document: Speech before the Chamber of Deputies, Jules Ferry, 1884

The policy of colonial expansion is a political and economic system . . . that can be connected to three sets of ideas: economic ideas; the most far-reaching ideas of civilization; and ideas of a political and patriotic sort.

In the area of economics, I am placing before you, with the support of some statistics, the considerations that justify the policy of colonial expansion, as seen from the perspective of a need, felt more and more urgently by the industrialized population of Europe and especially the people of our rich and hardworking country of France: the need for outlets [for exports]. . . . Yes, what our major industries [textiles, etc.], irrevocably steered by the treaties of 1861 into exports, lack more and more are outlets. Why? Because next door Germany is setting up trade barriers; because across the ocean the United States of America have become protectionists, and extreme protectionists at that; because not only are these great markets . . . shrinking, becoming more and more difficult of access, but these great states are beginning to pour into our own markets products not seen there before. . . . Nothing is more serious; there can be no graver social problem; and these matters are linked intimately to colonial policy.

Gentlemen, we must speak more loudly and more honestly! We must say openly that indeed the higher races have a right over the lower races. . . . I repeat, that the superior races have a right because they have a duty. They have the duty to civilize the inferior races. . . . In the history of earlier centuries these duties, gentlemen, have often been misunderstood; and certainly when the Spanish soldiers and explorers introduced slavery into Central America, they did not fulfill their duty as men of a higher race. . . . But, in our time, I maintain that European nations acquit themselves with generosity, with grandeur, and with sincerity of this superior civilizing duty.

I say that French colonial policy, the policy of colonial expansion, the policy that has taken us under the Empire, that has led us to Tunisia, to Madagascar—I say that this policy of colonial expansion was inspired by . . . the fact that a navy such as ours cannot do without safe harbors, defenses, supply centers on the high seas. . . .

Gentlemen, these are considerations that merit the full attention of patriots. The conditions of naval warfare have greatly changed. . . . At present, as you know, a warship, however perfect its design, cannot carry more than two weeks' supply of coal; and a vessel without coal is a wreck on the high seas, abandoned to the first occupier. Hence the need to have places of supply, shelters, ports for defense and provisioning. . . . And that is why we needed Tunisia; that is why we needed Saigon [in what is now Vietnam] and Indochina; that is why we need Madagascar . . . and why we shall never leave them!

Source: Halsall, P. (1998). Jules Ferry (1832–1893).
https://sourcebooks.fordham.edu/mod/1884ferry.asp

Comprehension Check:

1. Summarize Ferry's three goals in promoting colonization.
2. What is Ferry's criticism of Spanish colonizers in South America?

Activities:

1. Divide the class into small groups representing one of the goals of colonization. Create a poster showing the impact that French goals would have on colonized people in Indochina.
2. Would François Hollande (Lesson 3.1) agree with Ferry that France has the obligation to "civilize" people from other cultures? Use quotations from both documents to justify your answer.

Reflection: How would you have felt about France's "civilizing mission" if you were a person living in the area that it colonized? Why?

Resources:

Erenow. (n.d.). French and the civilizing mission. https://erenow.net/modern/modern-france
   -a-very-short-introduction/3.php

LESSON 3.11
How Did Meiji Japanese Leaders Define Civilization?

Historical Figure: Emperor Meiji

Event: Meiji Restoration, 1868–1912

Introduction: Is it better if civilizations adapt to current conditions, or keep their longtime traditions? Why?

Mini-Lecture:

- From 1603 to 1868, the region that is now Japan was under the rule of the Tokugawa Shogunate, a feudal kingdom in which peasants, samurai warriors, and nobles called daimyo who served the shogun, or military dictator appointed by the emperor.
- The Tokugawa Shogunate had a foreign policy that built relationships with other powers in East Asia but restricted trade or relationships outside the region.
- In the 19th century, after U.S. Commander Matthew Perry visited the shogunate with large warships and tried to start a trading relationship, Japanese leaders concluded that they needed to develop relationships with other regions.
- In 1868, the emperor Meiji oversaw the Meiji Restoration, a change in Japan's political, economic, and social system.
- Itō Hirobumi, politician and later prime minister, visited the United States and European countries to research their constitutions, and decided on a political system of constitutional monarchy influenced by the British parliamentary system and the Kingdom of Prussia.
- Our document, the Meiji Constitution, was written by Itō Hirobumi with the help of Prussian legal scholars and other foreign advisors; it outlines the role of the emperor and of the Imperial Diet, or parliament.

Vocabulary:

by virtue of: because of
lineal succession: a throne that is passed down from parent to child
faculties: abilities
vigilance: watchfulness and care
promulgate: pass a law
in pursuance of: in line with
rescript: official announcement

inviolable: something that must be respected
sovereignty: power over a country or area
give sanction to: approve
amenable to: agree to
abode: home
prejudicial: interfering with

Document: Meiji Constitution, 1889

Having, by virtue of the glories of Our Ancestors, ascended the Throne of a lineal succession unbroken for ages eternal; desiring to promote the welfare of, and to give development to the moral and intellectual faculties of Our beloved subjects, the very same that have been favored with the benevolent care and affectionate vigilance of Our Ancestors; and hoping to maintain the prosperity of the State, in concert with Our people and with their support, We hereby promulgate, in pursuance of Our Imperial Rescript of the 12th day of the 10th month of the 14th year of Meiji, a fundamental law of State, to exhibit the principles, by which We are to be guided in Our conduct, and to point out to what Our descendants and Our subjects and their descendants are forever to conform. . . .

Chapter 1, Article I. The Empire of Japan shall be reigned over and governed by a line of Emperors unbroken for ages eternal.

    Article II. The Imperial Throne shall be succeeded to by Imperial male descendants, according to the provisions of the Imperial House Law.

    Article III. The Emperor is sacred and inviolable.

    Article IV: The Emperor is the head of the Empire, combining in Himself the rights of sovereignty, and exercises them, according to the provisions of the present Constitution.

    Article V. The Emperor exercises the legislative power with the consent of the Imperial Diet.

    Article VI. The Emperor gives sanction to laws and orders them to be promulgated and executed. . . .

    Article XI. The Emperor has the supreme command of the Army and Navy. . . .

    Article XIII. The Emperor declares war, makes peace, and concludes treaties. . . .

Chapter 2, Article XX. Japanese subjects are amenable to service in the Army or Navy, according to the provisions of law.

    Article XXI. Japanese subjects are amenable to the duty of paying taxes, according to the provisions of law.

    Article XXII. Japanese subjects shall have the liberty of abode and of changing the same within the limits of law.

    Article XXIII. No Japanese subject shall be arrested, detained, tried, or punished, unless according to law.

    Article XXVIII. Japanese subjects shall, within limits not prejudicial to peace and order, and not antagonistic to their duties as subjects, enjoy freedom of religious belief.

    Article XXIX. Japanese subjects shall, within the limits of law, enjoy the liberty of speech, writing, publication, public meetings, and associations. . . .

Chapter 3, Article XXXIII. The Imperial Diet shall consist of two Houses, a House of Peers and a House of Representatives.

Article XXXIV. The House of Peers shall, in accordance with the Ordinance concerning the House of Peers, be composed of members of the Imperial Family, of the orders of nobility, and of those persons who have been nominated thereto by the Emperor.

Article XXXV. The House of Representatives shall be composed of Members elected by the people, according to the provisions of the Law of Election.

Source: Asia for Educators. (n.d.). Excerpts from the Meiji Constitution of 1889. http://afe.easia.columbia.edu/ps/japan/meiji_constitution.pdf

Comprehension Check:

1. Who does the "We" or "Our" mentioned in the first section refer to?
2. List some duties and rights of Japanese subjects in your own words.

Activities:

1. With a partner, underline the parts of the constitution that reference or preserve Japan's traditions, and circle the parts that show new influences.
2. In the late 18th century, the Qianlong emperor (Lesson 3.8) kept foreign "barbarians" from outside the region separated from his people, whereas in the late 19th century, Emperor Meiji welcomed interaction with and ideas of Europeans and Americans. Research some possible reasons for this difference and share your findings with the class.

Reflection: Many countries still have royal families, such as Japan, England, and Thailand. What do you think should be the role of these royal families today?

Resources:

Asia for Educators. (2009). The Meiji Restoration and modernization. http://afe.easia .columbia.edu/special/japan_1750_meiji.htm

Atsushi, K. (2018). The Meiji Restoration. https://www.nippon.com/en/views/b06902/the -meiji-restoration-the-end-of-the-shogunate-and-the-building-of-a-modern-japanese -state.html

---

LESSON 3.12

What Kind of Civilization Did Hitler Envision for the World?

Historical Figure: Adolf Hitler

Event: Nazi Third Reich, 1933–1945

Introduction: Can barbarism only be prevented with barbarism? Or can civilized people stop barbarism from spreading?

Mini-Lecture:

* In 1933, the Nazi Party, a group of far-right fascists led by Adolf Hitler, took control of Germany and began the Third Reich, or third German empire.
* The Nazis wanted to establish a worldwide dictatorship in which Aryan (White) people had power; they believed that Aryan people needed more living space, or lebensraum.
* In 1938, the Nazis claimed control over an area in Czechoslovakia, and as part of European leaders' policy of "appeasement" (doing anything to avoid war), French president Édouard Daladier and British prime minister Neville Chamberlain went to Munich and agreed not to interfere with the Nazi takeover.
* In 1939, Germany made plans to invade Poland by having German soldiers in Polish uniforms attack German territory in order to pretend Polish soldiers started the conflict.
* Our document comes from a speech Hitler gave at his home in Obersalzberg to his inner circle of supporters shortly before the invasion.
* Hitler references Mongol leader and supposed "barbarian" Chinggis Khan (see Lesson 5.4); the Ottoman Empire's genocide of over 1 million Armenians and other Christians during World War I; and Josef Stalin (Lesson 8.10), dictator of the Soviet Union.
* The invasion of Poland began World War II, during which the Nazis killed over 11 million Jews and other religious minorities; communists and other political opponents; LGBTQ people; disabled people; and other groups.

Vocabulary:

asserts: claims
of no account: doesn't matter
blockade: blocking goods from entering or leaving a country to express criticism of its leaders' actions

autarchy: autocracy, dictatorship
is indifferent: doesn't matter
depopulated: remove people from a place

Document: Obersalzberg Speech, Adolf Hitler, 1939

Our strength lies in our quickness and in our brutality; Genghis Khan has sent millions of women and children into death knowingly and with a light heart. History sees in him only the great founder of States. As to what the weak Western European civilization asserts about me, that is of no account. I have given the command and I shall shoot everyone who utters one word of criticism, for the goal to be obtained in the war is not that of reaching certain lines but of physically demolishing the opponent. And so for the present only in the East I have put my death-head formations [a division of the Nazi army] in place with the command relentlessly and without compassion to send into death many women and children of Polish origin and language. Only thus we can gain the living space [lebensraum] that we need. Who after all is today speaking about the destruction of the Armenians? . . .

I experienced those poor worms Daladier and Chamberlain in Munich. They will be too cowardly to attack. They won't go beyond a blockade. Against that we have our autarchy and the Russian raw materials.

Poland will be depopulated and settled with Germans. My pact with the Poles was merely conceived of as a gaining of time. As for the rest, gentlemen, the fate of Russia will be exactly the same as I am now going through with in the case of Poland. After Stalin's death—he is a very sick man—we will break the Soviet Union. Then there will begin the dawn of the German rule of the earth. . . .

The attack upon and the destruction of Poland begins Saturday early. I shall let a few companies in Polish uniform attack in Upper Silesia or in the Protectorate. Whether the world believes it is quite indifferent. The world believes only in success.

For you, gentlemen, fame and honor are beginning as they have not since centuries. Be hard, be without mercy, act more quickly and brutally than the others. The citizens of Western Europe must tremble with horror. That is the most human way of conducting a war. For it scares the others off.

Source: Halsall, P. (1998). Adolf Hitler: The Obersalzberg speech.
https://sourcebooks.fordham.edu/mod/hitler-obersalzberg.asp

Comprehension Check:

1. What did Hitler think that France and Britain would do when he invaded Poland? Why did he think that?
2. Why did Hitler want to take over Poland, the Soviet Union, and other countries?

Activities:

1. Hitler was partly right—although Britain and France did declare war on Germany after his invasion of Poland, they did not act quickly enough to prevent the Nazis from taking over Poland; the United States did not enter the war until two years later. Research one of those countries' reasons for not getting involved, and connect them to ideas about civilization and barbarism.
2. Look back at the historical figures in this unit. Which one do you think most closely shared Hitler's ideas about civilization and barbarism? Quote from the documents to support your answer.

Reflection: Hitler argues that few people remember genocides, or act to prevent them. Is he right? Give examples to support your view.

Resources:

Encyclopedia Britannica. (n.d.). Third Reich. https://www.britannica.com/place/Third-Reich
PBS News Hour. (2019). Holocaust Remembrance Day lesson plans and activities. https://www.pbs.org/newshour/extra/lessons-plans/holocaust-day-of-remembrance-lesson-plans-and-activities/

LESSON 3.13

How Does the Universal Declaration of Human Rights Describe a Civilized Society?

Historical Figure: Charles Malik

Event: Universal Declaration of Human Rights, 1948

Introduction: Brainstorm the rights that you think everyone should have in a civilized society.

Mini-Lecture:

- The United Nations was founded in 1945, after the end of World War II, as a group of member countries (at first 51, now 193) that agree to work together for peace and to improve people's lives.
- In 1946, the United Nations brought together nine leaders from Australia, Canada, Chile, China, France, Lebanon, the United Kingdom, the United States, and the USSR to write a Universal Declaration of Human Rights (UDHR).
- One of these leaders was Charles Malik, a Lebanese diplomat, academic, and Christian theologian.
- The UDHR, from which our document was taken, includes 30 articles describing rights that all people have regardless of where they live.

Vocabulary:

whereas: because
inherent: something one is born with
dignity: worthiness of respect
inalienable: cannot be taken away
contempt: hatred
advent: beginning
want: not having what one needs
to have recourse to: use a strategy or tactic

observance of: following a law or guideline
endowed with: given
security of person: being safe
degrading: humiliating
incitement to: encouragement of
suffrage: right to vote

Document: Universal Declaration of Human Rights, 1948

> Whereas recognition of the inherent dignity and of the equal and inalienable rights of all members of the human family is the foundation of freedom, justice and peace in the world, Whereas disregard and contempt for human rights have resulted in barbarous acts which have outraged the conscience of mankind, and the advent of a world in which human beings shall enjoy freedom of speech and belief and freedom from fear and want has been proclaimed as the highest aspiration of the common people, Whereas it is essential, if man is not to be compelled to have recourse, as a last resort, to rebellion against tyranny and oppression, that human rights should be protected by the rule of law,
>
> Whereas it is essential to promote the development of friendly relations between nations, Whereas the peoples of the United Nations have in the

Charter reaffirmed their faith in fundamental human rights, in the dignity and worth of the human person and in the equal rights of men and women and have determined to promote social progress and better standards of life in larger freedom, Whereas Member States have pledged themselves to achieve, in cooperation with the United Nations, the promotion of universal respect for and observance of human rights and fundamental freedoms, Whereas a common understanding of these rights and freedoms is of the greatest importance for the full realization of this pledge,

Article 1 All human beings are born free and equal in dignity and rights. They are endowed with reason and conscience and should act towards one another in a spirit of brotherhood. . . .

Article 3 Everyone has the right to life, liberty and security of person.

Article 4 No one shall be held in slavery or servitude; slavery and the slave trade shall be prohibited in all their forms.

Article 5 No one shall be subjected to torture or to cruel, inhuman or degrading treatment or punishment. . . .

Article 7 All are equal before the law and are entitled without any discrimination to equal protection of the law. All are entitled to equal protection against any discrimination in violation of this Declaration and against any incitement to such discrimination. . . .

Article 18 Everyone has the right to freedom of thought, conscience and religion; this right includes freedom to change his religion or belief, and freedom, either alone or in community with others and in public or private, to manifest his religion or belief in teaching, practice, worship and observance. . . .

Article 21 (1) Everyone has the right to take part in the government of his country, directly or through freely chosen representatives. (2) Everyone has the right to equal access to public service in his country. (3) The will of the people shall be the basis of the authority of government; this will shall be expressed in periodic and genuine elections which shall be by universal and equal suffrage and shall be held by secret vote or by equivalent free voting procedures.

Source: UN. (2015). Universal Declaration of Human Rights. https://www.un.org/en/udhrbook/pdf/udhr_booklet_en_web.pdf

Comprehension Check:

1. What is the purpose of this declaration?
2. Divide the class into seven groups and have each group create an illustration of one of the rights listed here.

Activities:

1. Divide the class into teams representing each of the historical figures in this unit. After reviewing the document or information, they should explain how that figure upheld or violated the rights in the UDHR.

2. Look at the full UDHR, and then revise it by adding or revising rights to match your own idea of a "civilized" society.

Reflection: Do you think it makes sense to evaluate historical figures from the past according to an idea of human rights from the 20th century? Why or why not?

Resources:

Georges-Khoury, A. (n.d.). Charles Malik. https://hvli.org/models/charles-malik/

UN. (n.d.). History of the document. https://www.un.org/en/sections/universal-declaration/history-document/index.html

Conflict

Unit Question: What Is Worth Fighting For?

This unit allows students to explore the causes and effects of war, as well as possibilities for peace. They begin with some statistics from UN Office for the Coordination of Humanitarian Affairs (OCHA) on the conflict in Yemen, which has led to one of the worst recent humanitarian crises in the world—and, if by the time this book reaches you, this has changed, feel free to substitute a more current conflict. Starting with the effect of war on civilians is important, because the rest of the documents don't dwell on it. Themistocles's account of the Greco-Persian War and Polybius's description of Hannibal's conquest of Rome help students to consider the merits of making alliances and carrying cross-generational grievances forward. At the same time, both of these documents introduce students to historiographical questions that will recur throughout the unit. Aśoka's disavowal of war makes an interesting counterpoint to many of the other documents they read. The Bayeux Tapestry's portrayal of the Norman conquest of England shows how wars live on in the popular imagination. Bernard de Clairvaux's letter on the Second Crusade brings up religiously motivated wars, while an enquiry into King Leopold II's atrocities in the Congo provides an example of the economic and racist justifications for colonizers' violence. Napoleon's speeches at the Battle of Austerlitz raise the question of how military commanders motivate soldiers to risk their lives. Nationalism is thematized in the Constitution of the Black Hand as students explore the causes of World War I. In an echo of Aśoka's sentiments thousands of years earlier, students learn about Costa Rica's decision to abolish its military. Theodor Herzl's *The Jewish State* prepares students to understand the Israeli-Palestinian conflict, which they explore further by reading Yasser Arafat's famous "gun and olive branch" speech. The unit closes with an inquiry into the causes of the Rwandan genocide.

This unit can bring up complex emotions for students, especially those who come from military families or those who have experienced violence themselves. Teachers may wish to speak with these students and their families before the unit begins. Learning about the war in Yemen could disturb any student, and teachers should consider whether exposing them to images of this conflict is wise or not. Additionally, teachers should take special care with students who identify as Jewish or Arab; the Israeli-Palestinian conflict is one of the most contentious issues of our time, and difficult to bring into the classroom—but, I believe, extremely worthwhile. The underlying issues of religion, nationalism, and human rights, which are echoed in other documents, make for productive, if delicate, discussions.

LESSON 4.1
WHAT ARE THE EFFECTS OF THE WAR IN YEMEN ON CIVILIANS?

Historical Figure: Tawakkol Karman

Event: Civil war in Yemen begins, 2015

Introduction: What impact do you think war has on civilians? Give some examples.

Mini-Lecture:

- In 2011, Yemeni people staged a peaceful revolution against the dictator Ali Abdullah Saleh, and voted a new president, Abdrabbah Mansour Hadi, into office.
- A rebel group called the Houthis, apparently supported by the government of Iran, took over part of Yemen in 2015 in an attempt to reinstall Saleh as dictator.
- Saudi Arabia, the United Arab Emirates, and other countries in the region, supported by the United States and the United Kingdom, formed a coalition to fight back against the Houthi rebels.
- Both sides have caused civilians to die and be displaced from their homes; the Saudi-led coalition blockaded Yemen's main port in order to prevent Iran from supplying the Houthi rebels with weapons and resources, but this resulted in a humanitarian crisis (a problem causing widespread human suffering).
- The UN Office for the Coordinator of Humanitarian Affairs (OCHA) has been providing assistance to Yemeni civilians and produced our document in order to publicize the crisis there.
- Tawakkol Karman is a Yemeni journalist and human rights activist who was co-recipient of the Nobel Peace Prize in 2011 for her role in the Yemeni revolution and her work protecting freedom of the press; she was the first Arab woman to win the prize.
- Karman has spoken out against the war in Yemen and criticized the Saudi-led coalition and the Houthi rebels for the humanitarian crisis.

Vocabulary:

humanitarian: related to human welfare
lactating: breastfeeding
malnourished: illness resulting from not getting enough healthy food
indiscriminate: targeting anyone
unexploded ordnance: bombs that have fallen but not yet gone off,
endangering people who find them later
governorates: provinces
cholera: water- and food-borne disease that causes diarrhea, dehydration, and possibly death
alleviate: make better

Document: Eleven facts about the Yemen crisis, UN Humanitarian, 2019

1. The humanitarian situation in Yemen is still the worst in the world. Now in its fourth year of conflict, more than 22 million people—or three-quarters of the population—need humanitarian aid and protection, making Yemen the world's worst humanitarian crisis.

2. Some 8.4 million people in Yemen don't know where they will get their next meal. Last year, humanitarians scaled up dramatically to provide emergency food assistance to more than 7 million people per month. But this year we need to do even more. Ensuing families have the food they need to survive is the top priority for humanitarians.

3. Every ten minutes, a child under 5 in Yemen dies of preventable causes. Nearly 3 million children under 5 and pregnant or lactating women are acutely malnourished. This includes 400,000 children who are severely malnourished and nine times likelier to die than their healthier peers.

4. Civilians are bearing the brunt of the violence. Civilians face indiscriminate attacks, bombing, snipers, unexploded ordnance, cross-fire, kidnapping, rape and arbitrary detention, and other dangers. In February alone, at least 53 children were killed and 92 maimed in 12 governorates. All parties must respect international humanitarian law and international human rights law at all times.

5. Women and children are subject to widespread protection violations. Children are being forcibly recruited by the parties to the conflict; are being married off early and forced to work, to help their families survive. About one quarter of school-aged children are out of school, and 2,500 schools have been damaged or are not able to run.

6. Some 3 million people have been displaced. Internally displaced people are more vulnerable to exploitation and abuse. . . .

7. Ending the conflict is the only way to resolve the humanitarian crisis. All warring parties and their backers must work towards a negotiated political settlement.

8. Half of all health facilities are damaged or unable to function. Those that remain face severe shortages of staff and equipment.

9. Millions of Yemenis do not have access to safe drinking water, and cholera could resurge. In the last year, more than 1 million people suffered from cholera or watery diarrhea. Water and sanitation systems struggle to keep pace. As the rainy season approaches, there is high risk of another cholera epidemic breaking out.

10. Humanitarian response faces a nearly $2 billion funding gap. To alleviate suffering on a massive scale, the Yemen humanitarian response plan calls for $2.69 billion to assist 13 million people. Donors, particularly Saudi Arabia and the United Arab Emirates, have already been generous, but a nearly $2 billion funding gap remains.

11. Keeping the ports and other access channels open is crucial to deliver aid. Ports, which were blockaded through part of 2017, are now open to humanitarian and commercial shipments. All ports must remain open both to humanitarian cargo and commercial cargo to ensure local markets have food and other essential goods. . . .

Source: UNOCHA. (2019). Eleven facts about the Yemen crisis. https://unocha.exposure.co/eleven-facts-about-the-yemen-crisis

Comprehension Check:

1. List the different ways that Yemeni civilians are dying or at risk of dying, according to this document.
2. View the photos that accompany the online version of this document. Choose one to look at more closely and explain to the class how it illustrates one of the problems described in the document.

Activities:

1. Divide the class in half and debate this statement from the document: "All parties must respect international humanitarian law and international human rights law at all times."
2. Read and/or listen to the part of the interview with Tawakkol Karman in the Resources section (6:45-13:05). Write a response to UNOCHA's document from her perspective.

Reflection: Tawakkol Karman is the only woman featured in this unit, and one of the only advocates for peace; most of the conflicts described here were initiated by men. Why do you think that is?

Resources:

BBC. (2019). Yemen in crisis: Why is there a war? https://www.bbc.co.uk/news/world-middle-east-29319423

Council on Foreign Relations. (2018). Yemen in crisis: A conversation with Tawakkol Karman. https://www.cfr.org/event/yemen-crisis-conversation-tawakkol-karman

---

LESSON 4.2

HOW DID THE GREEKS TRY TO CONVINCE THE IONIANS TO JOIN THEIR FIGHT AGAINST THE PERSIANS?

Historical Figure: Themistocles

Event: Greco-Persian wars, 499–449 BCE

Introduction: How should nations or groups decide who are their allies and who are their enemies?

Mini-Lecture:

- In the 5th century BCE, the Persian Empire, centered in what is now Iran and stretching from Central Asia to Northern Africa, tried to invade what is now Greece.
- The Athenians, who called themselves and other Greek-speakers Hellenes, and who called their land Hellas, united with the Spartans against the Persians.
- The Ionians, a Greek-speaking people who lived in what is now Turkey, had unsuccessfully revolted against Persian king Darius early in the 5th century, and the Greeks had supported them.
- The Phoenicians, who lived in what is now Lebanon, and the Carians, who lived in what is now Turkey, were also included in the Persian Empire.
- Themistocles was an Athenian general who fought against the Persian king Xerxes in a series of battles in 480 BCE, which resulted in Athens remaining independent.
- Herodotus was a Greek historian who was born in Halicarnassus (now in Turkey) in the 5th century BCE; he wrote a history of the Greco-Persian Wars, from which our document is taken.

Vocabulary:

prosperity: wealth
seaworthiest: best for sailing
entreat: beg

fast bound: required
constrained: not able to

Document: Themistocles' appeal to the Ionians, Herodotus, 440 BCE

This is the display of the inquiry of Herodotus of Halicarnassus, so that things done by man not be forgotten in time, and that great and marvelous deeds, some displayed by the Hellenes, some by the barbarians, not lose their glory, including among others what was the cause of their waging war on each other. The Persian learned men say that the Phoenicians were the cause of the dispute. . . . But the Phoenicians do not tell the same story. . . .

For my part, I shall not say that this or that story is true, but I shall identify the one who I myself know did the Greeks unjust deeds, and thus proceed with my history, and speak of small and great cities of men alike. For many states that were once great have now become small; and those that were great in my time were small before. Knowing therefore that human prosperity never continues in the same place, I shall mention both alike. . . .

Themistocles thought that if the Ionian and Carian nations were removed from the forces of the barbarians, the Greeks might be strong enough to prevail over the rest. . . .

Themistocles . . . picked out the seaworthiest Athenian ships and made his way to the places where drinking water could be found. Here he engraved on the rocks words which the Ionians read on the next day when they came to Artemisium. This was what the writing said: "Men of Ionia, you do wrongly to fight against the land of your fathers and bring slavery upon Hellas. It would be best for you to join yourselves to us, but if that should be impossible for you, then at least now withdraw from the war, and entreat the Carians to do the same as you. If neither of these things may be and you are fast bound by such constraint that you cannot rebel, yet we ask you not to use your full strength in the day of battle. Remember that you are our sons and that our quarrel with the barbarian was of your making in the beginning." To my thinking Themistocles wrote this with a double intent, namely that if the king knew nothing of the writing, it might induce the Ionians to change sides and join with the Greeks, while if the writing were maliciously reported to Xerxes, he might thereby be led to mistrust the Ionians and keep them out of the sea-fights.

> *Source:* Perseus Digital Library. (n.d.). Herodotus, *The Histories.* http://www.perseus.tufts
> .edu/hopper/text?doc=Perseus:abo:tlg,0016,001:8

Comprehension Check:

1. Explain in your own words the three steps that Themistocles asks the Ionians to take, in order of what he prefers most to least.
2. What is Herodotus's theory about the two reasons that Themistocles wrote those words on the rocks?

Activities:

1. How you would react to Themistocles's message if you were an Ionian? Write a message back to him.
2. Herodotus is often called "the Father of History," because he introduced methods of writing history that historians still use today. What do you think he did that was different from earlier writers of history? Highlight the sentences that show his methods.

Reflection: Do you think groups should decide on their allies based on how similar their cultures are, or how close their relations have been in the past? Or should they decide based on what they think is right in the current situation? Why?

Resources:

Gill, N. S. (2019). A short summary of the Persian Wars. https://www.thoughtco.com
   /introduction-to-the-greco-persian-wars-120245
TEDEd. (n.d.). Why is Herodotus called the "Father of History"? https://ed.ted.com/lessons
   /why-is-herodotus-called-the-father-of-history-mark-robinson

---

LESSON 4.3

WHY DID KING AŚOKA WANT TO STOP WARS?

Historical Figure: Aśoka

Event: Mauryan Empire, 322–180 BCE

Introduction: Do you think leaders ever felt guilty about all the death and suffering they caused while expanding their empires? Why or why not?

Mini-Lecture:

- The Mauryan Empire was based in what is now India starting in the 4th century BCE; it was one of the largest empires of its time, connecting South Asia in a network of trade and administration.
- Chandragupta Maurya, who founded the empire, practiced Jainism, a religion based on nonviolence that has similarities with Hinduism and Buddhism.
- King Aśoka (also spelled Ashoka), who ruled from 268 to 232 BCE, conquered groups including the Kalingas, expanding the empire to its greatest size.
- Aśoka later became a devout Buddhist, sent out Buddhist monks to spread their teachings, and pledged to stop fighting wars in order to live in line with the dharma (also spelled dhamma), or Buddha's teachings, including nonviolence.
- Aśoka spread the news of his conversion in "rock edicts," or announcements that he had inscribed in stone throughout his empire; our document is taken from these inscriptions.

Vocabulary:

deported: sent away from their homes
inclination: liking for
remorse: feeling sorry
Brahman: Hindu of the highest caste
ascetic: person who gives up luxuries in order to pursue a spiritual life

householder: an ordinary person who owns a home
impartiality: fairness
yojana: unit to measure distance equivalent to about eight miles
forbearance: tolerance

Document: Rock edicts, Aśoka, 2nd century BCE

Beloved-of-the-Gods, King [Aśoka], conquered the Kalingas eight years after his coronation. One hundred and fifty thousand were deported, one hundred thousand were killed and many more died (from other causes). After the Kalingas had been conquered, Beloved-of-the-Gods came to feel a strong inclination towards the Dhamma, a love for the Dhamma and for instruction in Dhamma. Now Beloved-of-the-Gods feels deep remorse for having conquered the Kalingas.

   Indeed, Beloved-of-the-Gods is deeply pained by the killing, dying and deportation that take place when an unconquered country is conquered. But Beloved-of-the-Gods is pained even more by this—that Brahmans, ascetics, and householders of different religions who live in those countries, and who are respectful to superiors, to mother and father, to elders, and who behave properly and have strong loyalty towards friends, acquaintances, companions, relatives, servants and employees—that they are injured, killed or separated from their loved ones. Even those who are not affected (by all this) suffer when they see friends, acquaintances, companions and relatives affected. These misfortunes befall all (as a result of war), and this pains Beloved-of-the-Gods. . . .

Therefore the killing, death or deportation of a hundredth, or even a thousandth part of those who died during the conquest of Kalinga now pains Beloved-of-the-Gods. Now Beloved-of-the-Gods thinks that even those who do wrong should be forgiven where forgiveness is possible.

Even the forest people, who live in Beloved-of-the-Gods' domain, are entreated and reasoned with to act properly. They are told that despite his remorse Beloved-of-the-Gods has the power to punish them if necessary, so that they should be ashamed of their wrong and not be killed. Truly, Beloved-of-the-Gods desires non-injury, restraint and impartiality to all beings, even where wrong has been done.

Now it is conquest by Dhamma that Beloved-of-the-Gods considers to be the best conquest. And it (conquest by Dhamma) has been won here, on the borders, even six hundred yojanas away, where the Greek king Antiochos rules, beyond there where the four kings named Ptolemy, Antigonos, Magas and Alexander rule, likewise in the south among the Cholas, the Pandyas, and as far as Tamraparni. . . . This conquest has been won everywhere, and it gives great joy—the joy which only conquest by Dhamma can give. But even this joy is of little consequence. Beloved-of-the-Gods considers the great fruit to be experienced in the next world to be more important.

I have had this Dhamma edict written so that my sons and great-grandsons may not consider making new conquests, or that if military conquests are made, that they be done with forbearance and light punishment, or better still, that they consider making conquest by Dhamma only, for that bears fruit in this world and the next. May all their intense devotion be given to this which has a result in this world and the next.

Source: Colorado State University. (n.d.). The edicts of King Ashoka.
https://www.cs.colostate.edu/~malaiya/ashoka.html

Comprehension Check:

1. Why is Aśoka sad about the conquests he made in the past?
2. What kind of conquest does Aśoka want to make in the future?

Activities:

1. Divide the class in half and debate the following statement: It is possible to build a great empire without making military conquests.
2. Aśoka mentions Alexander the Great (Lesson 3.3). How do you think he would have responded to Aśoka's rock edicts? Write a dialogue between them in comic strip form.

Reflection: Do you think it is right for a ruler to spread their own religion the way Aśoka did? Why or why not?

Resources:

Lumen Learning. (n.d.). The Maurya Empire. https://courses.lumenlearning.com/boundless
   -worldhistory/chapter/the-maurya-empire/

Rattini, K. B. (2019). Who was Ashoka? https://www.nationalgeographic.com/culture/people
   /reference/ashoka/

LESSON 4.4

WHY DID HANNIBAL ATTACK THE ROMAN EMPIRE?

Historical Figure: Hannibal Barca

Event: Punic Wars, 264–146 BCE

Introduction: Do you think wars are more often started because of the economic and political needs of a country, or because of the personal feelings of rulers? Give some examples.

Mini-Lecture:

- The Punic Wars occurred between Carthage—an empire based in North Africa and extending into Iberia (now Spain)—and the Roman Empire.
- During the first Punic War, Rome won control of the island of Sicily, and Carthage, under the leadership of Hamilcar Barca, retained control of Sardinia, but had to pay a fine to Rome as part of the treaty.
- Hamilcar's son Hannibal Barca led Carthage in the Second Punic War; he carried out a siege in the Roman territory of Saguntum and broke a treaty that Carthage had made with Rome by crossing the River Ebro.
- Hannibal was famous for leading a force that included horses and elephants over the high mountains of the Pyrenees to invade Rome; however, in the end, he was unable to conquer Rome.
- Polybius was a Greek historian who lived from 208 to 125 BCE, who wrote *The Histories*, about the Roman Republic, from which our document is taken.
- Polybius interviewed survivors from Hannibal's army to gather details about the war.

Vocabulary:

pronouncement: claim	*bade:* asked
distinction: difference	*exasperated:* annoyed
indignation: humiliation	*libation:* a drink offered to the gods
Zeus: Greek and Roman god	*exorbitancy:* expensiveness

Document: *The Histories*, Polybius, 2nd century BCE

Some of those authors who have dealt with Hannibal and his times, wishing to indicate the causes that led to the above war between Rome and Carthage, allege as its first cause the siege of Saguntum by the Carthaginians and as its second their crossing, contrary to treaty, the river [Ebro]. I should agree in stating that these were the beginnings of the war, but I can by no means allow that they were its causes, . . . These are pronouncements of men who are unable to see the great and essential distinction between a beginning and a cause or purpose, these being the first origin of all, and the beginning coming last. . . .

To return to the war between Rome and Carthage . . . we must regard its first cause as being the indignation of Hamilcar surnamed Barcas, the actual father of Hannibal. . . .

[Hannibal] said that at the time when his father was about to start with his army on his expedition to Spain, he himself, then nine years of age, was standing by the altar, while Hamilcar was sacrificing to Zeus. When, on the omens being favorable, Hamilcar had poured a libation to the gods and performed all the customary rites, he ordered the others who were attending the sacrifice to withdraw to a slight distance and calling Hannibal to him asked him kindly if he wished to accompany him on the expedition. On his accepting with delight, and, like a boy, even begging to do it besides, his father took him by the hand, led him up to the altar, and bade him lay his hand on the victim and swear never to be the friend of the Romans. . . .

We must consider, then, the causes of the [Punic] War to have been those I have stated, while its beginnings were as follows. The Carthaginians could ill bear their defeat in the war for Sicily, and, as I said above, they were additionally exasperated by the matter of Sardinia and the exorbitancy of the sum they had been last obliged to agree to pay. Therefore, when they had subjugated the greater part of Iberia, they were quite ready to adopt any measures against Rome which suggested themselves. . . .

[Hannibal] advanced on the day he had fixed with an army of about ninety thousand foot and twelve thousand horse. Crossing the Ebro, he set about subduing the tribes of the Ilurgetes, Bargusii, Aerenosii, and Andosini as far as the Pyrenees. . . .

The Romans protested against his attacking Saguntum, which they said was under their protection, or crossing the Ebro, contrary to the treaty engagements. . . .

Source: Thayer, B. (n.d.). Polybius, the histories.
http://penelope.uchicago.edu/Thayer/E/Roman/Texts/Polybius/3*.html

Comprehension Check:

1. According to Polybius, what was one main cause of the Punic Wars?
2. According to Polybius, what was the beginning of the Punic Wars?

Activities:

1. The basis for Polybius's theory about the cause of the war is a story Hannibal told to someone else, which was then reported to Polybius. Make a list of evidence that could corroborate or contradict Polybius's theory.
2. With a partner, choose a war or conflict. Do some research to find out the underlying cause(s) as well as the beginning, and present them to the class.

Reflection: Do you think that loyalty to family is a worthy reason to start a war? Why or why not?

Resources:

Ball, P. (2016). The truth about Hannibal's trip across the Alps. https://www.theguardian.com /science/2016/apr/03/where-muck-hannibals-elephants-alps-italy-bill-mahaney-york -university-toronto

History.com. (2019). Punic Wars. https://www.history.com/topics/ancient-history/punic-wars

---

LESSON 4.5

WHY DID THE NORMANS ATTACK THE ANGLO-SAXONS IN THE BATTLE OF HASTINGS?

Historical Figure: William the Conqueror

Event: Battle of Hastings, 1066

Introduction: Would you fight out of loyalty to a certain leader? Why or why not?

Mini-Lecture:

- In 1066, William the Conqueror, who was the Duke of Normandy (now in France), succeeded in taking over the Anglo-Saxons, in what is now England.
- In 1064, King Edward the Confessor of Saxony had told his brother-in-law Harold Godwinson to go to Normandy and offer William the English throne.
- However, after King Edward died, Harold claimed the English throne for himself.
- William attacked the Anglo-Saxons in the Battle of Hastings in 1066, and won.
- Our document comes from the Bayeux Tapestry, a 230-foot-long piece of fabric showing scenes from the war.
- Historians are not sure who commissioned the tapestry to be made, but it ended up in a cathedral in Bayeux, France, and is now housed in the Bayeux Museum.
- The scenes were embroidered in wool thread on linen cloth by an unknown number of female needleworkers.

Vocabulary:

Harold Rex interfectus est (Latin): King Harold is killed

Document: Bayeux Tapestry, 11th century, female needleworkers (see Figure 4.1)

Figure 4.1. Detail of the Bayeux Tapestry, 11th century

Source: The Bayeux Museum. The Bayuex Tapestry. www.bayeuxmuseum.com
Image reprinted with special permission from the City of Bayeux

Comprehension Check:

1. Historians have debated whether Harold is the figure holding an arrow that has pierced his eye (between the O and the L in Harold), or the figure in the scene to his left being stabbed with a sword, or whether Harold is represented by both of those figures. What do you think? What evidence in the tapestry supports your position?
2. What do you see in the lower border of the tapestry?

Activities:

1. As a result of the Norman conquest of Anglo-Saxony, the English language evolved to be close to what it is today. Brainstorm other unintended effects of French-speaking Normans taking over and ruling what is now England.
2. Research a war or conflict going on now, print out pictures from the Internet, and collage a "tapestry" that shows what has happened.

Reflection: Do you think it is important for artists to depict what happens in wars? Why or why not?

Resources:

Bayeux Museum. (2019). Discover the Bayeux Tapestry. https://www.bayeuxmuseum.com
/en/the-bayeux-tapestry/discover-the-bayeux-tapestry/

English Heritage. (n.d.). 1066 and the Norman Conquest. https://www.english-heritage.org
.uk/learn/1066-and-the-norman-conquest/

LESSON 4.6

How Did Christians Justify the Crusades?

Historical Figure: Bernard of Clairvaux

Event: Second Crusade, 1147–1149

Introduction: Is there any cause that you would be willing to fight and die for? What would it be, and why?

Mini-Lecture:

- The Crusades were a series of wars in the 11th to 13th centuries in which Christians tried to gain control of the "Holy Land" (now located in Jordan, Israel, Lebanon, Palestine, and Syria) from Muslim rulers, who had ruled it since the 7th century.
- This area, and in particular the city of Jerusalem, is sacred to Christians, Muslims, and Jews, and is the site of many religious landmarks; those groups sometimes fought, and sometimes coexisted peacefully in this area.
- Bernard of Clairvaux was a Christian abbot (head of a monastery) who lived in what is now France from 1090 to 1153.
- Clairvaux was close to several popes (leaders of the Roman Catholic Church), including Pope Eugenius III, who called for the Second Crusade.
- Our document comes from a letter Clairvaux sent to Christian leaders in France and Bavaria (now in Germany) encouraging them to recruit people to fight in the Crusades.
- Clairvaux uses several metaphors from the Bible: the "spotless lamb with purple blood" symbolizes Jesus Christ, and "cast pearls before swine" means sharing the Christian teachings with those who do not value them.

Vocabulary:

clergy: religious authorities
abound: have plenty of
behold: observe
brethren: brothers
consecrate: make holy
resurrection: coming back from the dead (as Christians believe Jesus Christ did)
blaspheming: saying things that go against a certain religion

alas: sadly
defilement: making something dirty or impure
heathen: negative term some Christians use for people who are not Christian
purged: made clean
robust: strong
gird up your loins: get ready
prudent: wise
contrite: apologetic

Document: Letter on the Second Crusade, Bernard de Clairvaux, 1147

To the Lords and very dear Fathers, the Archbishops and Bishops, with the whole clergy and the faithful people of Eastern France and Bavaria: Bernard, called Abbot of Clairvaux, desires that they may abound in the spirit of strength.

I write to you with respect to a matter which concerns the service of Christ, in whom is our salvation. . . .

Behold, brethren, now is the accepted time, now is the day of salvation. The earth also is moved and has trembled, because the God of heaven has begun to destroy the land which is his: his, I say, in which the word of the Father was taught, and where he dwelt for more than thirty years, a man among men; his, for he enlightened it with miracles, he consecrated it with his own blood; in it appeared the first fruits of his resurrection. And now, for our sins, the enemies of Cross have raised blaspheming heads, ravaging with the edge of the sword the land of promise. For they are almost on the point, if there be not One to withstand them, of bursting into the very city of the living God, of the holy places of the spotless Lamb with purple blood. Alas! They rage against the very shrine of the Christian faith with blasphemous mouths, and would enter and trample down the very couch on which, for us, our Life lay down to sleep in death.

What are you going to do then, O brave men? What are you doing, O servants of the Cross? Will you give what is holy to the dogs, and cast your pearls before swine? How many sinners there, confessing their sins with tears, have obtained pardon, after the defilement of the heathen had been purged by the swords of your fathers! . . .

Since, therefore, your land is fruitful in brave men, and is known to be full of robust youth, since your praise is in the whole world, and the fame of your valor has filled the entire earth, gird up your loins manfully, and take up arms in zeal for the Christian name. Let not your former warlike skill cease, but only that spirit of hatred in which you are accustomed to strike down and kill one another and in turn be overcome yourselves. . . .

But now, O brave knight, now, O warlike hero, here is a battle you may fight without danger, where it is glory to conquer and gain to die. If you are a prudent merchant, if you are a desirer of this world, behold I show you some great bargains; see that you lose them not. Take the sign of the cross and you shall gain pardon for every sin that you confess with a contrite heart.

Source: Council of Centers on Jewish-Christian Relations. (2008). Bernard of Clairvaux, the Jews and the Second Crusade (1146). https://www.ccjr.us/dialogika-resources /primary-texts-from-the-history-of-the-relationship/bernard-of-clairvaux

Comprehension Check:

1. According to Clairvaux, why is the Crusade necessary at this time?
2. According to Clairvaux, why is fighting in the Crusades a "bargain" for soldiers?

Activities:

1. Write a letter back to Clairvaux from King Aśoka (Lesson 4.3).
2. Divide the class in half and debate the following proposition: "Religion is worth fighting for."

Reflection: ISIS (Lesson 3.1) refers to the French and other Europeans as "Crusaders," and uses these 12th-century battles as a justification for their attacks. Do you think Bernard de Clairvaux still would have supported the Crusades if he had known that ISIS would use these former conflicts as a reason to attack Paris in 2015? Why or why not?

Resources:

New World Encyclopedia. (n.d.). Bernard of Clairvaux. https://www.newworldencyclopedia
    .org/entry/Bernard_of_Clairvaux
Sullivan, M. (2017). Why Muslims see the Crusades so differently from Christians. https://
    www.history.com/news/why-muslims-see-the-crusades-so-differently-from-christians

LESSON 4.7

How Did Napoleon Motivate Soldiers to Fight for Him?

Historical Figure: Napoleon

Event: Napoleonic Wars, 1803–1815

Introduction: If you were a military commander, how would you motivate your soldiers to fight, especially if some had been drafted into the army rather than choosing to join?

Mini-Lecture:

- Napoleon Bonaparte was the emperor of France between 1804 and 1815.
- The Napoleonic Wars were a series of conflicts that occurred between 1803 and 1815 between France and various alliances of European powers (often led by Britain) as Napoleon tried to expand his territory.
- The Third Coalition was an alliance that Britain, Russia, and the Austrian Empire created to oppose Napoleon.
- The Third Coalition had been defeated by Napoleon at the battles of Hollabrunn and Ulm.
- In the Battle of Austerlitz, in 1805, the French beat a larger force of Russians and Austrians, bringing about the end of the Third Coalition.
- Our document comes from a series of speeches that Napoleon made to his troops before and after that battle.

Vocabulary:

formidable: strong

flank: side of a military force

expose himself: make himself vulnerable to

strokes: attacks   *fatigues:* tiredness
intrepidity: bravery   *vindicate:* prove that one is right
dispersed: scattered   *effect:* carry out
vanquished: defeated

Document: Speeches on the Battle of Austerlitz, Napoleon, 1805

Proclamation to the Soldiers before the Battle of Austerlitz: December 1, 1805

Soldiers: The Russian army has presented itself before you to revenge the disasters of the Austrians at Ulm. They are the same men that you conquered at Hollabrunn, and on whose flying trails you have followed. The positions which they occupy are formidable. While they are marching to turn my right, they must present their flank to your blows.

   Soldiers: I will myself direct all your battalions. I will keep myself at a distance from the fire, if, with your accustomed valor, you carry disorder and confusion into the enemies' ranks. But should victory appear for a moment uncertain, you will see your Emperor expose himself to the first strokes. Victory must not be doubtful on this occasion.

Proclamation after the Battle of Austerlitz: December 3, 1805

Soldiers: I am satisfied with you. In the Battle of Austerlitz you have justified all that I expected from your intrepidity. You have decorated your eagles with immortal glory. An army of one hundred thousand men, commanded by the Emperors of Russia and Austria, has been, in less than four hours, either cut in pieces or dispersed. Thus in two months the third coalition has been vanquished and dissolved. Peace cannot now be far distant. But I will make only such a peace as gives us guarantee for our future, and secures rewards to our allies. When everything necessary to secure the happiness and prosperity of our country is obtained, I will lead you back to France. My people will behold you again with joy. It will be enough for one of you to say, "I was at the battle of Austerlitz"; for all your fellow citizens to exclaim, "There is a brave man."

Address to the Soldiers on the Signing of Peace with Austria: December 26, 1805

Peace has just been signed by the Emperor of Austria. You have in the last autumn made two campaigns. You have seen your Emperor share your dangers and your fatigues. I wish also that you should see him surrounded by the grandeur and splendor which belong to the sovereign of the first people in the world. You shall all be there. We will celebrate the names of those who have died in these two campaigns in the field of honor. The world shall ever see us ready to follow their example. We will even do more than we have yet done, if necessary to vindicate our national honor, or to resist the efforts of those who are the eternal enemies of peace upon the continent. During the three months which are necessary to effect your return to France, prove the example for all armies. You have now to give testimonies, not of courage and intrepidity, but of strict discipline. Conduct yourself like children in the bosom of their family.

Source: The Napoleon Series. (2005). Napoleon's addresses:
The Austerlitz campaign, 1805.
https://www.napoleon-series.org/research/napoleon/speeches/c_speeches5.html

Comprehension Check:

1. Under what circumstances did Napoleon plan to enter the battle himself?
2. According to Napoleon, how would French people treat the returning soldiers?

Activities:

1. Create a T-chart comparing and contrasting Napoleon's methods of motivating soldiers with Bernard of Clairvaux's (Lesson 4.6).
2. Write a letter to Napoleon from one of the soldiers who fought in the Battle of Austerlitz; then switch with a partner and discuss how your perspectives are similar or different.

Reflection: How are veterans treated in your community? Why do you think that is?

Resources:

Encyclopedia Britannica. (2019). The Napoleonic Wars. https://www.britannica.com/event/Napoleonic-Wars

Foundation Napoleon. (2020). Timeline: Consulate/1st French Empire. https://www.napoleon.org/en/young-historians/napodoc/timeline-consulate1st-french-empire/

LESSON 4.8

WHY DID KING LEOPOLD II FIGHT FOR CONTROL OF THE CONGO?

Historical Figure: King Leopold

Event: King Leopold announces creation of the Congo Free State, 1885

Introduction: Do you know of any wars that have been fought at least partly for economic reasons? Give examples.

Mini-Lecture:

- Leopold II was king of Belgium from 1865 to 1909.
- In 1885, he set up a corporation in which he was the primary stakeholder, and which established the Congo Free State, a private colony in Central Africa (now the Democratic Republic of Congo).
- The Congo Free State was rich in natural resources including ivory and rubber; King Leopold ordered the Indigenous people to pay "prestations," or taxes, by harvesting the rubber, and he enforced these orders with violence.

- These policies caused the death of what historians believe may be as many as 10 million people, or half the population of the Congo.
- King Leopold established the Force Publique, an army with European officers commanding soldiers (called "sentries") from the Congo and surrounding areas; the sentries were paid for each person that they killed, and they had to cut off and present the hands of their victims to prove they had killed them.
- Leopold used the wealth he gained from selling the Congo's resources to build monuments in his home city of Brussels, including the Royal Museum for Central Africa and the Cinqantenaire victory arch.
- Our document comes from a commission of enquiry that was launched by the Belgian government to investigate claims of abuses against the Indigenous people of the Congo by King Leopold's corporation.

Vocabulary:

Negro: person of African heritage
aversion: dislike
compulsion: forcing someone to do something
induce: force
coercion: forcing someone to do something
detention: holding someone in prison
sentinel: soldier
prestation: tax
forthcoming: available
mortality: death
post: town
lash: whip
furnish: provide
impost: tax
excess: too much

sentries: soldiers
abuse: harsh treatment
deduce: conclude
considerations: details
abolished: stopped
might: power
confound: confuse
compel: force
regrettable: too bad
extremity: worst possible situation
beat the bush: to search through the forest
ascribed: blamed on
punitive: in order to punish
inflict: cause suffering
exemplary: make an example of someone or something

Document: Report of the Congo Commission of Enquiry, 1905

The dislike of the negro for all kinds of work; his especial aversion to the rubber gathering . . . ; all of these circumstances have made compulsion necessary to induce the native to gather rubber.

Until recent years this coercion has been exercised in different ways, such as, the taking of hostages, the detention of chiefs and the institution of sentinels or bosses and the sending of armed expeditions. . . . The prestations were due from the village as a whole; when they were not forthcoming the chiefs were arrested and some of the inhabitants taken at random, often the women were held as hostages. . . .

From the statements of witnesses and the official documents that we saw, we found that this detention may have been continued, in certain cases, for several months. . . . We have been told that the places in which the prisoners were kept were sometimes in a bad condition, that they often lacked the necessities and that the mortality amongst them was very great.

Some chiefs of posts, assuming a right that never belonged to them administer the lash to those who fail to furnish the complete imposts. Some have carried this to excess, as is shown by the record of their punishment by the courts. . . .

The Sentries: One means by sentries . . . , the black overseers, armed with a muzzle-loading gun, who have the official duty of directing the work of the natives in the forest. . . . It is not possible for us to say, even approximately, how many abuses these sentries have committed. . . . One [chief] declared that in his village one hundred and twenty had been killed during the past years. . . .

It would undoubtedly be wrong to deduce from these considerations the idea that all coercion should be abolished. The native can understand and respect nothing but might and with this he confounds right. The State ought to assure the triumph of law and, consequently, compel the black to work. But if it wishes to avoid the regrettable consequences which we have pointed out, it should, according to our ideas, make use of this authority only in the last extremity. . . .

State Expeditions: . . . It is the abusive military operations having a warlike nature, which we feel ought to be mentioned. . . . It most frequently happens that the natives flee at the approach of the troops without offering any resistance. . . . One of the plans usually followed in such cases is to send out search parties and beat the bush, with instructions to bring such natives as they may find. . . . It is during this service that most of the murders are committed which are ascribed to the State. . . .

The military expedition sometimes takes on a character still more repressive. We shall now speak of those operations which have been called "punitive expeditions," whose purpose is to inflict an exemplary punishment upon a village or a group of natives who have been guilty of some crime or serious resistance against the authority of the State. . . .

The Mutilations: . . . other mutilated persons said about as follows: "The soldiers (or sentries) came to make war in our village. I had been wounded and had fallen unconscious upon the ground. A soldier (or sentry) thinking me dead, cut off my hand."

Source: Project Gutenberg. (2008). The Congo: A report of the commission of enquiry appointed by the Congo Free State government. https://archive.org/stream /congoreportofcom00congrich/congoreportofcom00congrich_djvu.txt

Comprehension Check:

1. List four things that could happen to people in the Congo whose villages did not provide enough rubber to the authorities.
2. What does the Commission of Enquiry recommend to King Leopold II?

Activities:

1. Highlight the words and phrases in this document that are racist (that establish the superiority of White European people over African people). Then compare your document with a partner and discuss differences or similarities between the words and phrases you chose.
2. Write one word on a Post-it to describe what the Congo Free State led by King Leopold did. Stick your Post-it on the board alongside the responses of other students, and discuss as a class.

Reflection: Today, the Royal Museum of Africa that King Leopold II built contains objects that were taken from Congo during colonial rule. What do you think should happen to art and artifacts that were seized during wars by colonial powers—should they be returned to the areas where they originated, or should they remain in the colonizing countries' museums? Why?

Resources:

Arke, L. (2016). A lasting legacy of the Builder King in Brussels. https://theculturetrip.com /europe/belgium/articles/a-lasting-legacy-of-the-builder-king-in-brussels/

Hochschild, A. (2019). King Leopold II. https://www.britannica.com/biography/Leopold-II -king-of-Belgium

LESSON 4.9

WHY DID SERBIAN NATIONALISTS IGNITE WORLD WAR I?

Historical Figure: Gavrilo Princip

Event: Assassination of Archduke Franz Ferdinand, 1914

Introduction: Do you feel you have more in common with people who come from the same country as you, speak the same language as you, come from the same racial or ethnic group, or practice the same religion? Why?

Mini-Lecture:

*   Serbians are an ethnic group who live in what is now Serbia, as well as throughout the Balkan region; along with groups including Croatians, Russians, Poles, and Slovaks, their language belongs to the Slavic family and they may identify as Slavs.
*   Serbians lived under the rule of the Ottoman Empire from the 15th century until the late 19th century, when they gained an independent country of their own.
*   Serbia had close economic and political ties to the Austro-Hungarian Empire, which was expanding its territory in the early 20th century; but many Serbians resented the empire's influence, as well as its annexation in 1908 of Bosnia and Herzegovina, home to other Slavs.

- In the early 20th century, nationalism (identification with one's own nation over others, and the desire to protect its interests and independence) increased among Serbians and other Slavs, who wanted to form a Slavic nation independent of foreign influence.
- A group called the Black Hand formed to promote the unification of Serbia and Bosnia-Herzegovina as "Serbdom"; our document comes from the constitution of this group, which was written in 1911.
- In 1914, Gavrilo Princip, a member of the Black Hand, assassinated Archduke Franz Ferdinand, the heir to the Austro-Hungarian throne, while he was visiting Bosnia-Herzegovina.
- The Austro-Hungarian Empire declared war on Serbia, with the backing of Germany, and Russia (along with Great Britain, France, and Belgium) came to its aid, sparking World War I.

Vocabulary:

irrespective of: without differences among
revolutionary: trying to change a government
striving: efforts
raison d'etre: reason for existing

strata: levels
exploit: use unfairly
coat of arms: design that symbolizes a group or individual
phial: small bottle

Document: Constitution of the Black Hand, 1911

Article 1. For the purpose of realizing the national ideals—the Unification of Serbdom—an organization is hereby created, whose members may be any Serbian irrespective of sex, religion, place or birth, as well as anybody else who will sincerely serve this idea.

Article 2. The organization gives priority to the revolutionary struggle rather than relies on cultural striving, therefore its institution is an absolutely secret one for wider circles.

Article 3. The organization bears the name: [The Black Hand].

Article 4. In order to carry into effect its task the organization will do the following things: (1) Following the character of its raison d'etre it will exercise its influence over all the official factors in Serbia . . . as also over all the strata of the State and over the entire social life in it: (2) It will carry out a revolutionary organization in all the territories where Serbians are living: (3) Beyond the frontiers, it will fight with all means against all enemies of this idea: (4) It will maintain friendly relations with all the States, nations, organizations, and individual persons who sympathize with Serbia and the Serbian race: (5) It will give every assistance to those nations and organizations who are fighting for their own national liberation and unification. . . .

Article 30. On entering into the organization, every member must know that by joining the organization he loses his own personality; he must not expect any glory for himself, nor any personal benefit, material or moral. Consequently the member who should dare to try to exploit the organization for his personal, or class, or party interests shall be punished by death. . . .

Article 34. The Organization's official seal is thus composed: In the center of the seal there is a powerful arm holding in its hand an unfurled flag on which—as a coat of arms—there is a skull with crossed bones; by the side of the flag, a knife, a bomb and a phial of poison. Around, in a circle, there is the following inscription, reading from left to right: "Unification or Death," and in the base: "The Supreme Central Directorate."

Source: About WWI Document Archive. (2009). Constitution of the Black Hand. https:// wwi.lib.byu.edu/index.php/Constitution_of_the_Black_Hand

Comprehension Check:

1. With whom would the Black Hand be allied, and who would be its enemies?
2. Draw the seal of the Black Hand.

Activities:

1. Polybius (Lesson 4.4) makes a distinction between the causes of a war and its beginning. Work with a small group and use this document, the mini-lecture, and background readings to create a poster showing the causes versus the beginning of World War I.
2. After World War I, a country called Yugoslavia was formed, which included many different Slavic groups. Yet this country eventually broke into smaller countries: Bosnia Herzegovina, Croatia, Kosovo, Montenegro, North Macedonia, Slovenia, and Serbia. Work with a partner to research one of these countries and outline what the people there have in common with each other that they do not share with others from the former Yugoslavia.

Reflection: Would you join an organization like the Black Hand if a foreign power took over your country? If yes, why, and if not, what would you do instead?

Resources:

Dzidic, D. et al. (2014). Gavrilo Princip—Hero or villain? *The Guardian.* https://www .theguardian.com/world/2014/may/06/gavrilo-princip-hero-villain-first-world-war -balkan-history
History.com. (2019). World War I. https://www.history.com/topics/world-war-i/world-war-i -history

LESSON 4.10

WHY DID COSTA RICA ABOLISH ITS MILITARY?

Historical Figure: José Figueres Ferrer

Event: Costa Rica abolishes its military, 1948

Introduction: Would you like to live in a country that had no military? Why or why not?

Mini-Lecture:

- In 1948, there was a civil war in Costa Rica after the government annulled, or canceled, the results of an election won by an opposition candidate; historians believe that in less than two months, more than 2,000 people died.
- José Figueres Ferrer led a rebel army that defeated the government, and then became president.
- Ferrer helped to write a new constitution, from which our document is taken; this constitution abolished the "standing army," or any military forces that are active outside of wartime.
- Costa Rica has not been engaged in a war since 1949, and it is home to the University for Peace, a UN-organized institution that promotes conflict resolution; however, it has had border disputes with Nicaragua and has struggled to control the drug trade in the region.

Vocabulary:

republic: country in which people elect representatives to lead them
sovereignty: power
usurp: take away
treason: betraying a country
continental shelf: a seabed around a landmass that is higher than the rest of the sea floor
surveillance: secretly watching people
continental agreement: agreement with other countries in the continent
subordinate to: under the control of
civil: nonmilitary

deliberate: discuss important decisions
comprehensive: including all stages
correlated: connected
compulsory: mandatory
diversified education level: education beyond high school (e.g., university, professional, vocational schools)
expenditure: amount of money spent
per annum: per year
gross domestic product: the value of goods and services produced in a country over the course of one year

Document: Costa Rican Constitution, 1948

Article 1. Costa Rica is a free and independent democratic Republic.
Article 2. Sovereignty resides exclusively in the Nation.
Article 3. No one may usurp sovereignty; anyone who does it commits the crime of treason to the Nation. . . .
Article 5. The national territory is bounded by the Caribbean Sea, the Pacific Ocean, and the Republics of Nicaragua and Panama. . . .
Article 6. The State exercises complete and exclusive sovereignty over the air space above its territory, over its territorial waters within a distance of twelve miles measured from the low-tide mark along its shores, over its continental shelf and its insular undersea base, in accordance with principles of International Law. . . .

Article 12. The Army as a permanent institution is abolished. There shall be the necessary police forces for surveillance and the preservation of the public order. Military forces may only be organized under a continental agreement or for the national defense; in either case, they shall always be subordinate to the civil power: they may not deliberate or make statements or representations individually or collectively. . . .

Article 77. Public education shall be organized as a comprehensive process correlated in its various phases, from preschool to university education.

Article 78. Preschool education and general basic education are compulsory. These levels and the diversified education level are, in the public system, free and supported by the Nation.

Public expenditure in State education, including higher education, shall not be less than six percent (6%) per annum of the gross domestic product, in accordance with the law. . . . The State shall facilitate the pursuit of higher studies by persons who lack monetary resources. The Ministry of Public Education, through the organization established by law, shall be in charge of awarding scholarships and assistance.

Source: Costa Rica Law. (n.d.). Costa Rica Constitution in English.
https://costaricalaw.com/costa-rica-legal-topics/constitutional-law
/costa-rica-constitution-in-english/

Comprehension Check:

1. Under what circumstances could Costa Rica organize an army? What restrictions would be placed on it?
2. What does Costa Rica promise to fund instead of devoting money to an army?

Activities:

1. Work with a partner to list Costa Rica's possible responses if a person violated Article 3, or if a country violated Article 6.
2. Line up on an "opinion cline" (a physical line representing a spectrum of opinion) based on how much you agree with the following statement: The world would be more peaceful if all countries abolished their standing armies. Talk with someone near you, and then someone with a different opinion.

Reflection: If your country were to abolish its military, what would you think it should spend that money on instead?

Resources:

Badri-Maharaj, S. (2017). Costa Rica's challenge: Maintaining internal security without an army. https://idsa.in/idsacomments/costa-rica-challenge-maintaining-internal-security _sbmaharaj_230317
Trejos, A. (2018). Why getting rid of Costa Rica's army 70 years ago has been such a success. https://www.usatoday.com/story/news/world/2018/01/05/costa-rica-celebrate-70-years -no-army/977107001/

LESSON 4.11

WHY WERE JEWISH PEOPLE WILLING TO FIGHT FOR A COUNTRY OF THEIR OWN?

Historical Figure: Theodor Herzl

Event: State of Israel created, 1948

Introduction: If your religious group were persecuted in every country in the world, what would you do? Why?

Mini-Lecture:

- Throughout history, Jewish people have faced discrimination from other religious and ethnic groups; in many societies they were banned from holding certain jobs, prevented from owning property, unfairly blamed for spreading diseases, forced to leave their homes, and sometimes killed.
- Discrimination against Jewish people is called anti-Semitism, because many Jews belong to a larger collection of ethnic groups called Semites.
- Zionism is the idea that Jewish people need a country of their own in order to be safe from discrimination.
- Theodor Herzl was a journalist born in the Austro-Hungarian Empire (in what is now Hungary) who witnessed anti-Semitism while living in France in the late 19th century.
- In 1895, Herzl wrote a short book called *The Jewish State*, from which our document is taken; in it, he argued in favor of Zionism and explained how he thought a Jewish country could be established.
- Many Jews in Europe agreed with Herzl's argument, especially after more than 6 million Jews were killed during the Holocaust between 1933 and 1945 due to the anti-Semitism of Adolf Hitler and the Nazis.

Vocabulary:

gravity: seriousness
perceptible: able to be seen
persecuted: made to suffer
statute: law
dead letter: not effective
debarred: forbidden
enunciated: spoken
resignation: accepting the situation

mercifully disposed toward: having compassion for
covertly: secretly
execution: putting into action
potency: power
rampart: defense
Christendom: relating to Christianity
extra-territorial: separate from the territory of a nation

Document: *The Jewish State*, Theodor Herzl, 1895

No one can deny the gravity of the situation of the Jews. Wherever they live in perceptible numbers, they are more or less persecuted. Their equality before the law, granted by statute, has become practically a dead letter. They are debarred from filling even moderately high positions, either in the army, or in any public or private capacity. And attempts are made to thrust them out of business also: "Don't buy from Jews!"

Attacks in Parliaments, in assemblies, in the press, in the pulpit, in the street, on journeys—for example, their exclusion from certain hotels—even in places of recreation, become daily more numerous. . . .

Everything tends, in fact, to one and the same conclusion, which is clearly enunciated in that classic Berlin phrase: "Juden Raus!" (Out with the Jews!)

I shall now put the Question in the briefest possible form: Are we to "get out" now and where to? Or, may we yet remain? And, how long?

Let us first settle the point of staying where we are. Can we hope for better days, can we possess our souls in patience, can we wait in pious resignation till the princes and peoples of this earth are more mercifully disposed towards us? I say that we cannot hope for a change in the current of feeling. . . . The nations in whose midst Jews live are all either covertly or openly Anti-Semitic. . . .

The Plan: . . . Let the sovereignty be granted us over a portion of the globe large enough to satisfy the rightful requirements of a nation; the rest we shall manage for ourselves. . . . The plan, simple in design, but complicated in execution, will be carried out by two agencies: The Society of Jews and the Jewish Company. The Society of Jews will do the preparatory work in the domains of science and politics, which the Jewish Company will afterwards apply practically. . . . Let all who are willing to join us, fall in behind our banner and fight for our cause with voice and pen and deed. . . .

Shall we choose Palestine or Argentina? We shall take what is given us, and what is selected by Jewish public opinion. . . . Palestine is our ever-memorable historic home. The very name of Palestine would attract our people with a force of marvelous potency. . . . We should there form a portion of a rampart of Europe against Asia, an outpost of civilization as opposed to barbarism. We should as a neutral State remain in contact with all Europe, which would have to guarantee our existence. The sanctuaries of Christendom would be safeguarded by assigning to them an extra-territorial status such as is well-known to the law of nations. . . .

Let me repeat once more my opening words: The Jews who wish for a State will have it.

We shall live at last as free men on our own soil, and die peacefully in our own homes.

The world will be freed by our liberty, enriched by our wealth, magnified by our greatness.

And whatever we attempt there to accomplish for our own welfare, will react powerfully and beneficially for the good of humanity.

Source: Project Gutenberg. (2008). The Jewish State. http://www.gutenberg.org/files /25282/25282-h/25282-h.htm#I_Introduction

Comprehension Check:

1. According to Herzl, why do Jews need a country of their own?
2. Explain two reasons why Herzl thinks Palestine would be a good place to establish the Jewish State.

Activities:

1. With a partner, list some pros and cons of Herzl's plan.
2. Imagine you are a 19th-century Jewish person living in a place where you are persecuted. List reasons why you would support or oppose Herzl's plan to create a Jewish State.

Reflection: Herzl mentions fighting "with voice and pen and deed." Do you think military fighting would be necessary as well to realize his plan? Why or why not?

Resources:

History.com. (2019). State of Israel proclaimed. https://www.history.com/this-day-in-history/state-of-israel-proclaimed

MJL. (n.d.). Theodor Herzl. My Jewish learning. https://www.myjewishlearning.com/article/theodor-herzl/

LESSON 4.12

WHY HAVE PALESTINIANS FOUGHT AGAINST ISRAEL?

Historical Figure: Yasser Arafat

Event: Creation of the Palestinian Liberation Organization, 1964

Introduction: What do you know about the struggle between Israelis and Palestinians? Where did you learn it?

Mini-Lecture:

- In 1917, the British, who had colonized Palestine, issued the Balfour Declaration, which stated that they supported "the establishment in Palestine of a national home for the Jewish people," while preserving the rights of Palestinian Arabs already living there.
- Jewish people inspired by Zionism had begun moving to Palestine in the 19th century, and their numbers increased in the 1930s due to persecution by the Nazis; by 1947 there were about 650,000 Jewish people and 1.3 million Palestinian Arabs there.
- In 1947, the British asked the United Nations to make a plan to divide Palestine, and they decided to give about half the territory to Israel; but when Israel was established, in 1948, war between Jews and Palestinians ended with Israel controlling more than three-quarters of the former Palestinian territory.

- During 1948, Jewish militias and/or the fear they inspired forced about half of the Palestinian Arabs to flee to the remaining Palestinian territories or to become refugees in Lebanon, Jordan, or Syria; Palestinians call this the Nakba, or the Catastrophe.
- In 1964, a group called the Palestinian Liberation Organization (PLO) was formed, its goal being "the liberation of Palestine" through armed struggle.
- Yasser Arafat was chairman of the PLO from 1969 to 2004; our document comes from a speech he made at the United Nations in 1974.

Vocabulary:

scheme: plan
raided: took valuables from
usurpation: taking by force
partition resolution: the United Nations's
   plan for dividing Palestinian territory
   in 1947

obliterating: destroying
exile: living away from one's home, not
   by choice
consecrated: protected

Document: Speech to the UN General Assembly, Yasser Arafat, 1974

The roots of the Palestinian question reach back into the closing years of the nineteenth century, in other words, to that period we call the era of colonialism and settlement as we know it today. This is precisely the period during which Zionism as a scheme was born; its aim was the conquest of Palestine by European immigrants, just as settlers colonized, and indeed raided, most of Africa. . . .

The Jewish invasion of Palestine began in 1881. Before the first large wave of immigrants started arriving, Palestine had a population of half a million; most of the population was either Muslim or Christian, and only 20,000 were Jewish. Every segment of the population enjoyed the religious tolerance characteristic of our civilization. . . . Between 1882 and 1917 the Zionist movement settled approximately 50,000 European Jews in our homeland. . . .

Over a period of 30 years after the Balfour Declaration, the Zionist movement, together with its colonial ally, succeeded in bringing about the immigration of more European Jews and the usurpation of the lands of the Arabs of Palestine. . . . Furthermore, even though the partition resolution granted the colonialist settlers 54 per cent of the land of Palestine, their dissatisfaction with the decision prompted them to wage a war of terror against the civilian Arab population. They occupied 81 per cent of the total area of Palestine, uprooting a million Arabs. Thus, they occupied 524 Arab towns and villages, of which they destroyed 385, completely obliterating them in the process. Having done so, they built their own settlements and colonies on the ruins of our farms and our groves. The roots of the Palestine question lie here. Its causes do not stem from any conflict between two religions or two nationalisms. Neither is it a border conflict between neighboring States. It is the cause of people deprived of its homeland, dispersed and uprooted, and living mostly in exile and in refugee camps. . . .

We do distinguish between Judaism and Zionism. While we maintain our opposition to the colonialist Zionist movement, we respect the Jewish faith. . . .

Those who call us terrorists wish to prevent world public opinion from discovering the truth about us and from seeing the justice on our faces. . . . The difference between the revolutionary and the terrorist lies in the reason for which each fights. For whoever stands by a just cause and fights for the freedom and liberation of his land from the invaders, the settlers and the colonialists cannot possibly be called terrorist, otherwise the American people in their struggle for liberation from the British colonialists would have been terrorists; the European resistance against the Nazis would be terrorism, the struggle of the Asian, African and Latin American peoples would also be terrorism, and many of you who are in this Assembly hall were considered terrorists. This is actually a just and proper struggle consecrated by the United Nations Charter and by the Universal Declaration of Human Rights. . . .

I appeal to you to enable our people to establish national independent sovereignty over its own land. Today I have come bearing an olive branch and a freedom-fighter's gun. Do not let the olive branch fall from my hand.

Source: UN. (n.d.). Agenda Item 108: The question of Palestine.
https://unispal.un.org/unispal.nsf/9a798adbf322aff38525617b006d88d7
/a238ec7a3e13eed18525624a007697ec?OpenDocument
From Agenda Item 180: The Question of Palestine, by Yasser Arafat, ©1974, United Nations.
Reprinted with the permission of the United Nations.

Comprehension Check:

1. Does Arafat recognize Israel's right to exist? If so, highlight the part of the speech where he does so.
2. Make a T-chart with headings for Palestinian Arabs and Israeli Jews. To whom does Arafat compare each of these groups? Make a list.

Activities:

1. With a partner, go through the speech and highlight words that display Arafat's bias for Palestinians and against Israelis (e.g., "invasion"). Then change those words to reflect Herzl's bias for Israelis and against Palestinians. Finally, see if you can find more neutral words to replace the ones Arafat and Herzl would use.
2. Write a response to Arafat's speech from Gavrilo Princip (Lesson 4.9).
3. Access the full version of the UDHR (Lesson 3.13). List the rights of Palestinian people that were violated according to Arafat. Then list the rights of Jewish people that were violated according to Theodor Herzl in Lesson 4.11. What similarities and differences do you see?

Reflection: What do you think are the differences between the versions of history learned by Israeli Jewish children and Palestinian children? What could be the result of these differences?

Resources:

NobelPrize.org. (2019). Yasser Arafat—Biographical. https://www.nobelprize.org/prizes/peace /1994/arafat/biographical/

UN. (n.d.). History of the question of Palestine. https://www.un.org/unispal/history/

LESSON 4.13

WHY WERE HUTUS WILLING TO KILL TUTSIS IN RWANDA?

Historical Figure: Hassan Ngeze

Event: Rwandan genocide, 1994

Introduction: Why do you think genocides happen? What would cause one ethnic or religious group to want to exterminate another?

Mini-Lecture:

- Rwanda is inhabited by several ethnic groups who speak the same language but tend to have slightly different appearances—the minority Tutsis are thought to be taller, thinner, and have lighter skin than the majority Hutus.
- Belgian colonizers, who ruled Rwanda from 1919 to 1962, treated the Tutsis better than the Hutus, allowing them better educational and professional opportunities.
- In 1959, Hutus rebelled against Belgian rule and the Tutsi elite in what was called the "Social Revolution"; over 100,000 Tutsis fled the country.
- In 1961, shortly before Rwanda became an independent country, a referendum was held in which voters chose to abolish the monarchy, which had traditionally been dominated by Tutsis; voters then chose Hutu-dominated parties to rule Rwanda.
- Between October 1990 and 1994, there was a civil war in which Tutsi rebels challenged the government of President Juvénal Habyarimana, who was Hutu.
- Hutu Power was an extremist group created in 1990 by journalist Hassan Ngeze, who developed the "Hutu Ideology," expressed in the "Hutu Ten Commandments," which is our document.
- Ngeze published these Ten Commandments in his newspaper and broadcasted them on the radio.
- In April 1994, President Habyarimana died when his plane was shot down; the Hutu Power movement blamed Tutsi rebels, although they denied responsibility.
- Over the next three months, 800,000 Rwandans (mostly Tutsis) were killed (by mostly Hutus).

Vocabulary:

concubine: romantic partner
protégée: someone who is given support
 and professional encouragement

strategic: important for reasons of political power
prevail: exist

Document: Hutu Ten Commandments, 1990

1. Every Hutu must know that the Tutsi woman, wherever she may be, is working for the Tutsi ethnic cause. In consequence, any Hutu is a traitor who: Acquires a Tutsi wife; Acquires a Tutsi concubine; Acquires a Tutsi secretary or protégée.

2. Every Hutu must know that our Hutu daughters are more worthy and more conscientious as women, as wives and as mothers. Aren't they lovely, excellent secretaries, and more honest!

3. Hutu women, be vigilant and make sure that your husbands, brothers and sons see reason.

4. All Hutus must know that all Tutsis are dishonest in business. Their only goal is ethnic superiority. We have learned this by experience from experience. In consequence, any Hutu is a traitor who: Forms a business alliance with a Tutsi; Invests his own funds or public funds in a Tutsi enterprise; Borrows money from or loans money to a Tutsi; Grants favors to Tutsis (import licenses, bank loans, land for construction, public markets . . .).

5. Strategic positions such as politics, administration, economics, the military and security must be restricted to the Hutu.

6. A Hutu majority must prevail throughout the educational system (pupils, scholars, teachers).

7. The Rwandan Army must be exclusively Hutu. The war of October 1990 has taught us that. No soldier may marry a Tutsi woman.

8. Hutu must stop taking pity on the Tutsi.

9. Hutu wherever they be must stand united, in solidarity, and concerned with the fate of their Hutu brothers. Hutu within and without Rwanda must constantly search for friends and allies to the Hutu Cause, beginning with their Bantu brothers. Hutu must constantly counter Tutsi propaganda. Hutu must stand firm and vigilant against their common enemy: the Tutsi.

10. The Social Revolution of 1959, the Referendum of 1961 and the Hutu Ideology must be taught to Hutu of every age. Every Hutu must spread the word wherever he goes. Any Hutu who persecutes his brother Hutu for spreading and teaching this ideology is a traitor.

Source: University of Wisconsin Oshkosh. (n.d.). The "Hutu Ten Commandments."
 http://www.uwosh.edu/faculty_staff/henson/188/rwanda_kangura_ten.html

Comprehension Check:

1. In what ways are Hutus and Tutsis allowed or encouraged to interact in these Commandments? Highlight the parts of the document that describe this interaction.
2. Which past experiences with Tutsis were cited as evidence that Hutus should not trust them, and why?

Activities:

1. Work with a small group to make a mind map including any individuals or groups that could be considered responsible for the Rwandan genocide. Discuss with your group which of these people or groups bears most responsibility, and present your answer to the class.
2. The United Nations makes a distinction between "hate speech" (any communication that expresses discrimination against a particular racial, ethnic, religious, or other identity group), and "incitement to violence" (which is intended to inspire people to act on those discriminatory ideas). Decide which category fits this document, and underline the parts that influenced your decision.

Reflection: Do you think anything could have been done, either inside or outside Rwanda, to prevent the genocide? Why or why not?

Resources:

BBC. (2018). Rwanda Profile—Timeline. https://www.bbc.com/news/world-africa-14093322

UN. (2019). UN Strategy and Plan of Action on hate speech. https://www.un.org/en /genocideprevention/documents/UN%20Strategy%20and%20Plan%20of%20 Action%20on%20Hate%20Speech%2018%20June%20SYNOPSIS.pdf

Equality vs. Hierarchy

UNIT QUESTION: What Should Be the Balance Between
Social Equality and Social Hierarchy?

This unit allows students to explore the divisions and hierarchies that exist within societies, as well as people's attempts to equalize those disparities. They start by reading quotations from ordinary people from South Sudan, the world's newest country, which introduce them to the idea of intersectionality, or how forms of discrimination and privilege interact. This is important, as most of the other documents focus on just one aspect of social hierarchy. The oldest document is Aristotle's justification of the master-slave relationship, which laid the foundations for more recent inequalities. A Maya carving introduces students to classical forms of social hierarchy, and a description of Mongol society shows them how the nomadic pastoral lifestyle influenced people's relations. A description of the Inca *allyu* system allows a contrast with the Spanish encomienda system that followed it, and an account of feudalism under the Tokugawa Shogunate enables comparison with medieval European societies with which students may be more familiar. An excerpt from the *Communist Manifesto* illustrates one attempt to abolish economic stratification—although a later glimpse of the Khmer Rouge provides a cautionary tale about how this ideology could be violently executed with tragic results. Racial and religious inequalities are explored through the examples of apartheid South Africa and the Dalits' struggle for rights in India.

This unit as well can bring up complex feelings in students. Socioeconomic or other status distinctions can be less visible than other differences, and students may find that their reactions to these documents vary according to aspects of their identities that they have not discussed with peers. Students' or their families' political orientations may become relevant, especially when discussing Marxist ideology. It is important for teachers to convey that reading these documents is not an attempt at indoctrination, but a quest to understand the ideas that have influenced world history. If students are unfamiliar with the terms "intersectionality," "discrimination," and "privilege," an activity like "Privilege for Sale" <http://www.socialjusticetoolbox.com/activity/privilege -for-sale/> can be useful. It is also good to remind students that although the introduction and reflection questions ask them about their personal experiences, they aren't obligated to share unless they feel comfortable doing so.

LESSON 5.1

HOW ARE ORDINARY PEOPLE IN SOUTH SUDAN WORKING TOGETHER FOR JUSTICE?

Historical Figure: Lilian Riziq

Event: South Sudan becomes an independent country, 2011

Introduction: Do you think that high-status or well-connected people in your society who commit crimes are less likely to be punished? Give examples to prove your point.

Mini-Lecture:

- In 2011, after a long civil war, South Sudanese people voted to become independent of the Republic of Sudan, making it the world's newest country; Juba is its capital.
- South Sudan is inhabited by ethnic groups including the Dinka, Nuer, Azande, Bari, and Madi; there are also divisions between people with more and less political and social power; and women are struggling for equal rights with men.
- Between 2013 and 2018, there was a civil war between rival political factions, which sometimes aligned with ethnic identity.
- Lilian Riziq is the founder of the South Sudanese Women's Empowerment Network, which increases women's participation in politics and protects their rights; she has also served as a government minister and helped to write the Constitution of South Sudan.
- Our document consists of quotations from ordinary South Sudanese people that were collected by the organization Justice Africa, which held workshops in 2017 in which people discussed the problems the new country was facing.

Vocabulary:

nepotism: when a leader gives jobs or other benefits to their own family members

tribalism: bias in favor of people from one's own tribe or ethnic group

super power: power that is held by one person instead of being distributed in the community

brigadier: officer in the army

Document: Quotations on justice, peace, and equality from ordinary people in South Sudan, 2017

"Justice means treating people equally. What's needed is for justice to be put in place. To tackle nepotism, and tribalism, at least the high-ranking leaders should bring peace through political dialogue, so the issue of tribe is not there. Everyone should be called South Sudanese."

"Unless we accept unity in diversity we will stay in crisis [.] [I]f a Madi, Dinka, Bari, etc. cannot stay together we will stay in conflict of diversity. If we don't accept ourselves and look at ourselves without divisions we will not establish peace. We need to feel safe with other tribes."

"It is very important for us to say, 'I am South Sudanese' without emphasis on where you're from—together we are all agents of change and we will take the same message to the grassroots."

"[We should] organize a conference where all the tribes sit together for open space discussion without restriction. . . . This is how constitutions are written in other countries. . . . Here they sit a few people and approve as if the nation approved. People write their interests not the interests of the society. It should be the ideas of the citizens that contribute to constitution not one person."

"One of the challenges is super power. If someone is arrested immediately he's taken where I can't see him . . . maybe he's a brigadier there is nothing I can do . . . if the arrested has a brother who's a general he is released."

"Super power is one thing we face . . . one of our teachers was on the ground with us. Some big general military man sent soldiers to the site and he was taken by force. It was very difficult to follow up because they can arrest you in the same way. He was taken to the barracks in Juba, we followed it up. He was taken to the police. Once he was taken to the police the one who was pushing his arrest disappeared so he was released because there was no case."

"Peace is not something we are waiting for someone to bring; it is the responsibility of everyone. If we contribute, that peace will be there. This peace, there are some laws that if implemented it will contribute to a good environment; there will be respect to the dignity of human beings and human rights."

"Women should be involved or represented as much as men are to prevent and resolve conflicts [and create] peace."

"Women can spread peace very fast, even if the implementation will take long. My sister can take what we talk about to other women, and they can understand. Now there are some women that do not understand themselves— there are women with different thoughts. We have to make them understand that they are one, and to teach our children that we are one—they need to know themselves that they are South Sudanese. If you talk about negative things with your children daily, after the conference, you might change the way that you talk to them."

Source: Justice Africa. (n.d.). Welcome to the voices of South Sudan. http://justiceafrica
.org/pages/voices-of-south-sudan/

Comprehension Check:

1. List as many kinds of social differences as you can find referenced in these quotations.
2. Put into your own words the problem that some people quoted describe as "super power."

Activities:

1. "Intersectionality" describes the way that people experience multiple forms of discrimination or privilege, based on their gender, race or ethnicity, socioeconomic class, and other factors. Based on your answer to the first Comprehension Question, work with a small group to create a visual representation showing who would experience the most and least privilege in South Sudan.
2. Watch the video of Lilian Riziq's speech from the Resources section. Take notes, and then discuss with the class what you learned about social hierarchy and equality in South Sudan.

Reflection: Which factors do you think affect the discrimination or privilege you experience in your society, and how do they intersect or interact?

Resources:

BBC. (2018). South Sudan country profile. https://www.bbc.com/news/world-africa -14069082

Kroc School. (2019). Women peacemaker event 2019: Lilian Riziq. https://www.youtube .com/watch?time_continue=14&v=2_YEebUeNbA&feature=emb_logo

---

LESSON 5.2

How Did Athenian Democrats Justify Slavery?

Historical Figure: Aristotle

Event: Athenian democracy, 5th–4th century BCE

Introduction: Can democracy coexist with slavery? Why or why not?

Mini-Lecture:

*   Aristotle was a philosopher who lived in in Greece from 384 to 322 BCE.
*   Our document is from Aristotle's book *Politics*, in which he tries to explain why slavery was not morally wrong.
*   In Athens, where Aristotle lived and wrote, slavery was common, and owning enslaved persons was a status symbol for middle class and "noble," or wealthy, families.
*   A person could become enslaved by being captured in war, kidnapped, by falling into debt, by being sold into slavery, or by being born into slavery.
*   Enslaved people, like women and foreigners, could not vote in the direct democracy that existed in Athens.
*   Slavery did not have a racial basis, but Greeks made a distinction between themselves ("Hellenes") and "barbarians," who did not speak Greek; some enslaved people fell into each category.

Vocabulary:

attain: get
necessaries: necessities
instrument: tool
expedient: appropriate
subjection: being under the control of
    other people
apprehend: understand

minister: take care of
servile: serving others
latter: the last group referred to
convention: tradition
jurists: experts on law
impeach: deny

Document: *Politics*, Aristotle, 5th century BCE

Let us first speak of master and slave, looking to the needs of practical life and also seeking to attain some better theory of their relation than exists at present. . . . Property is a part of the household, and the art of acquiring property is a part of the art of managing the household; for no man can live well, or indeed live at all, unless he be provided with necessaries. And so, in the arrangement of the family, a slave is a living possession, and property a number of such instruments; and the slave is himself an instrument which takes precedence of all other instruments. . . .

But is there any one thus intended by nature to be a slave, and for whom such a condition is expedient and right, or rather is not all slavery a violation of nature? There is no difficulty in answering this question, on grounds both of reason and of fact. For that some should rule and others be ruled is a thing not only necessary, but expedient; from the hour of their birth, some are marked out for subjection, others for rule. . . . Again, the male is by nature superior, and the female inferior; and the one rules, and the other is ruled; this principle, of necessity, extends to all mankind. Where then there is such a difference as that between soul and body, or between men and animals (as in the case of those whose business is to use their body, and who can do nothing better), the lower sort are by nature slaves, and it is better for them as for all inferiors that they should be under the rule of a master. . . .

Whereas the lower animals cannot even apprehend a principle; they obey their instincts. And indeed the use made of slaves and of tame animals is not very different; for both with their bodies minister to the needs of life. Nature would like to distinguish between the bodies of freemen and slaves, making the one strong for servile labor, the other upright, and although useless for such services, useful for political life in the arts both of war and peace. . . . It is clear, then, that some men are by nature free, and others slaves, and that for these latter slavery is both expedient and right.

There is a slave or slavery by law as well as by nature. The law of which I speak is a sort of convention—the law by which whatever is taken in war is supposed to belong to the victors. But this right many jurists impeach . . . : they detest the notion that, because one man has the power of doing violence and is superior in brute strength, another shall be his slave and subject. . . .

Hellenes do not like to call Hellenes slaves, but confine the term to barbarians. . . . The same principle applies to nobility. Hellenes regard themselves as noble everywhere, and not only in their own country, but they deem the barbarians noble only when at home [in their place of origin]. . . .

Source: Halsall, P. (1996). Documents on Greek slavery. https://sourcebooks.fordham.edu /ancient/greek-slaves.asp

Comprehension Check:

1. According to Aristotle, what is the difference between a slave by law and a slave by nature?
2. What is Aristotle's argument for why it is better for slaves to be ruled by their master?

Activities:

1. Aristotle claims that men are naturally superior to women, and also that some men are naturally superior to other men. With a partner, list some evidence he might use to support his points. Then list some evidence you could use to refute those points.
2. Aristotle points out that it is easier to see a person as an "animal" incapable of higher thoughts if they are in some way different from us (in the case of "barbarians," speaking a language other than Greek). Work with a small group to generate examples of how this tendency has influenced slavery in other times and places.

Reflection: Which idea bothers you more, slavery by law or slavery by nature? Why?

Resources:

Amadio, A. H., & Kenny, A. J. P. (2019). Aristotle. https://www.britannica.com/biography /Aristotle

Cartwright, M. (2018). Ancient Greek society. https://www.ancient.eu/article/483/ancient -greek-society/

LESSON 5.3

WHAT SOCIAL CLASSES EXISTED IN THE MAYA EMPIRE?

Historical Figure: Bird Jaguar IV

Event: Maya Empire, c. 250–900

Introduction: Would you rather live in a society where social classes were strictly separated but social mobility (moving from one class to another) was possible, or a society in which social classes could mix freely, but one could not change one's social class? Why?

Mini-Lecture:

- The Maya, or Mayan, people are indigenous to what is now Mexico, Guatemala, and Belize, and had an empire there between 250 and 900.
- Maya society was divided into nobles (government officials, military leaders, priests, plantation managers); commoners (farmers, artisans, laborers, servants); serfs (who farmed the land belonging to a ruler); and enslaved persons (who had been captured in war, fallen into debt, or punished for a crime).
- Maya social classes were strictly divided, but mobility among them was possible; children of enslaved persons did not become slaves themselves, and commoners could rise into the nobility through military service.
- Our document is an image of a carved relief showing the king of the Maya city-state of Yaxchilan, which is now in Chiapas, Mexico; it was carved in limestone and was used as a lintel, or stone above a doorway.
- The glyphs, or pictographic symbols, in the carving state that the three captives were presented to the king on the date in the Mayan calendar corresponding to August 23, 783; they also state the name of the artist who carved this panel.
- Bird Jaguar IV ruled Yaxchilan from 752 to 768; more is known about him than his son and successor Itzamnaaj B'alam III, who is shown in this relief.

Document: Presentation of captives to a Maya ruler, c. 785 (see Figure 5.1)

Comprehension Check:

1. This carving shows a king, his *sahal* (military chief), and three captives. Point them out. How can you tell?
2. What does the captive in front seem to be holding? What clue does it give about his occupation?

Activities:

1. Write a narrative from the perspective of one of the captives, explaining what social class they belonged to before being captured, and what class they would belong to after being captured.
2. With a small group, discuss the social classes in your society today. What would you call them, and who falls into them? Create a poster to illustrate your discussion.

Reflection: How easy and how common is mobility among social classes in your society? Why do you think this is?

Resources:

Ancientpages.com. (2018). On this day in history: Mayan King Bird Jaguar IV assumes the throne. http://www.ancientpages.com/2016/05/03/day-history-mayan-king-bird-jaguar -iv-assumes-throne-may-3-752/

Tarlton Law Library. (2018). Maya social structure. https://tarlton.law.utexas.edu/aztec-and -maya-law/maya-social-structure

**Figure 5.1. Ancient American, Presentation of Captives to a Maya Ruler, c. 785, limestone
    with traces of paint**

Source: Kimbell Art Museum. (n.d.). Presentation of captives to a Maya ruler.
https://www.kimbellart.org/collection/ap-197107
Image courtesy of Kimbell Art Museum, Fort Worth, Texas

LESSON 5.4

HOW DID MONGOL PASTORALISTS ORGANIZE THEIR NOMADIC SOCIETY?

Historical Figure: Chinggis Khan

Event: Chinggis Khan proclaims the Mongol Empire, 1206

Introduction: Who do you think would have high status in a nomadic, pastoral society in which people moved from place to place herding animals? Why?

Mini-Lecture:

- The Mongols are a nomadic (moving around), pastoral (animal-herding) people who have lived in what is now Mongolia and China for thousands of years; traditionally, they bring their horses, sheep, camels, goats, and yaks to new pastures several times per year.
- The basic unit in ancient Mongol society was the tribe, a group of clans (each made up of families) that traveled together; within these tribes, people had higher status who owned many animals or who could communicate with the spirit world in the Mongols' shamanistic religion.
- In the early 13th century, the Mongols began expanding their territory, eventually bringing together the largest contiguous (connected) empire in world history, which stretched from what is now China to Europe, and included most of central Asia and parts of the Middle East.
- Chinggis (also spelled Genghis) Khan started this expansion in 1206 and ruled until 1227; he is known for supporting the development of a written language for Mongols, and creating a code of laws.
- The Mongol Empire was open to foreign ideas, allowing foreigners to live in their court, valuing the skills of foreign artisans, facilitating trade, and practicing religious tolerance.
- Giovanni da Pian del Carpini, or John Plano of Carpini, was a diplomat from Italy who was sent by Pope Innocent IV in 1245 to Mongolia to ask that the Mongols (who he calls the Tartars) stop expanding into Europe and to try to convert them to Christianity.
- Our document comes from a book Carpini wrote when he returned describing the Mongol society.

Vocabulary:

seculars: people who are not religious
lightly: easily
contend: fight
scorn: treat badly
naught: worthless

low born: born into a less powerful social class
assigned: chosen to supervise
base-born: born into a less powerful social class
morsels: bits

Document: The Mongol Mission, Giovanni da Pian del Carpini, 1247

These men, that is to say the Tartars, are more obedient to their masters than any other men in the world, be they religious or secular; they show great respect to them nor do they lie lightly to them. They rarely or never contend with each other in word, and in action never. Fights, brawls, wounding, murder are never met with among them. Nor are robbers and thieves who steal on a large scale found there; consequently their dwellings and the carts in which they keep their valuables are not secured by bolts and bars. If any animals are lost, whoever comes across them either leaves them alone or takes them to men appointed for this purpose; the owners of the animals apply for them to these men and they get them back without any difficulty. They show considerable respect to each other and are very friendly together, and they willingly share their food with each other, although there is little enough of it. . . . No one scorns another but helps him and promotes his good as far as circumstances permit.

Now that the good characteristics of the Tartars have been described, it is time for something to be said about their bad. They are most arrogant to other people and look down on all, indeed they consider them as naught, be they of high rank or low born.

For at the Emperor's court we saw Jerozlaus, a man of noble birth, a mighty duke of Russia, also the son of the King and Queen of Georgia, and many important sultans; the chief also of the Solangi received no fitting honor from them, but the Tartars who were assigned to them, however base-born they were, went ahead of them and always had the first and highest place; indeed they were often obliged to sit behind their backs. . . .

They have neither bread nor herbs nor vegetables nor anything else, nothing but meat, of which, however, they eat so little that other people would scarcely be able to exist on it. They make their hands very dirty with the grease of meat, but when they eat they wipe them on their leggings or the grass or some such thing. It is the custom for the more respectable among them to have small bits of cloth with which they wipe their hands when they eat meat. One of them cuts the morsels and another takes them on the point of a knife and offers them to each, to some more, to some less, according to whether they wish to show them greater or less honor. . . . In winter, moreover, unless they are wealthy, they do not have mare's milk.

Source: Brill. (2016). John of Plano Carpini.
https://brill.com/view/book/edcoll/9789004216358/B9789004216358-s013.xml

Comprehension Check:

1. What is Carpini's evidence that the Mongols look down on other people?
2. According to Carpini, how do the lives of the higher-status people in Mongol society differ from those of lower-status people?

Activities:

1. Although there was a hierarchy, historians believe that Mongol society in this period was relatively free from conflict among people of different status levels. Work with a partner to brainstorm economic, political, social, religious, or other reasons for this.
2. Divide the class in half and debate this proposition: People from one society should respect the social class divisions of other societies.

Reflection: Is there a social hierarchy among the students in your school? If so, what is it based on? If not, how can you tell?

Resources:

Asia for Educators. (2004). The Mongols in world history. http://afe.easia.columbia.edu
/mongols/main/transcript.pdf

History.com. (2019). Genghis Khan. https://www.history.com/topics/china/genghis-khan

LESSON 5.5

How Did the Incan *Allyu* System Work?

Historical Figure: Pachacuti Inca Yupanqui

Event: Inca Empire, 14th–16th century

Introduction: How might an empire keep records and organize society if it had no written language?

Mini-Lecture:

- The Inca Empire expanded along the western coast of South America between 1483 and 1533, including portions of what is now Ecuador, Peru, Chile, Bolivia, and Argentina; it included Quechua peoples, as well as other Indigenous groups.
- Quechua and other Indigenous peoples organized their society into *allyus*, kinship groups of hundreds of families who intermarried and believed they had a common ancestor.
- The Inca created a class of nobles to administer the *allyus* and built a system of roads to connect their empire.
- When the Sapa Inca (emperor) took over a territory, he required each *allyu* to send tribute (a payment to a ruler showing loyalty; like a tax) in the form of gold, silver, or other valuable goods to the capital at Cuzco.
- A quipu is a tool made of knotted string that Incan officials used to keep track of the labor capacity of each *allyu* based on the number of able-bodied men it contained; the Inca did not have a written language.
- Pachacuti Inca Yupanqui ruled the Inca Empire from 1438 to c. 1471; he is known for expanding and reorganizing the empire, and rebuilding Cuzco.
- Our document comes from a book called *Chronicles of the Incas*, written by Spanish conquistador Pedro de Cieza de León, who participated in colonizing Peru.

Vocabulary:

league: measurement of distance equal to about four miles

tribute: payment of goods to a ruler showing loyalty

fraud: cheating someone out of money or goods

meted out: carried out

conspirators: people plotting against a government

lean year: time when harvests were not good

Document: *Chronicles of the Incas*, Pedro de Cieza de León, 1540

It is told for a fact of the rulers of this kingdom that in the days of their rule they had their representatives in the capitals of all the provinces, for in all these places there were larger and finer lodgings than in most of the other cities of this great kingdom, and many storehouses. They served as the head of the provinces or regions, and from every so many leagues around the tributes were brought to one of these capitals, and from so many others, to another. This was so well-organized that there was not a village that did not know where it was to send its tribute. . . .

The tribute paid by each of these provinces, whether gold, silver, clothing, arms and all else they gave, was entered in the accounts of those who kept the quipus and did everything ordered by the governor in the matter of finding the soldiers or supplying whomever the Inca ordered, or making delivery to Cuzco; but when they came from the city of Cuzco to go over the accounts, or they were ordered to go to Cuzco to give an accounting, the accountants themselves gave it by the quipus, or went to give it where there could be no fraud, but everything had to come out right. . . .

At the beginning of the new year the rulers of each village came to Cuzco, bringing their quipus, which told how many births there had been during the year, and how many deaths. In this way the Inca and the governors knew which of the Indians were poor, the women who had been widowed, whether they were able to pay their taxes, and how many men they could count on in the event of war, and many other things they considered highly important. The Incas took care to see that justice was meted out, so much so that nobody ventured to commit a felony or theft. This was to deal with thieves, rapists, or conspirators against the Inca. . . .

If there came a lean year, the storehouses were opened and the provinces were lent what they needed in the way of supplies; then, in a year of abundance, they paid back all they had received. No one who was lazy or tried to live by the work of others was tolerated; everyone had to work. Thus on certain days each lord went to his lands and took the plow in hand and cultivated the earth, and did other things. Even the Incas themselves did this to set an example. And under their system there was none such in all the kingdom, for, if he had his health, he worked and lacked for nothing; and if he was ill, he received what he needed from the storehouses. And no rich man could deck himself out in more finery than the poor, or wear different clothing, except the rulers and the headmen, who, to maintain their dignity, were allowed great freedom and privilege.

Source: Halsall, P. (2019). Pedro de Cieza de León.
https://sourcebooks.fordham.edu/mod/1540cieza.asp

Comprehension Check:

1. What was de León's purpose in writing this document, and what attitude did he have toward the Inca?

2. According to de León, why did the lords, or nobles, plough the fields alongside the people?

Activities:

1. Create a visual representation of the Inca administration and social structure based on de Leon's account.
2. Spanish conquistadors destroyed Inca administrative structures and imposed the encomienda system, in which Spanish rulers brutally forced Indigenous people to work in mines or on farms. Research the encomienda system and create a visual representation to contrast the one you made for the Inca Empire.

Reflection: Given de León's apparent respect for the Inca Empire, why do you think he and other conquistadors participated in destroying it?

Resources:

Cartwright, M. (2016). Daily life in the Inca Empire. https://www.ancient.eu/article/953/daily-life-in-the-inca-empire/

Minster, C. (2019). Spain's American colonies and the encomienda system. https://www.thoughtco.com/spains-american-colonies-encomienda-system-2136545

New World Encyclopedia. (2019). Pachacuti. https://www.newworldencyclopedia.org/entry/Pachacuti

---

LESSON 5.6

HOW DID THE TOKUGAWA SHOGUNATE PRACTICE FEUDALISM?

Historical Figure: Tokugawa Ieyasu

Event: Tokugawa Shogunate, 1603–1868

Introduction: Do you think the work done by people at the bottom of the social hierarchy in your society is valued? Why or why not?

Mini-Lecture:

- The Tokugawa Shogunate was a feudal military government that ruled what is now Japan during the Edo period, from 1603 to 1868.
- The emperor and his court, who did not have much political power, were at the top of the social hierarchy; the shogun, or military leader, supervised the daimyo, or lords, each of whom controlled a territory as well as some samurai warriors (who could also work as government bureaucrats), farmers, artisans, and merchants (who had the lowest status).
- Social mobility was forbidden, a complex bureaucratic administration kept track of people's duties, and Confucian values guided the government.
- Tokugawa Ieyasu founded the shogunate and ruled it from 1603 to 1616 by fighting other daimyo for supremacy, thus putting an end to the "Warring States" period of military competition.

Vocabulary:

vices: bad deeds
dispel: get rid of
in the throes of: in the middle of
martial: military
proverbial: famous

husked: outer shell taken off
steward: caretaker (in this case, *daimyo*)
sustenance: nourishment
partaking of: eating

Document: Tokugawa Ieyasu, Military government and the social order, c. 1610

Once, Lord [Ieyasu] conversed with Honda, Governor Sado, on the subject of the emperor, the Shogun, and the farmer. "Whether there is order or chaos depends on the virtues and vices of these three. The emperor, with compassion in his heart for the needs of the people, must not be remiss in the performance of his duties—from the early morning worship of the New Year to the monthly functions of the court. Secondly, the shogun must not forget the possibility of war in peacetime, and must maintain his discipline. He should be able to maintain order in the country; he should bear in mind the security of the sovereign; and he must strive to dispel the anxieties of the people. One who cultivates the way of the warrior only in times of crisis is like a rat who bites his captor in the throes of being captured. The man may die from the effects of the poisonous bite, but to generate courage on the spur of the moment is not the way of the warrior. To assume the way of the warrior upon the outbreak of war is like a rat biting his captor. Although this is better than fleeing from the scene, the true master of the way of the warrior is one who maintains his martial discipline even in times of peace. Thirdly, the farmer's toil is proverbial—from the first grain to a hundred acts of labor. He selects the seed from last fall's crop, and undergoes various hardships and anxieties through the heat of the summer until the seed grows finally to a rice plant. It is harvested and husked and then offered to the land steward. The rice then becomes sustenance for the multitudes. Truly, the hundred acts of toil from last fall to this fall are like so many tears of blood. Thus, it is a wise man who, while partaking of his meal, appreciates the hundred acts of toil of the people. Fourthly, the artisan's occupation is to make and prepare wares and utensils for the use of others. Fifthly, the merchant facilitates the exchange of goods so that the people can cover their nakedness and keep their bodies warm. As the people produce clothing, food, and housing, which are called the 'three treasures,' they deserve our every sympathy.

Source: Asia for Educators. (n.d.). Tokugawa Ieyasu on military government and the social order. http://afe.easia.columbia.edu/ps/japan/ieyasu_four_classes.pdf

Comprehension Check:

1. Fill in a diagram like this with the social classes Ieyasu describes as well as the ones mentioned in the mini-lecture; for each one, list its primary duties.

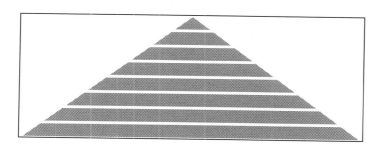

Activities:

1. Write a letter from Aristotle (Lesson 5.2) to Tokugawa Ieyasu explaining his views on the Japanese feudal system.
2. Research feudalism in medieval Europe, and compare and contrast it with feudalism during the Tokugawa Shogunate.

Reflection: Do you think the farmers, artisans, and merchants thought the feudal system was fair? Why or why not?

Resources:

Asia for Educators. (n.d.). Tokugawa Japan. http://afe.easia.columbia.edu/at/tokugawa/tj01 .html

Snell, M. (2019). The problem with feudalism. https://www.thoughtco.com/the-f-word -feudalism-1788836

Totman, C. D. (2019). Tokugawa Ieyasu. https://www.britannica.com/biography/Tokugawa -Ieyasu

---

LESSON 5.7

WHY DID KARL MARX ENVISION A CLASSLESS SOCIETY?

Historical Figure: Karl Marx

Event: *Communist Manifesto* published, 1848

Introduction: Would you want to live in a society where there were no rich or poor people, but everyone had enough to meet their basic needs? Why or why not?

Mini-Lecture:

- Communism is a social and economic theory that argues that wealth should be distributed evenly and property should be shared; there should be no socioeconomic classes (rich and poor, high status and low status), but everyone should have what they need to survive.
- Karl Marx was a German philosopher who lived from 1818 to 1883, and whose writings contributed to the ideas of communism.

- The Industrial Revolution began in Great Britain (now the United Kingdom) in the 18th century; instead of living on farms and producing most of what they needed themselves, many people moved to cities and worked in factories where machines made possible a "division of labor" in which each worker did a small part of the job of producing goods.
- Marx believed that this system of producing goods created greater divisions between two classes of people: the proletariat, who worked in these factories and barely got enough money to survive; and the bourgeoisie, who made money from the work of the proletariat.
- Marx believed it was unfair that the bourgeoisie owned the "means of production" (the land, machinery, and capital—or wealth—needed to produce goods), while the proletariat sold their labor (ability to work) and only had the property necessary for their daily survival.
- Our document comes from *The Communist Manifesto*, written by Karl Marx and Friedrich Engels (another German philosopher) in 1848 in order to bring together the proletariat from different countries in support of communism.

Vocabulary:

manifesto: statement of beliefs

hitherto: up until now

guild-master: the leader of an organization of artisans

journeyman: someone with job skills who works for a daily wage

reconstitution: something built up again

contending: competing

antagonisms: conflicts

epoch: era

wage labor: working for payment by the hour or day instead of having a steady income

appendage: extension

monotonous: boring

subsistence: survival

maintenance: the ability to continue

propagation: having children

commodity: a valuable product

appropriating: taking

exploitation: when a more powerful person takes advantage of a less powerful one

surplus: extra

wherewith: with which

accumulated: collected

disdain to: don't want to

forcible: using force

Document: *The Communist Manifesto*, Karl Marx and Friedrich Engels, 1848

The history of all hitherto existing society is the history of class struggles. Freeman and slave, patrician and plebeian, lord and serf, guild-master and journeyman, in a word, oppressor and oppressed, stood in constant opposition to one another, carried on an uninterrupted, now hidden, now open fight, a fight that each time ended, either in a revolutionary reconstitution of society at large, or in the common ruin of the contending classes. . . . The modern bourgeois society that has sprouted from the ruins of feudal society has not done away with class antagonisms. It has but established new classes, new conditions of oppression, new forms of struggle in place of the old ones.

Our epoch, the epoch of the bourgeoisie, possesses, however, this distinct feature: it has simplified class antagonisms. Society as a whole is more and more splitting up into two great hostile camps, into two great classes directly facing each other—Bourgeoisie and Proletariat. (By bourgeoisie is meant the class of modern capitalists, owners of the means of social production and employers of wage labor. By proletariat, the class of modern wage laborers who, having no means of production of their own, are reduced to selling their labor power in order to live.—Engels, 1888 English edition. . . .

Owing to the extensive use of machinery, and to the division of labor, the work of the proletarians has lost all individual character, and, consequently, all charm for the workman. He becomes an appendage of the machine, and it is only the most simple, most monotonous, and most easily acquired knack, that is required of him. Hence, the cost of production of a workman is restricted, almost entirely, to the means of subsistence that he requires for maintenance, and for the propagation of his race. But the price of a commodity, and therefore also of labor, is equal to its cost of production. In proportion, therefore, as the repulsiveness of the work increases, the wage decreases. . . .

The immediate aim of the Communists is the same as that of all other proletarian parties: formation of the proletariat into a class, overthrow of the bourgeois supremacy, conquest of political power by the proletariat. . . . The distinguishing feature of Communism is not the abolition of property generally, but the abolition of bourgeois property. But modern bourgeois private property is the final and most complete expression of the system of producing and appropriating products, that is based on class antagonisms, on the exploitation of the many by the few. . . .

We by no means intend to abolish this personal appropriation of the products of labor, an appropriation that is made for the maintenance and reproduction of human life, and that leaves no surplus wherewith to command the labor of others. All that we want to do away with is the miserable character of this appropriation, under which the laborer lives merely to increase capital, and is allowed to live only in so far as the interest of the ruling class requires it. In bourgeois society, living labor is but a means to increase accumulated labor. In Communist society, accumulated labor is but a means to widen, to enrich, to promote the existence of the laborer. . . .

The Communists disdain to conceal their views and aims. They openly declare that their ends can be attained only by the forcible overthrow of all existing social conditions. Let the ruling classes tremble at a Communistic revolution. The proletarians have nothing to lose but their chains. They have a world to win. Working men of all countries, unite!

Source: Marxist Internet Archive. (2010). *The Communist Manifesto.*
https://www.marxists.org/archive/marx/works/download/pdf/Manifesto.pdf

Comprehension Check:

1. According to Marx and Engels, what has stayed the same throughout history about class relationships, and what has recently changed? Why?
2. What kind of property do Marx and Engels want to abolish, and why?

Activities:

1. What would Tokugawa Ieyasu (Lesson 5.6) say about Marx's classless society? Write their conversation in the form of a comic strip.
2. Divide the class in half and debate the following proposition: Society would be fairer if bourgeois private property was abolished.

Reflection: No country has yet been able to establish a communist society as Marx envisioned it. Why do you think that is?

Resources:

Hoyt, A. (2008). How Communism works. https://people.howstuffworks.com/communism .htm

McClellan, D. T., & Feuer, L. S. (2019). Karl Marx. https://www.britannica.com/biography /Karl-Marx

---

LESSON 5.8

HOW DID WHITE SOUTH AFRICANS JUSTIFY APARTHEID RULE?

Historical Figure: Nelson Mandela

Event: Apartheid rule in South Africa, 1948–1994

Introduction: Do you have close friends from another racial or ethnic group? Why do you think that is?

Mini-Lecture:

- In the 17th century, Dutch settlers colonized territory in what is now South Africa, which was inhabited by Indigenous peoples including the Zulu and Xhosa.
- In the late 19th and early 20th century, colonial powers engaged in a "scramble for Africa," in which they competed for land; the British fought the Dutch and won control of the country they called South Africa.
- Hendrik F. Verwoerd was the prime minister of South Africa from 1958 to 1966; he promoted the policy of apartheid, meaning keeping racial groups apart.
- Our document comes from a speech Verwoerd gave in 1948 in Parliament in support of apartheid.
- Under apartheid, South African Whites (the minority) set up a White supremacist hierarchy in which they ruled over populations they called "Coloured" (multiracial), "Indian" (of South Asian descent), and "Black" (of African descent, also called "Native").

- Whites forced Blacks, Indians, and Coloured people to live in separate areas with fewer resources, forbade them from traveling freely in White areas, and perpetrated discrimination as well as human rights abuses.
- Nelson Mandela was a Black South African activist who opposed apartheid; the government imprisoned him for almost 30 years, but he served as president from 1994 to 1999, after domestic and international pressure ended apartheid in the early 1990s.

Vocabulary:

friction: conflict

tram: kind of public transportation

reserves: areas of land set aside for a certain purpose

benevolent: kind

Document: The policy of apartheid, Hendrik F. Verwoerd, 1948

The apartheid policy has been described as what one can do in the direction of what one regards as ideal. Nobody will deny that for the Native as well as for the European, complete separation would have been the ideal if it had developed that way historically. If we had had a white South Africa in the sense in which we have a white England and a white Holland and a white France, and if there had been a Native state somewhere for the Natives, and if this white state could have developed to a self-supporting condition as those European states have developed by themselves, then we should certainly not have had the friction and the difficulties which we have today. . . .

What is the situation as it exists? Europeans and non-Europeans scattered and mingled about the whole South Africa; Europeans and non-Europeans travelling mixed in the trams and in the trains; Europeans and non-Europeans mixing are already in hotels and places where meals are served; engaged more and more in taking possession of the theatres and the streets; engaged in devastating the reserves; engaged in seeking learning which they do not use in the service of their own people, but which they use in order to try to cross the border line of European life, to become traitors to their own people and to desert their own people. . . .

I want to state here unequivocally . . . that South Africa is a white man's country and we are not prepared to allow the Natives to be the masters; we are not masters there. But within the European areas, we, the white people in South Africa, are and shall remain the masters. . . .

Firstly, we want to have in the reserves the national home of the various tribal groups; only there can the brains and intelligence that are developing among them find their expression; to the reserves there should go those who are seeking education, for whom the opportunities will exist there. And as far as those who remain in the towns of the Europeans are concerned, they will have their local rights there. In the field of transport there will be separation, so that the mixing on the European stations is restricted to a minimum. The main object is the removal of friction. . . .

Indeed, it is not the Native whose future is being threatened, it is that of the Europeans; the European is really the person who should say: "My rights must be protected". . . .

Where we are prepared to accord to non-Europeans the right to their own opportunities of development, where we bring it about not by means of the sword, but through the benevolent hand of the Europeans who are in the country, then do not . . . do not arouse the suspicion of the world that there is oppression, but show them that there is a policy which seeks rights and justice towards all.

Source: Hendrick Verwoerd Blogspot. (n.d.). The policy of apartheid. http://hendrikverwoerd.blogspot.com/2010/12/september-3-1948-policy-of-apartheid-hf .html

Comprehension Check:

1. According to Verwoerd, what problems existed in South Africa without the policy of apartheid?
2. According to Verwoerd, why is the policy of apartheid necessary?

Activities:

1. How do you think Nelson Mandela would respond to Verwoerd? Add marginal notations and comments to the speech from his perspective.
2. Verwoerd was inspired by the U.S. policy of "separate but equal" facilities for White and Black people. Research the similarities and differences between segregation in the United States and in South Africa and create a Venn diagram comparing them.

Reflection: Do you see evidence of racial segregation or integration in your community today? Give some examples.

Resources:

Blakemore, E. (2019). The harsh reality of life under apartheid in South Africa. https://www .history.com/news/apartheid-policies-photos-nelson-mandela
Nelson Mandela Foundation. (n.d.). Biography of Nelson Mandela. https://www .nelsonmandela.org/content/page/biography

---

LESSON 5.9

HOW DID DALIT PEOPLE SEEK EQUALITY IN INDIA?

Historical Figure: B. R. Ambedkar

Event: Mass conversion of Dalits to Buddhism, 1950s

Introduction: Do you think a social hierarchy based on economics, race, or religion would be hardest to change? Why?

Mini-Lecture:

- In the region where India is located today, a social hierarchy called the caste system has operated for thousands of years; when the British colonized the region in the 18th century, they reinforced the boundaries of the caste system in order to rule the people more easily.
- According to some interpretations of ancient scriptures, Hindus are born into four main castes: Brahmans, the highest-status group, who serve as spiritual leaders; Kshatriyas, who can be warriors or rulers; Vaishyas, who can be farmers or merchants; and Shudras, workers of the lowest caste.
- At the very bottom of this hierarchy are the Dalits, once called the "Untouchables" because they have no caste and some Hindus consider it inappropriate to interact with them; other castes restricted Dalits to what they considered unclean work, such as handling dead bodies and animal carcasses.
- People from higher-status castes have discriminated against members of lower-status castes in education, work, and society; some families discourage young people from marrying outside their caste.
- B. R. Ambedkar was a Dalit man who overcame these obstacles, becoming a lawyer and helping to write the Indian Constitution, which took effect in 1950.
- Our document comes from a speech Ambedkar gave in 1935 urging Dalits to convert to another religion; he later argued that Buddhism was the best choice, and in 1956, he arranged a mass conversion of almost 400,000 Dalits (including himself).

Vocabulary:

atrocities: abuses
tyranny: unfair rule
feud: fight
on par with: on the same level as

dictates: rules
shoulder: take on
intercourse: interaction
discharge: fulfill

Document: Why go for conversion, B. R. Ambedkar, 1935

There are two aspects of conversion; social as well as religious; material as well as spiritual. . . . In order to have a clear understanding of untouchability and its practice in real life, I want you to recall the stories of the atrocities perpetrated against you. . . . What is at the root cause of their tyranny? . . . This is not a feud between rival men. The problem of untouchability is a matter of class struggle. It is the struggle between caste Hindus and the Untouchables. That is not a matter of doing injustice against one man. This is a matter of injustice being done by one class against another. . . . This struggle starts as soon as you start claiming equal treatment with others.

The reason for their [caste Hindus'] anger is very simple. Your behaving on par with them insults them. The untouchability is not a short or temporary feature; it is a permanent one. . . . It is eternal, because the religion which has placed you at the lowest level of the society is itself eternal, according to the belief of the Hindu caste people. . . . And unless you think over it, there is no way out. Those who desire to live in obedience to the dictates of the Hindus, those who wish to remain their slaves, they do not need to think over this problem. But those who wish to live a life of self-respect, and equality, will have to think over this. . . .

To reform the Hindu society is neither our aim nor our field of action. Our aim is to gain freedom. . . . If we can gain freedom by conversion, why should we shoulder the responsibility of reforming the Hindu religion? And why should we sacrifice our strength and property for that? . . .

According to me, this conversion of religion will bring happiness to both the Untouchables as well as the Hindus. So long as you remain Hindus, you will have to struggle for social intercourse, for food and water, and for inter-caste marriages. And so long as this quarrel continues, relations between you and the Hindus will be of perpetual enemies. By conversion, the roots of all the quarrels will vanish. . . .

The Hindu religion does not appeal to my conscience. It does not appeal to my self-respect. However, your conversion will be for material as well as for spiritual gains. . . .

I tell you all very specifically, religion is for man and not man for religion. To get human treatment, convert yourselves. Convert, for getting organized. Convert, for becoming strong. Convert, for securing equality. Convert, for getting liberty. Convert, for that your domestic life may be happy. . . . It is now for you to decide and discharge your responsibility.

Source: Velivada. (2019). Why go for conversion? https://velivada.com /2017/06/01/why-go-for-conversion-speech-by-dr-b-r-ambedkar/

Comprehension Check:

1. List the benefits of conversion for Untouchables, according to Ambedkar.
2. According to Ambedkar, why shouldn't Untouchables try to reform Hinduism?

Activities:

1. Ambedkar and Marx (Lesson 5.7) both use the term "class struggle." Create a T-chart distinguishing between the way these two authors use the term.
2. Ambedkar says, "religion is for man and not man for religion." What does this mean, and does it ring true for you? Write your reaction to this quote on a sticky note, then put it on the board and read other students' responses.

Reflection: If you were a Dalit, would you change your religion? Why or why not?

Resources:

BBC. (2019). What is India's caste system? https://www.bbc.com/news/world-asia-india -35650616

Queen, C. (1993). The great conversion. *Tricycle.* https://tricycle.org/magazine/great-conversion/

LESSON 5.10

How Did the Khmer Rouge Justify Violence in the Name of Equality?

Historical Figure: Pol Pot

Event: Khmer Rouge regime, 1975–1979

Introduction: If the ideology of communism were applied by people who embraced violence, what would you predict would happen?

Mini-Lecture:

- The Khmer Rouge was a communist dictatorship that ruled Cambodia from 1975 to 1979; the Khmer are the majority ethnic group, and "rouge" is the French word for red, a color associated with communism.
- The Khmer Rouge called the country the Democratic Republic of Kampuchea (which is the Khmer word for Cambodia); they also called themselves "Angkar."
- When the Khmer Rouge overthrew the existing government, they declared it was "Year Zero," and announced their plan to rebuild the country as a classless society; they abolished religion, separated families, reorganized everyone into "people's collectives," and forced them to work under brutal conditions.
- The Khmer Rouge was responsible for the deaths of between 1 and 3 million Cambodians; they killed well-educated people, ethnic minorities, and anyone who opposed was suspected of opposing their rule—and many Cambodians also died of starvation and disease.
- Pol Pot (1925–1998) was the leader of the Khmer Rouge and played a role in writing our document, which comes from the Constitution of the Democratic Republic of Kampuchea.

Vocabulary:

cadres: people who believe in an ideology, in this case, communism

strata: classes

borne: endured

non-aligned: not allied either to communists or capitalists in the Cold War (see Lesson 8.13)

territorial integrity: area foreigners can't invade

Document: Constitution of the Democratic Republic of Kampuchea, 1978

On the basis of the sacred and fundamental desires of the people, workers, peasants, and other laborers as well as those of the fighters and cadres of the Kampuchean Revolutionary Army; and Whereas a significant role has been played by the people, especially the workers, poor peasants, the lower middle peasantry, and other strata of laborers in the countryside and cities, who account for more than ninety-five percent of the entire Kampuchean nation, who assumed the heaviest responsibility in waging the war for the liberation of the nation and the people, made the greatest sacrifices in terms of life, property, and commitment, served the front line relentlessly, and unhesitatingly sacrificed their children and husbands by the thousands for the fight on the battlefield; Whereas great sacrifices have been borne by the three categories of the Kampuchean Revolutionary Army who fought valiantly, day and night, in the dry and rainy season, underwent all sorts of hardship and misery, shortages of food, medicine, clothing, ammunition, and other commodities in the great war for the liberation of the nation and the people; Whereas the entire Kampuchean people and the entire Kampuchean Revolutionary Army desire an independent, unified, peaceful, neutral, non-aligned, sovereign Kampuchea enjoying territorial integrity, a national society informed by genuine happiness, equality, justice, and democracy without rich or poor and without exploiters or exploited, a society in which all live harmoniously in great national solidarity and join forces to do manual labor together and increase production for the construction and defense of the country; . . .

Article 1: The State of Kampuchea is an independent, unified, peaceful, neutral, non-aligned, sovereign, and democratic State enjoying territorial integrity. The State of Kampuchea is a State of the people, workers, peasants, and all other Kampuchean laborers. . . .

Article 2: All important general means of production are the collective property of the people's State and the common property of the people's collectives. Property for everyday use remains in private hands. . . .

Article 5: Legislative power is invested in the representative assembly of the people, workers, peasants, and all other Kampuchean laborers. . . . The Kampuchean People's Representative Assembly shall be made up of 250 members, representing the people, the workers, peasants, and all other Kampuchean laborers and the Kampuchean Revolutionary Army. Of these 250, there shall be: Representing the peasants 150 Representing the laborers and other working people 50 Representing the revolutionary army 50. . . .

Article 12: Every citizen of Kampuchea enjoys full rights to a constantly improving material, spiritual, and cultural life. Every citizen of Democratic Kampuchea is guaranteed a living. All workers are the masters of their factories. All peasants are the masters of the rice paddies and fields. All other laborers have the right to work. There is absolutely no unemployment in Democratic Kampuchea.

Article 13: There must be complete equality among all Kampuchean people in an equal, just, democratic, harmonious, and happy society within the great national solidarity for defending and building the country together. Men and women are fully equal in every respect.

Source: Perspective Monde. (2019).
Constitution of the Democratic Republic of Kampuchea. http://perspective.usherbrooke
.ca/bilan/servlet/BMDictionnaire?iddictionnaire=1749

Comprehension Check:

1. Name as many social groups or professions as you can who are not mentioned in this constitution.
2. According to this constitution, who wants a society without social or economic classes?

Activities:

1. Write a letter from Karl Marx (Lesson 5.7) to Pol Pot praising or criticizing the Khmer Rouge's version of communism; quote from *The Communist Manifesto* to support your points.
2. Divide the class in half and debate the following proposition: It would have been possible for the Khmer Rouge to carry out the aims in this constitution without violence.

Reflection: The United Nations defines genocide as "intent to destroy, in whole or in part, a national, ethnical, racial or religious group, as such." Because most of the people who died under the Khmer Rouge were of the same national, ethnic, racial, and religious group as their killers, there has been controversy about whether what they did should be called a genocide or not. What do you think?

Resources:

BBC. (2018). Khmer Rouge: Cambodia's years of brutality. https://www.bbc.com/news/world-asia-pacific-10684399

Cambodian Tribunal Monitor. (n.d.). Khmer Rouge history. https://www.cambodiatribunal.org/history/cambodian-history/khmer-rouge-history/

Economics, Technology, and the Environment

UNIT QUESTION: How Should People Get the Resources They Need?

This unit builds on students' investigation of social hierarchy and brings together economics, technology, and the environment in humans' struggles to survive and thrive. We start with a timely exploration of climate change, an issue that has motivated youth around the globe. Moving back in time to the late Pleistocene era, students learn how Aboriginal Australians gained resources from their environment. Agricultural tools from the ancient world illustrate the Neolithic Revolution, and a hymn to the Nile River shows how civilizations fed their growing populations with the help of natural resources. A lesson on the Silk Road introduces trade and the cultural diffusion it promoted, while Ibn Battuta's description of the Mali Empire shows how civilizations could profit by creating conditions conducive to commerce. Leonardo da Vinci's drawings of an "ideal city" less prone to outbreaks of the plague help students understand both the challenges of medieval life and the solutions that the Renaissance hoped to provide—as well as to consider connections with COVID19. Students are likely to be shocked by the power and wealth of the Dutch East India Company, and its charter allows comparison with today's giant technology corporations. The Aztec Sun Stone shows how Mesoamericans' knowledge of astronomy enabled them to create an effective system of agricultural production. Mahommah G. Baquaqua's account of his life as a slave in Brazil illustrates the human costs of colonial wealth, while an excerpt of Adam Smith's *Wealth of Nations* shows how free-market capitalism is intended to work. The final two documents, on Mao's Great Leap Forward and the Chernobyl nuclear disaster, indicate some less successful attempts to meet the needs of growing populations and economies.

Before starting this unit, teachers may want to determine how controversial the reality of human-caused climate change will be in their classroom, and to provide students with additional information as necessary. Another document that may cause emotional distress—for good reason—is Baquaqua's biography. I have chosen to include it in this unit not to suggest that enslaved people were merely cogs in an economic machine, but rather to inject the realities of slavery and colonization into discussions of economic growth. This unit also offers a break from text-heavy units by including four visual sources; teachers may want to review Visual Thinking Strategies (2016) to ensure that these discussions have rigor. The interplay among Adam Smith, Mao Zedong, Mikhail Gorbachev, and a glance back at Karl Marx should create a healthy discussion about the pros and cons of communism, socialism, and capitalism, but it is also important to realize that these debates can become a proxy for contemporary political views. Teachers can encourage students to make connections to the present day, but also keep these documents well situated in their original contexts.

LESSON 6.1

What Did Greta Thunberg Ask World Leaders to Do About Climate Change?

Historical Figure: Greta Thunberg

Event: UN Climate Action Summit, 2019

Introduction: What do you know about climate change? Where did you learn it?

Mini-Lecture:

- The vast majority of scientists believe that the warming of the climate over the past century is due to human activities in which carbon dioxide (CO_2), methane, and nitrous oxide are emitted, or released into the environment.
- Top sources of these emissions are power plants that burn "fossil fuels" such as coal, oil, and natural gas; home appliances such as heaters and air conditioners; and transportation such as cars and airplanes.
- Scientists believe that effects of climate change include melting glaciers and rising sea levels as well as extreme weather events such as hurricanes and droughts; some people fear that these changes not only will affect humans, but could also cause a "mass extinction" of other species.
- In 2016, many countries ratified the Paris Agreement, a plan to reduce emissions in order to keep the increase in average global temperature below 2 degrees Celsius (from pre-Industrial Revolution levels) during this century.
- In 2018, Swedish teenager Greta Thunberg began leaving school each Friday to sit in front of the Parliament building in Stockholm as part of a "climate strike" to draw attention to the situation.
- In 2019, about 6 million people participated in "global climate strike" demonstrations in advance of the United Nations' Climate Action Network Meeting, which involved government and business leaders from around the world.

- Our document consists of a speech that Thunberg gave to the United Nations during this meeting.

Vocabulary:

ecosystem: interdependent group of organisms and their environment

mass extinction: extinction of 75% or more of species within a time span of several million years

CO_2 budget: amount of carbon dioxide that can be emitted while keeping within the goal of a less than 2-degree temperature rise

tipping point: when a series of small changes adds up to produce a larger change

feedback loop: when one change has effects that increase the speed of that change (e.g., when sea ice melts, it no longer bounces sunlight back into space, which increases the temperature and causes more sea ice to melt)

gigaton: 1 million tons (a ton is about 2,000 pounds)

Document: Speech to the UN Climate Action Network, Greta Thunberg, 2019

This is all wrong. I shouldn't be standing here. I should be back in school on the other side of the ocean. Yet you all come to me for hope? How dare you! You have stolen my dreams and my childhood with your empty words. And yet I'm one of the lucky ones. People are suffering. People are dying. Entire ecosystems are collapsing. We are in the beginning of a mass extinction. And all you can talk about is money and fairytales of eternal economic growth. How dare you!

For more than thirty years the science has been crystal clear. How dare you continue to look away and come here saying that you are doing enough, when the politics and solutions needed are still nowhere in sight. With today's emissions levels, our remaining CO_2 budget will be gone in less than 8.5 years. You say you "hear" us and that you understand the urgency. But no matter how sad and angry I am, I don't want to believe that. Because if you fully understood the situation and still kept on failing to act, then you would be evil. And I refuse to believe that. The popular idea of cutting our emissions in half in ten years only gives us a fifty per cent chance of staying below 1.5 degrees, and the risk of setting off irreversible chain reactions beyond human control. Maybe 50 percent is acceptable to you. But those numbers don't include tipping points, most feedback loops, additional warming hidden by toxic air pollution or the aspects of justice and equity. To have a 67 percent chance of staying below a 1.5 global temperature rise—the best odds given by the Intergovernmental Panel on Climate Change—the world had 420 gigatons of carbon dioxide left to emit back on January 1, 2018. Today that figure is already down to less than 350 gigatons. How dare you pretend that this can be solved with business-as-usual and some technical solutions. With today's emissions levels, that remaining CO_2 budget will be entirely gone in less than eight and a half years. There will not be any solutions or plans presented in line with these figures today. Because these numbers are too uncomfortable. And you are still not mature enough to tell it like it is. You are failing us. But the young people are starting to understand your betrayal. The eyes of all future generations are upon you. And if you choose to fail us I say we will never forgive you. We will not let you get away with this. Right here, right now is where we draw the line. The world is waking up. And change is coming, whether you like it or not.

Source: Kettley, S. (2019). Greta Thunberg speech in full.
https://www.express.co.uk/news/science/1183377/Greta-Thunberg-speech
-full-read-climate-change-UN-speech-transcribed-United-Nations

Comprehension Check:

1. Who is the "you" that Thunberg is addressing in this speech, and who is the "we"?
2. According to Thunberg, what is the problem with the existing plan to stop climate change?

Activities:

1. Line up on an "opinion cline" based on how concerned you are about climate change. First, talk with someone near you in line. Then, talk with someone far from you in line.
2. Take this quiz about the most effective ways to curb climate change at <https://edition.cnn.com/interactive/2019/04/specials/climate-change-solutions-quiz/>. Then discuss the results with the class. Which of these solutions are most and least realistic, and why?

Reflection: If you could choose one issue to address the United Nations about, what would it be and why?

Resources:

Allianz. (2019). 15 sources of greenhouse gases. https://www.allianz.com/en/press/extra/knowledge/environment/140912-fifteen-sources-of-greenhouse-gases.html

Frischmann, C. (2019). The young minds solving climate change. https://www.bbc.com/future/article/20190327-the-young-minds-solving-climate-change

NASA. (2019). Climate change: How do we know? https://climate.nasa.gov/evidence/

LESSON 6.2

HOW HAVE AUSTRALIAN ABORIGINAL PEOPLE INTERACTED WITH THEIR ENVIRONMENT?

Historical Figure: Essie Coffey

Event: Late Pleistocene era, c. 125,000 BCE–c. 10,000 BCE

Introduction: If all the grocery stores suddenly closed, what natural food sources could you find in your neighborhood?

Mini-Lecture:

- Archaeologists believe that Indigenous Aboriginal people have been living in Australia since about 60,000 BCE.
- Traditionally, Aboriginal people were seminomadic, moving seasonally within a defined territory, hunting and fishing, and gathering yams, fruits, nuts, and seeds; there is also evidence that they practiced agriculture and aquaculture (fish farming).
- Our documents are photos of artifacts that Aboriginal people used: a grinding stone used to grind seeds or plants into flour for baking, which have been dated to about 30,000 BCE; and fishhooks made of shell that have been dated to sometime in the last 1,000 years.
- When the British colonized Australia in 1788, they took Aboriginal people's land and disrupted their lifestyle; nonetheless, Aboriginal people continue their traditions while also finding new survival strategies.
- Essie Coffey (1941–1998) was an Aboriginal activist of the Muruwari people who cofounded both a legal service to help Aboriginal people gain ownership of their land, and the Brewarrina Aboriginal Cultural Museum, which preserves artifacts and helps visitors understand Aboriginal ways of life.

Document: Australian Aboriginal artifacts, c. 30,000 BCE–1000 CE (see Figures 6.1 and 6.2)

Figure 6.1. Grinding Stone made from Sandstone, Collected from the Marra Station on the Darling River, New South Wales*

Source: Australian Museum. (n.d.). Grindstones. https://australianmuseum
.net.au/learn/cultures/atsi-collection/cultural-objects/grindstones/
Photo by Stewart Humphreys for the Australian Museum

Figure 6.2. Shellfish Hooks (c. 1200), in Five Stages of Manufacture, Excavated at Botany Bay, New South Wales, in 1970*

Source: Australian Museum. (n.d.). Shellfish hooks. https://australian
.museum/learn/cultures/atsi-collection/cultural-objects/shellfish-hooks/
Photo Paul Ovenden for the Australian Museum

Comprehension Check:

1. What would the smaller rock in the image of the Grinding Stone be used for?
2. What does the sequence of shell pieces show in the image of Shellfish Hooks?

Activities:

1. With a partner, list some of the advantages and disadvantages of the Aboriginal people's methods of gaining resources from their environment.

---

*Please visit these links to see the images. The Australian Aboriginal people whose ancestors created these objects restrict the republishing of these images, but they have granted permission to the Australian Museum to display them on their website.

2. When the British colonized Australia, they did so on the basis that it was
    unoccupied. They argued that Aboriginal people were nomadic hunter-gatherers
    and thus could not own land, and moved inhabitants to reserves sometimes far
    from their original territories. Write a response to this argument from Essie Coffey.

Reflection: Around the world, people still hunt and gather food. Do you know
anyone who does so, or in what situations you could imagine doing so yourself?

Resources:

Australian Women's Archive Project. (2019). Essie Coffey. http://www.womenaustralia.info
    /biogs/IMP0121b.htm
Survival International. (2019). Aboriginal people. https://www.survivalinternational.org
    /tribes/aboriginals

LESSON 6.3

WHAT WERE THE CAUSES AND EFFECTS OF THE NEOLITHIC REVOLUTION?

Historical Figure: James Suzman

Event: Neolithic Revolution, c. 10,000 BCE

Introduction: Grain can be stored for long periods of time more easily than meat or
fresh plants. How do you think ancient human societies changed once they started
growing and storing grains such as barley, rice, and wheat?

Mini-Lecture:

- The Neolithic Revolution was a period between 15,000 and 10,000 BCE when
  societies in various places around the world began to practice agriculture and
  domesticate (keep for milk and meat) animals, instead of only hunting and
  gathering food.
- "Neolithic" means "new stone age," and the stone tools that people used for
  growing and harvesting food became smoother and more effective.
- Our document is a photo of several stone agricultural tools found in what is now
  Spain, which have been dated to the 5th century BCE.
- Several factors could have contributed to the development of agriculture,
  including a warming climate more suitable for farming, and humans and their
  societies evolving to the point where they could plan and carry out planting,
  harvesting, and storing.
- Historians believe that effects of the Neolithic Revolution include increases in
  surplus food, in the world's population, in the concentration of people in cities,
  in technologies of record-keeping and writing, and in larger states and empires.
- James Suzman (1970–) is a South African anthropologist who has argued that the
  Neolithic Revolution also led to increased social hierarchy and inequality; the more
  surplus food produced, the greater the difference was between rich and poor.

Figure 6.3. Agricultural Tools Found in the Iberian Settlement Bastida of Alcusses, c. Late 5th Century BCE

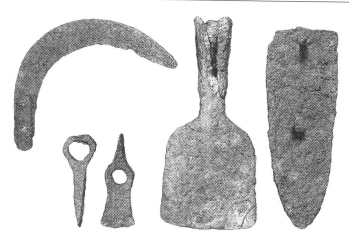

Source: Khan Academy. The Neolithic Revolution and early agriculture. https://www
.khanacademy.org/humanities/world-history/world-history-beginnings/birth-agriculture
-neolithic-revolution/a/where-did-agriculture-come-from
Carlos 1966, courtesy of Wikimedia Commons

Document: Agricultural tools, c. 5th century BCE (see Figure 6.3)

Comprehension Check:

1. Look at each of the tools above. How could people have used each of them in the planting and harvesting process?
2. What are the advantages and disadvantages of using stone tools over tools made of other materials?

Activities:

1. Look at the list of effects of the Neolithic Revolution in the mini-lecture. Work with a partner to create a poster connecting these effects.
2. Read the article by James Suzman from the Resources section. List reasons that you believe his theory, reasons you doubt it, and additional evidence that would help you decide.

Reflection: Would you rather have lived before the Neolithic Revolution or after it? Why?

Resources:

Suzman, J. (2017). How Neolithic farming sowed the seeds of modern inequality 10,000 years ago. https://www.theguardian.com/inequality/2017/dec/05/how-neolithic
-farming-sowed-the-seeds-of-modern-inequality-10000-years-ago

Blakemore, E. (2019). What was the Neolithic Revolution? https://www.nationalgeographic
    .com/culture/topics/reference/neolithic-agricultural-revolution/

LESSON 6.4

HOW DID ANCIENT EGYPTIANS USE THE NILE RIVER TO GAIN RESOURCES?

Historical Figure: Djoser

Event: Egypt's Old Kingdom, 2705–2213 BCE

Introduction: Do floods help or hurt people? Why?

Mini-Lecture:

- Around 5000 BCE, a civilization emerged in what is now Egypt, centered around the Nile River; historians call the years 2705 to 2213 BCE the "Old Kingdom," during which pharaohs (leaders) began building stone pyramids.
- Following monsoon rainstorms, the Nile River flooded regularly each year in August, fertilizing and irrigating the crops Egyptians grew.
- Egyptians worshipped many gods, including Hapi (god of the annual flooding of the Nile), Re (god of the sun), Seb (god of the earth), Nepera (god of grain), Ptah (god of craftspeople), Sobeth (god of fertility), and Neith (mother of all gods); they would prepare sacrifices to these gods by killing animals and, some historians argue, humans.
- Djoser was a pharaoh who ruled from 2650 to 2575 BCE, and he was known for building the first pyramid.
- Our document comes from a hymn, or religious song, that was sung in honor of the Nile.

Vocabulary:

manifest: appear
thy: your
issuing forth: appearing
whereon: when
inexhaustible: never running out
perpetuity: existing forever
waste away: starve

provisioning: storing food
herbage: plants
devoid: without
inundation: flood
immolated: burned
exalt: praise

Document: Hymn to the Nile, 2100 BCE

Hail to thee, O Nile! Who manifests thyself over this land, and comes to give life to Egypt! Mysterious is thy issuing forth from the darkness, on this day whereon it is celebrated. Watering the orchards created by Re, to cause all the cattle to live, you give the earth to drink, inexhaustible one! Path that descends from the sky, loving the bread of Seb and the first-fruits of Nepera, You cause the workshops of Ptah to prosper! . . .

You create the grain, you bring forth the barley, assuring perpetuity to the temples. If you cease your toil and your work, then all that exists is in anguish. If the gods suffer in heaven, then the faces of men waste away. . . .

He brings the offerings, as chief of provisioning; He is the creator of all good things, as master of energy, full of sweetness in his choice. If offerings are made it is thanks to Him. He brings forth the herbage for the flocks, and sees that each god receives his sacrifices. . . .

Where misery existed, joy manifests itself; all beasts rejoice. The children of Sobek, the sons of Neith, the cycle of the gods which dwells in him, are prosperous. No more reservoirs for watering the fields! He makes mankind valiant, enriching some, bestowing his love on others. . . .

If you have refused (to grant) nourishment, the dwelling is silent, devoid of all that is good, the country falls exhausted.

O inundation of the Nile, offerings are made unto you, men are immolated to you, great festivals are instituted for you. Birds are sacrificed to you, gazelles are taken for you in the mountain, pure flames are prepared for you. . . .

Men exalt him like the cycle of the gods, they dread him who creates the heat, even him who has made his son the universal master in order to give prosperity to Egypt. Come (and) prosper! Come (and) prosper! O Nile, come (and) prosper! O you who make men to live through his flocks and his flocks through his orchards!

Source: Halsall, P. (1998). Hymn to the Nile, c. 2100 BCE.
https://sourcebooks.fordham.edu/ancient/hymn-nile.asp

Comprehension Check:

1. Underline the positive effects of the Nile's flood, and circle the negative effects that would occur if the Nile did not flood.
2. Based on this document, what are some foods that Egyptians ate?

Activities:

1. Some scientists believe that climate change could cause the flooding of the Nile to become less predictable. Brainstorm effects that unpredictability would have had on the Old Kingdom's economy, as well as effects it could have on Egypt's economy today.
2. Research a recent weather or climate-related event (e.g., flood, drought, fire, storm) that impacted the economy in your region. What were its effects?

Reflection:
Ancient Egyptians gave credit to their gods for causing the annual flood of the Nile and the growth of crops. Do most people in your society see

weather events as caused by some divine force, by human causes, or by natural causes? Why?

Resources:

Encyclopedia Britannica. (2015). Djoser. https://www.britannica.com/biography/Djoser
Mark, J. J. (2016). Old Kingdom of Egypt. https://www.ancient.eu/Old_Kingdom_of_Egypt/

LESSON 6.5

HOW DID TRADE PROMOTE CULTURAL DIFFUSION ALONG THE SILK ROAD?

Historical Figure: Benjamin of Tudela

Event: Silk Road trade, 2nd century BCE–15th century CE

Introduction: Look at the things around you in the classroom. How many were made in the country where you live?

Mini-Lecture:

- The Silk Road was a network of trade routes over land used by merchants to bring goods back and forth over 4,000 miles between what is now Europe and China.
- The Silk Road was used between 130 BCE, when Han Dynasty China opened trade relations with European powers, and the 15th century, when the Ottoman Empire closed off these routes.
- In addition to silk and spices, goods including paper and gunpowder were transported from China to Europe along these routes, while horses and precious metals were brought to China.
- In addition to goods, religious beliefs, scientific knowledge, and languages were spread along these routes; the process by which ideas are spread is called cultural diffusion.
- Benjamin of Tudela was a rabbi (Jewish spiritual leader) from Spain; in the 12th century, he traveled along the Silk Road and wrote an account of his journey, from which our document is taken.
- In this document he writes about the city of Baghdad, now in Iraq, which was at that time ruled by the Abbasid Caliphate, a Muslim dynasty of kings who were known for their religious tolerance and their support of learning; they built a huge library called the House of Wisdom where scientific and philosophical books by Roman, Chinese, Persian, Indian, and African scholars were collected.

Vocabulary:

thence: there
Mohammedan religion: Islam
all manner: all kinds
partake of: use

coverlets: blankets
courtier: assistant to a king
proceeds thereof: money earned by selling something

trusty: trustworthy
arm: branch of a river

hospice: place where sick people can stay
sage: wise person

Document: Itinerary of Benjamin of Tudela, Benjamin of Tudela, 12th century

I journeyed first from my native town to the city of Saragossa, and thence by way of the River Ebro to Tortosa. . . . [From Okbara] it is two days to Bagdad, the great city and the royal residence of the Caliph Emir al Muminin al Abbasi of the family of Mohammed. He is at the head of the Mohammedan religion, and all the kings of Islam obey him; he occupies a similar position to that held by the Pope over the Christians. He has a palace in Bagdad three miles in extent, wherein is a great park with all varieties of trees, fruit-bearing and otherwise, and all manner of animals. The whole is surrounded by a wall, and in the park there is a lake whose waters are fed by the river Hiddekel. Whenever the king desires to indulge in recreation and to rejoice and feast, his servants catch all manner of birds, game and fish, and he goes to his palace with his counsellors and princes. There the great king, Al Abbasi the Caliph (Hafiz) holds his court, and he is kind unto Israel, and many belonging to the people of Israel are his attendants; he knows all languages, and is well versed in the law of Israel. He reads and writes the holy language (Hebrew). He will not partake of anything unless he has earned it by the work of his own hands. He makes coverlets to which he attaches his seal; his courtiers sell them in the market, and the great ones of the land purchase them, and the proceeds thereof provide his sustenance. He is truthful and trusty, speaking peace to all men. . . .

He built, on the other side of the river, on the banks of an arm of the Euphrates which there borders the city, a hospital consisting of blocks of houses and hospices for the sick poor who come to be healed. Here there are about sixty physicians' stores which are provided from the Caliph's house with drugs and whatever else may be required. Every sick man who comes is maintained at the Caliph's expense and is medically treated. . . . All this the Caliph does out of charity to those that come to the city of Bagdad, whether they be sick or insane. The Caliph is a righteous man, and all his actions are for good. In Bagdad there are about 40,000 Jews, and they dwell in security, prosperity and honor under the great Caliph, and amongst them are great sages, the heads of Academies engaged in the study of the law. . . .

Source: University of Washington. (n.d.). The itinerary of Benjamin of Tudela. http://depts.washington.edu/silkroad/texts/tudela.html

Comprehension Check:

1. Go through the document and underline all the goods mentioned that could be traded along the Silk Road. Then circle parts of the text describing ideas or knowledge that might be spread along the Silk Road.
2. According to Tudela, how are Jewish people treated in Baghdad?

Activities:

1. Look at the website about the Silk Road in the Resources section. Choose one of the goods listed there and explain its importance to people in the society who bought it.
2. How is the process of cultural diffusion different today than it was in the 12th century? Sketch out how this process occurs now.

Reflection: Was Tudela's description of Baghdad surprising to you? Why or why not?

Resources:

Jewish Virtual Library. (2019). Benjamin of Tudela. https://www.jewishvirtuallibrary.org /benjamin-of-tudela

Mark, J. J. (2018). The Silk Road. https://www.ancient.eu/Silk_Road/

LESSON 6.6

How Did the Mali Empire Profit From Trade in Gold and Salt?

Historical Figure: Mansa Musa

Event: Mali Empire, c. 1230–1670

Introduction: If you ruled a region without many natural resources, how would you gain wealth?

Mini-Lecture:

- From c. 1230 to 1670, the Mali Empire ruled territory in West Africa; its location between salt mines to the north and gold mines to the south enabled it to gain great wealth by taxing trade in these items.
- Mansa Musa ruled the Mali Empire from c. 1312 to c. 1337; he is known for being the richest person ever.
- Mansa Musa was Muslim, and he made a pilgrimage to the holy city of Mecca and brought back scholars, and with his wealth was able to create one of the greatest centers of learning in the world at that time.
- Ibn Battuta was a scholar from what is now Morocco who spent 30 years traveling through Africa and Asia; our document comes from a book he wrote about his journeys.

Vocabulary:

girth: size
company: large group
provisions: food
qadi: judge in an Islamic court
pilgrim: Muslim who has made the pilgrimage to Mecca

abhorrence: hatred
confiscate: take away lawfully
assiduous: dutiful
congregations: groups

Document: *Travels in Africa and Asia*, Ibn Battuta, 1354

When I decided to make the journey to [Mali], which is reached in twenty-four days from Iwalatan if the traveler pushes on rapidly, I hired a guide from the Massufa [people]—for there is no necessity to travel in a company on account of the safety of that road—and set out with three of my companions.

On the way there are many trees [baobabs], and these trees are of great age and girth; a whole caravan may shelter in the shade of one of them. There are trees which have neither branches nor leaves, yet the shade cast by their trunks is sufficient to shelter a man. Some of these trees are rotted in the interior and the rain-water collects in them, so that they serve as wells and the people drink of the water inside them. In others there are bees and honey, which is collected by the people. . . .

A traveler in this country carries no provisions, whether plain food or seasonings, and neither gold nor silver. He takes nothing but pieces of salt and glass ornaments, which the people call beads, and some aromatic goods. When he comes to a village the womenfolk of the blacks bring out millet, milk, chickens, pulped lotus fruit, rice, "funi" (a grain resembling mustard seed, from which "kuskusu" [couscous] and gruel are made), and pounded haricot beans. The traveler buys what of these he wants. . . .

Thus I reached the city of Malli, the capital of the king of the blacks. I stopped at the cemetery and went to the quarter occupied by the whites, where I asked for Muhammad ibn al-Faqih. I found that he had hired a house for me and went there. His son-in-law brought me candles and food, and next day Ibn al-Faqih himself came to visit me, with other prominent residents. I met the qadi of Malli, 'Abd ar-Rahman, who came to see me; he is a negro, a pilgrim, and a man of fine character. I met also the interpreter Dugha, who is one of the principal men among the blacks. All these persons sent me hospitality-gifts of food and treated me with the utmost generosity—may God reward them for their kindnesses! . . .

The negroes possess some admirable qualities. They are seldom unjust, and have a greater abhorrence of injustice than any other people. Their sultan shows no mercy to anyone who is guilty of the least act of it. There is complete security in their country. Neither traveler nor inhabitant in it has anything to fear from robbers or men of violence. They do not confiscate the property of any white man who dies in their country, even if it be uncounted wealth. On the contrary, they give it into the charge of some trustworthy person among the whites, until the rightful heir takes possession of it. They are careful to observe the hours of prayer, and assiduous in attending them in congregations, and in bringing up their children to them.

Source: Halsall, P. (2019). Ibn Battuta, *Travels in Asia and Africa 1325–1354.*
https://sourcebooks.fordham.edu/source/1354-ibnbattuta.asp

Comprehension Check:

1. List as many factors as you can that make the Mali Empire a good place for traders.
2. What serves as money in the Mali Empire?

Activities:

1. Divide the class into three groups: about half gold merchants, about half salt merchants, and two Mali Empire tax collectors, one for gold and one for salt. Each gold merchant should get five pieces of "gold," each salt merchant five blocks of "salt." As merchants enter Mali, tax collectors take one gold or one salt piece. See who has the most wealth after everyone has made their trades.
2. List actions that your government takes, using tax revenue, that creates a better environment for the buying and selling of goods in your country.

Reflection: Ibn Battuta makes a distinction between "whites" (including Arabs like himself) and "blacks," yet he gets along with people different from him. Why do you think that is?

Resources:

Berkeley ORIAS. (2019). The travels of Ibn Battuta. https://orias.berkeley.edu/resources -teachers/travels-ibn-battuta
Cartwright, M. (2019). Mansa Musa I. https://www.ancient.eu/Mansa_Musa_I/

LESSON 6.7
How Did Leonardo da Vinci Envision the Ideal City During the Renaissance?

Historical Figure: Leonardo da Vinci

Event: The Renaissance, c. 1300–1600

Introduction: Do you think that we should look to the past for solutions to our current problems? Why or why not?

Mini-Lecture:

*   The Renaissance is a term historians use to describe a period between 1300 and 1600 when scientists, artists, philosophers, writers, and architects revived ideas from Classical Greece and Rome (from about 500 BCE to about 400 CE).
*   One key idea during the Renaissance was humanism (the idea that people should make ethical decisions based on reason rather than on religious teachings, governmental authority, or traditions, and that the scientific method could guide people toward the truth).

- Leonardo da Vinci was an artist, inventor, architect, and scientist who lived in what is now Italy from 1452 to 1519.
- In the late 15th century, a disease called the bubonic plague, sometimes called the Black Death, killed about one-third of the people in Milan, where da Vinci was living; in the previous century, it had killed about one-third of the people in Europe.
- The bubonic plague was brought to Italy by traders returning from Asia and was spread by fleas, which lived on the rats that infested many medieval European cities and which also passed from human to human.
- Da Vinci did not know how the plague spread, but he was correct in suspecting that it was related to hygiene and sanitation, which was lacking in Milan and other medieval cities.
- Our document is a drawing from da Vinci's plan for a (never built) "ideal city," which would be cleaner and better designed, and thus less prone to outbreaks of disease.
- Da Vinci planned one underground network of canals for transportation and another for sewage and wastewater; on the ground floor level would be shops and roads for horse-carts, and the upper level would be for pedestrians.

Document: Ideal city drawings, Leonardo da Vinci, 1487 (see Figure 6.4)

Comprehension Check:

1. Label the parts of the drawing according to what you learned about da Vinci's plan from the mini-lecture.

Activities:

1. If da Vinci's ideal city represents a Renaissance humanist's response to the plague, how do you think Europeans in the earlier medieval era would have tried to solve the problem? Brainstorm solutions that don't involve using the scientific method.
2. Research the COVID19 pandemic. Then work with a small group to sketch out a plan for an "ideal city" that could prevent its spread.

Reflection: The plague is an example of how trade can bring dangers along with benefits. What are the dangers and benefits you see in global trade today?

Resources:

Dickson, A. (2017). Key features of Renaissance culture. https://www.bl.uk/shakespeare/articles/key-features-of-renaissance-culture

Liddell, D. (2018). The plague inspired da Vinci to design a city. We should steal his ideas. https://www.fastcompany.com/90163788/the-plague-inspired-da-vinci-to-design-a-city-we-should-steal-his-ideas

Figure 6.4. Plan for an Ideal City, Leonardo da Vinci, 1488–1490

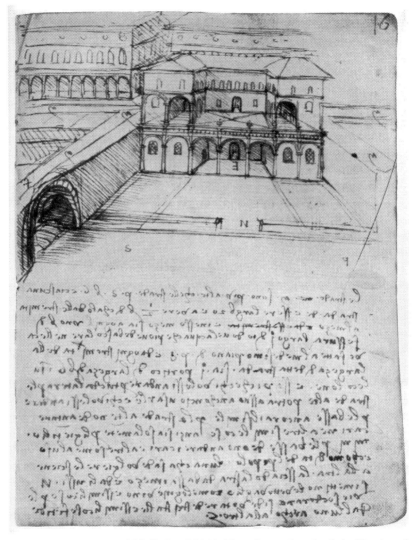

Source: Liddell, D. (2018). The plague inspired da Vinci to design a city. We should steal his ideas. https://www.fastcompany.com/90163788/the-plague -inspired-da-vinci-to-design-a-city-we-should-steal-his-ideas

Image courtesy of Alamy Stock Photos

LESSON 6.8

HOW DID THE NETHERLANDS PROFIT FROM COLONIZATION?

Historical Figure: Jan Pieterszoon Coen

Event: Dutch East India Company founded, 1602

Introduction: What would happen if companies such as Google, Apple, Microsoft, Facebook, and Amazon had armies, as well as the power to make laws and enslave people?

Mini-Lecture:

- In the 16th century, the Dutch, the Portuguese, and the British were competing for control over trade with Asia and Africa.
- In 1602, the Netherlands established the Dutch East India Company (abbreviated VOC based on its Dutch-language name), a corporation that conducted shipping and trading in Asia and Africa.
- The VOC was the world's first public company (in which people could buy stock), and it paved the way for the current globalized economic system.
- Our document comes from the charter, or founding document, of the VOC, which granted it a monopoly on the Dutch spice trade and gave it powers a government would usually have.
- The VOC engaged in the slave trade, bringing 50,000 enslaved people from Africa to work in its colonies; and it also mistreated both local people and its own employees.
- At its peak value, the VOC was worth almost $8 trillion, more than the current largest 20 companies combined.
- Jan Pieterszoon-Coen was an officer in the Dutch East India Company who served as the governor-general of the Dutch East Indies in the early 17th century; he established the capital city of Batavia and created military fortifications throughout what is now Indonesia.

Vocabulary:

therewith: with
aforementioned: previously mentioned
commitments: treaties
fortifications and strongholds: military defenses and bases
judiciary: courts
contravene: do not obey
subverters: people who break the law

corporal punishment: physical punishment
material sanctions: not getting goods or money
categorically: clearly
license: permission
contraventions: disobedience
desist: stop

Document: Charter of the Dutch East India Company, Alb Joachims, 1602

We let it be known that as the prosperity of the United Netherlands is principally a result of our shipping trade and commerce that has undergone praiseworthy increases from time to time and that the Netherlands have been involved therewith since the distant past, not only with neighboring kingdoms and regions, but also with those located further away than these, in Europe, Asia and Africa. . . .

The Directors [of the VOC] shall solemnly swear an oath on their honor and faith that they shall carry out the administration properly and honestly, keep good and honest accounts, and in collecting the moneys for the equipping and in the distribution of profits obtained from the return cargoes shall not favor the greater shareholders over the lesser ones. . . .

Similarly, east of the Cape of Good Hope and in and beyond the Straits of Magellan, representatives of the aforementioned Company shall be authorized to enter into commitments and enter into contracts with princes and rulers in the name of [the Netherlands] or the country's Government in order to build fortifications and strongholds.

They may appoint governors, keep armed forces, install Judicial officers and officers for other essential services so to keep the establishments in good order, as well as jointly ensure enforcement of the law and justice, all combined so as to promote trade. In respect to trade and commerce the abovementioned governors, the judiciary and military shall be required to swear an oath of loyalty to [the Netherlands], or to the abovementioned government and to the Company. These in turn may dismiss the abovementioned governors and members of the judiciary should it be found that they have acted corruptly and dishonestly, on the understanding that the aforementioned governors and officers shall not be prevented from coming forward to express to us or the Company their concerns and dissatisfactions should they have any. . . . Except with consent of the Company, none of the ships, cannon or ammunition that belong to the Company shall be used in the service of the country. . . .

All these points, liberties and benefits recorded above, we have ordered and do hereby order will be maintained and they shall be followed and complied with by each and every subjects and residents of [the Netherlands] without exception of any kind, either directly or indirectly and either inside or outside [the Netherlands] and in all possible ways.

Those who contravene this shall be punished as subverters of the better welfare of the country and as transgressors of our ordinances and shall be subjected to corporal punishment as well as material sanctions. We therefore categorically call upon and command all governors, members of the judiciary, officers, magistrates and the inhabitants of [the Netherlands] to permit the abovementioned Directors to quietly and peacefully enjoy the full effect of this our License, this mandate and this privilege that we have provided, while contraventions and difficulties to the contrary must desist, since we have found this license to be right for the country.

Source: Gerritson, R. (n.d.). Charter of the Dutch East India Company.
http://rupertgerritsen.tripod.com/pdf/published/VOC_Charter_1602.pdf

Comprehension Check:

1. List at least five powers that the VOC had.
2. What would happen to Dutch citizens who did not follow the VOC's rules?

Activities:

1. What do you think the richest ever man, Mansa Musa (Lesson 6.6), would say to the richest ever corporation, the VOC? Write Mansa Musa's response to the Charter of the VOC.
2. Divide the class in half and debate the following proposition: People throughout Europe who consumed the spices, silks, and other products imported by the VOC shared responsibility for the mistreatment of the VOC's employees and slaves.

Reflection: Do you think that government should limit the powers of large companies today? Why or why not?

Resources:

Coolhaas, W. P. (2019). Jan Pieterszoon-Coen. https://www.britannica.com/biography/Jan
    -Pieterszoon-Coen
Salomons, B. (2017). The Dutch East India Company was richer than Apple, Google, and
    Facebook combined. https://dutchreview.com/culture/history/how-rich-was-the-dutch
    -east-india-company/

LESSON 6.9
How Did Aztec Technology Aid Agriculture?

Historical Figure: Moctezuma II

Event: Aztec Empire, 1428–1521

Introduction: How do you think people kept track of time before the invention of clocks and calendars?

Mini-Lecture:

*   In the 15th century, the Nahua people established the Aztec Empire in what is now Mexico.
*   Like other Mesoamerican people including the Maya and Inca, the Aztec were skilled astronomers who observed the movement of stars and planets to create sophisticated calendars with both religious and practical significance.
*   The Aztec believed that time was cyclical rather than linear; they had a ritual calendar based on a 260-day cycle, and a solar calendar based on a 365-day year.
*   The solar calendar was divided into 20 months; many were named for the agricultural phase that corresponded to that part of the year, for instance, "eating maize and beans," "the fruit falls," "growth," and "drought."
*   By using this calendar, as well as innovative farming methods such as flooded fields called *chinampas*, the Aztec were able to produce enough crops to feed a growing population, as well as to store a surplus of corn and beans for years when the harvests were poor.

Figure 6.5. Aztec Calendar Stone, c. 1520

Source: Wikimedia Commons. Aztec calendar stone in National Museum of Anthropology, Mexico City. https://commons.wikimedia.org/wiki/File:Aztec_calendar_stone_in _National_Museum_of_Anthropology,_Mexico_City.jpg
Sasha Isachenko, 2012

- Our document is a photo of the Sun Stone, a calendar created during the reign of Moctezuma II (1466–1520), which shows the alignment of the ritual and solar calendars.

Document: Sun Stone, c. 1520 (see Figure 6.5)

Comprehension Check:

1. (Watch the video from the Resources section first.) Which part of the Sun Stone shows the solar calendar?
2. How did the Aztec calendar help farmers grow food?

Activities:

1. Create a T-chart showing similarities and differences between the ways that ancient Egyptians (Lesson 6.4) and Aztecs linked religion and agriculture.
2. Work with a partner to research one technology that farmers use today to get the most yield from their crops. Explain it to the class, describing its similarities and differences from Aztec farming methods.

Reflection: Do you think that people who grow and harvest food today get the respect they deserve for their contributions to our economy? Why or why not?

Resources:

Cartwright, M. (2019). The Aztec calendar. https://www.ancient.eu/article/896/the-aztec
-calendar/

Khan Academy. (2015). The Sun Stone. https://www.youtube.com/watch?time_continue
=380&v=Zn03u3-U1fk&feature=emb_title

LESSON 6.10

HOW DID ENSLAVED AFRICANS EXPERIENCE THE TRANSATLANTIC SLAVE TRADE?

Historical Figure: Mahommah G. Baquaqua

Event: Transatlantic slave trade, 16th–19th centuries

Introduction: If you were enslaved, what would you do—run away? Fight back? Do the work you were given? Why?

Mini-Lecture:

- The transatlantic slave trade was the exchange of African people for money and other goods from the Americas and Europe that took place between the 16th and 19th centuries.
- African people who had been enslaved as war captives by other Africans were initially sold to Europeans, but as the demand for slaves increased, European and African slave traders began actively seeking out people to enslave.
- Enslaved people had to endure the "Middle Passage," the weeks- to months-long journey by ship to the Americas; at least 1.5 million died of illness, suicide, or were killed by their captors along the way.
- Slave traders brought most enslaved people—about 9.5 million out of the 11 million who survived the Middle Passage—to the Portuguese colony of Brazil, they worked on plantations producing sugar or molasses.
- These goods were exported to the United States and Europe, where rum was produced and then traded, along with guns, gunpowder, and other goods, for more enslaved people from Africa.
- Mahommah G. Baquaqua was born in what is now Benin around 1824, and enslaved and sent to Brazil in 1845; when his master took him to the northern United States, where slavery was illegal, in 1847, he escaped and gained freedom with the help of abolitionists.
- Our document comes from a biography that Baquaqua wrote with the assistance of Samuel Moore in 1854, after pursuing higher education in the United States.

Vocabulary:

trepanned: trapped
consigned to: forced to stay in

hold: compartment below the decks of a ship where cargo is usually kept

benevolent: kind
noisome: having an unpleasant smell
thoroughgoing: complete
abolitionists: people who want to abolish,
   or outlaw, slavery

frame: body
unfaithful: not obedient
indolent: lazy

Document: *Biography of Mahommah G. Baquaqua,* Mahommah G. Baquaqua and
Samuel Moore, 1854

The Slave Ship. Its horrors, ah! who can describe? . . . Oh! friends of humanity,
pity the poor African, who has been trepanned and sold away from friends and
home, and consigned to the hold of a slave ship, to await even more horrors and
miseries in a distant land, amongst the religious and benevolent. Yes, even in
their very midst; but to the ship! We were thrust into the hold of the vessel in a
state of nudity, the males being crammed on one side and the females on the
other; the hold was so low that we could not stand up, but were obliged to
crouch upon the floor or sit down; day and night were the same to us, sleep
being denied as from the confined position of our bodies, and we became
desperate through suffering and fatigue. . . .

Let those humane individuals, who are in favor of slavery, only allow
themselves to take the slave's position in the noisome hold of a slave ship, just
for one trip from Africa to America, and without going into the horrors of
slavery further than this, if they do not come out thorough-going abolitionists,
then I have no more to say in favor of abolition. But I think their views and
feelings regarding slavery will be changed in some degree, however; if not, let
them continue in the course of slavery, and work out their term in a cotton or
rice field, or other plantation, and then if they do not say hold, enough! I think
they must be of iron frames, possessing neither hearts nor souls. . . .

I was soon placed at hard labor, such as none but slaves and horses are put
to. At the time of this man's purchasing me, he was building a house, and had to
fetch building stone from across the river, a considerable distance, and I was
compelled to carry them that were so heavy it took three men to raise them
upon my head, which burden I was obliged to bear for a quarter of a mile at
least, down to where the boat lay. . . .

Things went on worse and worse, and I was very anxious to change masters,
so I tried running away, but was soon caught, tied and carried back. I next tried
what it would do for me by being unfaithful and indolent; so one day when I
was sent out to sell bread as usual, I only sold a small quantity, and the money I
took and spent for whiskey, which I drank pretty freely, and went home well
drunk, when my master went to count the days, taking in my basket and
discovering the state of things, I was beaten very severely. I told him he must
not whip me anymore, and got quite angry, for the thought came into my head
that I would kill him, and afterwards destroy myself. I at last made up my mind
to drown myself; I would rather die than live to be a slave. I then ran down to

the river and threw myself in, but being seen by some persons who were in a boat, I was rescued from drowning.

Source: University of North Carolina. (2001). Biography of Mahommah G. Baquaqua. https://docsouth.unc.edu/neh/baquaqua/baquaqua.html

Comprehension Check:

1. What is Baquaqua's idea for how to turn supporters of slavery into abolitionists?
2. What four things does Baquaqua do or think of doing to get away from his master?

Activities:

1. Research the transatlantic slave trade and create a map showing the trade in enslaved people and goods.
2. Line up on an "opinion cline" based on how much you agree with Baquaqua's proposition: If the people who profited from slavery temporarily experienced life as an enslaved person, they would abolish slavery. Talk with a person near you, and then with a person with a different view.

Reflection: Baquaqua described enslaver in the Americas as "religious and benevolent." Why do you think he chose that phrase?

Resources:

Colonial Williamsburg Foundation. (2019). Transatlantic slave trade. http://slaveryandremembrance.org/articles/article/?id=A0002

Faal, C. (2009). Mahommah Gardo Baquaqua. https://www.blackpast.org/global-african-history/baquaqua-mahommah-gardo-1824-1857/

LESSON 6.11

HOW WAS FREE-MARKET CAPITALISM SUPPOSED TO WORK?

Historical Figure: Adam Smith

Event: Industrial Revolution, c. 1760–1840

Introduction: Do you think governments should play a large role in the economy? Or should they let businesses, consumers, and workers agree on prices, wages, and safety issues? Why?

Mini-Lecture:

• The Industrial Revolution began in Great Britain (now the United Kingdom) in the 18th century; instead of living on farms and producing most of what they needed themselves, many people moved to cities and worked in factories where machines made possible a "division of labor" in which each worker did a small part of the job of producing goods.

- Adam Smith (1723–1790) was Scottish philosopher known as the "father of economics," who believed that the Industrial Revolution could improve the situation of all people.
- Our document comes from his 1776 book, *The Wealth of Nations*, in which he describes an economic system that would later be called free-market capitalism.
- Free-market capitalism is an economic system in which businesses compete to make products consumers will buy, and workers decide which businesses to work for; the government does not intervene much except to protect the right to private property.

Vocabulary:

draws out: pulls out
straights: straightens
exerted themselves: worked hard
manufactory: factory
in consequence of: because of
owing to: because of
dexterity: skillfulness

species: kind
abridge: shorten
occasions: produces
universal opulence: wealth for everyone
are derived: come from
propensity: tendency

Document: *The Wealth of Nations*, Adam Smith, 1776

Of the Division of Labor: . . . To take an example, therefore, the trade of the pin-maker; a workman not educated to this business, nor acquainted with the use of the machinery employed in it, could . . . make one pin in a day, and certainly could not make twenty. But in the way in which this business is now carried on, . . . it is divided into a number of branches. . . . One man draws out the wire, another straights it, a third cuts it, a fourth points it, a fifth grinds it at the top. . . . I have seen a small manufactory of this kind where ten men only were employed, and where . . . they could, when they exerted themselves, make among them about twelve pounds of pins in a day. . . .

This great increase of the quantity of work which, in consequence of the division of labor, the same number of people are capable of performing, is owing to three different circumstances; *first*, to the increase of dexterity in every particular workman; *secondly*, to the saving of the time which is commonly lost in passing from one species of work to another; and *lastly*, to the invention of a great number of machines which facilitate and abridge labor, and enable one man to do the work of many. . . .

It is the great multiplication of the productions of all the different arts, in consequence of the division of labor, which occasions, in a well-governed society, that *universal opulence* which extends itself to the lowest ranks of the people. . . .

This division of labor, from which so many advantages are derived, is not originally the effect of any human wisdom. . . . It is the necessary, though very slow and gradual, consequence of a certain propensity in human nature . . . to truck, barter, and exchange one thing for another. . . . Give me that which I want, and you shall have this which you want, is the meaning of every such offer. . . . It is not from the benevolence of the butcher, the brewer, or the baker that we expect our dinner, *but from their regard to their own interest. . . .*

[The individual] . . . neither intends to promote the public interest, nor knows how much he is promoting it. . . . He intends only his own security; and by directing that industry in such a manner as its produce may be of the greatest value, he intends only his own gain, and he is in this, as in many other cases, led by an invisible hand to promote an end which was no part of his intention. . . . By pursuing his own interest he frequently promotes that of the society more effectually than when he really intends to promote it.

Source: Halsall, P. (1999). Adam Smith, *The Wealth of Nations*, 1776.
https://sourcebooks.fordham.edu/mod/adamsmith-summary.asp

Comprehension Check:

1. What does Smith believe are the effects of division of labor?
2. According to Smith, what causes people to make economic decisions that are best for society as a whole?

Activities:

1. How would Karl Marx (Lesson 5.7) respond to Smith's ideas? Draw their interaction in the form of a comic strip.
2. How would Mahommah Baquaqua (Lesson 6.10) react to Smith's idea of an "invisible hand" that brings about "universal opulence" for everyone? Write a letter from Baquaqua to Smith explaining his views on free-market capitalism.

Reflection: What do you think are the advantages and disadvantages of free-market capitalism?

Resources:

Blenman, J. (2019). Adam Smith and "The Wealth of Nations." https://www.investopedia
.com/updates/adam-smith-wealth-of-nations/

LESSON 6.12

What Were the Goals and Results of Mao Zedong's Command Economy?

Historical Figure: Mao Zedong

Event: Mao's "Great Leap Forward," 1959

Introduction: Do you think the economy would be more efficient and productive if someone planned it out, instead of letting producers and consumers do as they choose? Why or why not?

Mini-Lecture:

- In 1949, there was a communist revolution in China, after which the People's Republic of China was founded.
- Mao Zedong, who was the chairman of the Chinese Communist Party (CCP) from 1943 to 1976, played a key role in the revolution and also led the country afterward.
- As well as embracing Marx's view that a communist classless society was preferable to capitalism, Mao also supported socialism, the idea that property should be owned publicly rather than privately, and that people should cooperate to produce goods from which they would all benefit.
- When the CCP took power, they instituted land reform, in which the government took property from rich landlords and distributed it to poor peasants; the next step, according to socialist ideology, was to collectivize the land so that the people owned and farmed it together.
- Mao was the mastermind of the "Great Leap Forward," which made China into a "command economy"; the government created an economic plan and allocated resources to carry it out, deciding what and how much people should produce.
- Mao's plan was to collectivize agriculture and industrialize rural areas; peasants had to grow enough grain to meet the quotas that the CCP set or face punishment, and they also had to make steel in their villages.
- The Great Leap Forward did not work out as Mao had hoped; historians estimate that it resulted in the deaths of 45 million people, due to either starvation or government repression.
- Our document comes from a speech Mao made in 1955 as he was forming the plan for the Great Leap Forward; he makes reference to foot-binding, a tradition banned by the CCP, in which women's feet were broken and tightly bound with cloth in order to give them a way of walking perceived as more delicate.

Vocabulary:

upsurge: strengthening
comrades: members of a communist organization
taboos: things that are considered inappropriate

mou: unit of measurement equal to about 800 square yards
gales: windstorms
rudiments: first steps

Document: The Question of Agricultural Cooperation, Mao Zedong, 1955

A new upsurge in the socialist mass movement is in sight throughout the Chinese countryside. But some of our comrades are tottering along like a woman with bound feet, always complaining that others are going too fast. They imagine that by picking on trifles, grumbling unnecessarily, worrying continuously, and putting up countless taboos and commandments, they will guide the socialist mass movement in the rural areas along sound lines.

No, this is not the right way at all; it is wrong. The tide of social reform in the countryside—in the shape of cooperation—has already reached some places.

Soon it will sweep the whole country. This is a huge socialist revolutionary moment, which involves a rural population more than five hundred million strong, one that has very great world significance. We should guide this movement vigorously, warmly, and systematically, and not act as a drag on it. . . .

It is wrong to say that the present pace of development of the agricultural producers cooperatives has "gone beyond practical possibilities" or "gone beyond the consciousness of the masses." The situation in China is like this: its population is enormous, there is a shortage of cultivated land (only three *mou* of land per head, taking the country as a whole; in many parts of southern provinces, the average is only one *mou* or less), natural catastrophes occur from time to time—every year large numbers of farms suffer more or less from flood, drought, gales, frost, hail, or insect pests—and methods of farming are backward. As a result, many peasants are still having difficulties or are not well off. The well-off ones are comparatively few, although since land reform the standard of living of the peasants as a whole has improved. For all these reasons there is an active desire among most peasants to take the socialist road. . . .

We have been taking steps to bring about a gradual advance in the socialist transformation of agriculture. The first step in the countryside is to call on the peasants, in accordance with the principles of voluntariness and mutual benefit, to organize agricultural producers' mutual-aid teams. Such teams contain only the rudiments of socialism. Each one draws in a few households, though some have ten or more. The second step is to call on the peasants, on the basis of these mutual-aid teams and still in accordance with the principles of voluntariness and mutual benefit, to organize small agricultural producers' cooperatives semi-socialist in nature, characterized by the pooling of land as shares and by single management. Not until we take the third step will the peasants be called upon, on the basis of these small, semi-socialist cooperatives and in accordance with the same principles of voluntariness and mutual benefit, to unite on a larger scale and organize large agricultural producers' cooperatives completely socialist in nature. These steps are designed to raise steadily the socialist consciousness of the peasants through their personal experience, to change their mode of life step by step, and so minimize any feeling that their mode of life is being changed all of a sudden.

Source: Asia for Educators. (n.d.). "The question of agricultural cooperation." http://afe
.easia.columbia.edu/ps/cup/mao_zedong_agricultural_cooperation.pdf

Comprehension Check:

1. What criticism does Mao make of his fellow CCP members?
2. Sketch out the steps in agricultural collectivization that Mao describes.

Activities:

1. Mao states that collectivization should be based on "voluntariness and mutual benefit." Yet during the Great Leap Forward, peasants were forced to collectivize

their land and did not benefit much. Brainstorm reasons why the plan differed so much from the reality.

2. How would Adam Smith (Lesson 6.11) respond to Mao's plan? Annotate the sketch you made in response to Question 2 above with comments from Smith's perspective.

Reflection: Do you think your government strikes the right balance between controlling the economy and letting the people control it? Why or why not?

Resources:

Amadeo, K. (2019). Command economy, its characteristics, pros, and cons. https://www
    .thebalance.com/command-economy-characteristics-pros-cons-and-examples-3305585
Clickview. (2018). Communist China: The Great Leap Forward. https://www.youtube.com
    /watch?v=bkR-uIXXcHo

LESSON 6.13

WHAT WERE THE EFFECTS OF THE CHERNOBYL NUCLEAR DISASTER?

Historical Figure: Mikhail Gorbachev

Event: Chernobyl nuclear power plant explosion, 1986

Introduction: If the electric power grid failed, how would it affect your daily activities? How would it affect the economy as a whole?

Mini-Lecture:

- In the 1970s, countries throughout the world, including the USSR, the United States, and countries in Europe began relying on nuclear power plants to meet their growing needs for energy in order to feed economic growth.
- The USSR had a command economy, in which the Communist Party planned the production of goods and directed workers and industries.
- On April 26, 1986, there was an explosion at the Chernobyl nuclear power plant in the Ukraine, USSR.
- Although toxic radiation was being emitted from the plant, the authorities denied the seriousness of the accident and waited for 36 hours to evacuate people from the nearest town of Pripyat and surrounding areas.
- Our document is a secret notice written by the USSR's government the day after the accident.
- At least 30 people died as a direct result of the accident, and thousands more died from cancers in the following years due to radiation exposure.
- Mikhail Gorbachev was the general secretary of the Communist Party of the USSR and leader of the country from 1985 to 1991; he later said that the Chernobyl disaster eventually led to the fall of communism, because people started to express their lack of faith in their leaders and in the economic system.

Vocabulary:

gamma radiation: kind of radiation that results from a nuclear bomb or accident at a nuclear power plant

microroentgens: measure of radiation exposure that was used in the 1980s

KGB: USSR's security service

covert: secret

sabotage: purposeful destruction for political or military purposes

Document: Untitled notice on levels of radiation in Chernobyl NPP and steps taken in response, 1986

As of 8 o'clock on April 27th, 1986, changes were detected in the radiation environment in the 3rd and 4th energy blocks of the Chernobyl atomic energy station.

The level of gamma radiation particles is up to 1000 microroentgens per second. On the rest of the territory of the station it is up to 15–200 microroentgens per second, and at the city limit it is up to 6–18 microroentgens per second.

There are 100 persons in the medical institutions of Pripyat, of whom two are in a critical condition. According to a decision by the Commission of the USSR Ministry of Health, 26 injured persons have been sent by airplane to Moscow for additional examination and treatment.

According to a decision by the Government Commission headed by the USSR Council of Ministers Deputy Chair Comrade B. E. Shcherbinoi, [operation at] energy blocks # 1 and 2 has been halted with a shut-down cooling of the reactors.

On the 26th of April, 1986 a criminal case was opened by the Prosecutor of Kiev Oblast on the accident at the Chernobyl atomic energy station. An intelligence investigation team is continuing its work with members of the 6th Administration [handwritten above: "and Investigation Department"] of the KGB in cooperation with the Special Departments, offices of the Ministry of Internal Affairs and the prosecutor's office with the use of covert agents and trusted individuals.

No information about possible sabotage or responsibility for the accident was received from the units' records management or persons verified by signals.

Necessary measures have been taken by Party and Soviet agencies for the possible evacuation of the city. In particular, 1,100 buses and 2 Diesel trains have been prepared and concentrated in the area of Chernobyl. A reserve of 1,500 police officers has been established as an escort to ensure safety and order.

Covert teams from the KGB Administration and UVD [Administration of Internal Affairs] were sent into the Polesskoe and Chernobyl districts, and outlying areas of evacuation.

According to an agreement with Party agencies, measures were taken to prevent distribution of information about the occurrence and panicky rumors.

Measures are being taken to determine the center of the accident with the use of helicopters. Radiation and chemical defense troops have been activated for this same purpose.

We are controlling the situation in Pripyat and the surrounding area. Information has been given to the KGB of the USSR.

Source: Wilson Center. (n.d.). Untitled notice on levels of radiation in Chernobyl NPP and steps taken in response. https://digitalarchive.wilsoncenter.org/document/134297

Comprehension Check:

1. Who made the decisions for what would be done related to health, safety, and justice respectively?
2. Why didn't the authorities let the public know what had happened at Chernobyl?

Activities:

1. Read Gorbachev's reflections on the Chernobyl accident in the Resources section. Underline the parts of our document that corroborate his version of events, and circle parts that contradict it.
2. Some scientists believe that nuclear power could be an important source of energy as the world tries to reduce reliance on fossil fuels in order to slow global warming. Work with a small group to research the risks and benefits of nuclear power and decide which are greater.

Reflection: Given that (1) fossil fuels like coal and oil contribute to climate change, (2) nuclear power can be dangerous, and (3) solar, wind, and other renewable sources are not yet able to support people's needs, what do you think people should do to meet (or reduce) their needs for electric power?

Resources:

Gorbachev, M. (2006). Turning point at Chernobyl. https://www.japantimes.co.jp/opinion/2006/04/21/commentary/world-commentary/turning-point-at-chernobyl/#.Xeq405NKhdB

Gray, R. (2019). The true toll of the Chernobyl nuclear disaster. https://www.bbc.com/future/article/20190725-will-we-ever-know-chernobyls-true-death-toll

Gender

UNIT QUESTION: What Should Be the Roles of Women and Men in Society?

This unit brings women, who are often in the background of history, to the fore. Students start investigating gender roles with the 21st-Century Issue of gender identity by reading an interview with a young Thai transgender man. Going back in time to Ancient Rome, students hear Hortensia argue for the rights of upper-class women in times of war. A focus on classical ideas continues with Ibn Rushd's commentary on Plato's *Republic*, which argues that women can take on roles equal to men. Queen Elizabeth I provides our first example of a female head of state; her speech to her troops sets up the archetype of a female leader presenting herself with masculine qualities. West African queen Nzinga, on the other hand, comes up with a unique strategy of military and economic diplomacy in her negotiations with the Portuguese. A painting of Catherine the Great as well as Mary Wollstonecraft's classic text *A Vindication of the Rights of Women* illustrates how women applied Enlightenment ideals. Qiu Jin's appeal to Chinese women shows the power of a female revolutionary in a male-dominated society. Violet Carruthers's appeal against universal suffrage, on the other hand, provides an important counterpoint to the other views in this unit. A print by artist Käthe Kollwitz helps students consider the effects of war on women. Huda Sha'arawi's argument for pan-Arab feminism helps us understand how women lobbied for multiple causes, an insight that is extended as students see how Jamaican writer Una Marson expands the boundaries of the international women's movement.

Some students may question devoting an entire unit to gender, while others may notice how much the histories they have studied before leave out women's voices. The unit ends with a question of how to define "women's issues," and whether it is a useful category; to prepare them for this outcome, teachers may wish to begin the unit with explanations of sexism, feminism, and patriarchy. The 21st-Century Issue for this unit may prove controversial in many contexts, and teachers have the option to replace it with another relevant topic. If transgender issues are explored in class, teachers will want to investigate in advance whether any students or their family members identify as transgender or nonbinary, in order to discuss with them how to keep them comfortable during these discussions.

LESSON 7.1
HOW ARE TRANSGENDER PEOPLE CHALLENGING ASSUMPTIONS ABOUT WOMEN AND MEN?

Historical Figure: Paravee Argasnoum

Event: World Health Organization (WHO) states that being transgender is not a mental disorder, 2019

Introduction: What do you know about transgender people? Where did you learn it?

Mini-Lecture:

- Transgender (or trans) describes people whose gender identity does not match the sex they were assigned at birth.
- Sex refers to biological status assigned at birth based on biology and anatomy; gender refers to socially constructed roles and behaviors considered appropriate for males or females in a given culture.
- A transgender woman is someone who was assigned the sex of male at birth but lives as a woman; a transgender man is someone who was assigned the sex of female at birth but lives as a man.
- Transgender people may also be "nonbinary," which means that they do not identify as male or female, or "gender non-conforming," which means they do not behave in accordance with their culture's gender roles.
- In the past, psychologists considered being transgender a mental disorder; but in 2019, the World Health Organization announced its position that being transgender is not a mental disorder.
- The rights of transgender people are often considered alongside other groups that experience discrimination because of their sexual orientation or gender identity, including people who are lesbian, gay, bisexual, queer or questioning, intersex, or asexual; these groups are often referred to by acronyms such as LGBTI or LGBTQIA+.
- Our document comes from an interview that an LGBTI activist from Thailand did with a transgender man named Paravee Argasnoum, or Evan.

Vocabulary:

queer: anyone whose gender identity or sexual orientation does not match their society's expectations
gender-neutral: available for any gender

alienation: feeling separate from one's community
phobia: fear

Document: Interview with Paravee Argasnoum, Thanita Wongprasert, 2018

Paravee Argasnoum (Evan), 19, is a young trans and gender-nonconforming activist in Thailand. He represents the new generation in LGBTI activism. As a trans queer youth, it is his genuine passion and personal experience that drives him to advocate for the rights he wishes to see in his country. . . .

> *Interviewer:* You've just entered university as a freshman, what inspires you to be an LGBTI activist on the side? How does it make you feel?
>
> *Evan:* The inspiration comes from my very own personal interest since high school. It was the time I came to the realization that my gender does not conform to the mainstream. I used social media as a platform to enter the field. Although I had a limited amount of experience, I became an active member of the Non-Binary community group. When opportunities knock at my door, I answer them. . . .
>
> *Interviewer:* There are several aspects to LGBTI rights and issues, which of them do you prioritize and why?
>
> *Evan:* I would start with something fundamental which is the general acceptance of LGBTI people. I want the perception of them to be positive, for them to be taken seriously and treated as ordinary humans. Members of society need to be aware that LGBTI people are not for comedy value and deserve respect. . . . Another issue that I have been particularly involved in is gender-neutral toilets. It is important because we use toilets every day and should feel safe and not discriminated against. . . .
>
> *Interviewer:* What have you achieved that contributes to significant changes in this field?
>
> *Evan:* I write a lot online. The feedback I have received is mostly positive. I hope for my stories to inspire and empower LGBTI people. Body positivity, for example, is the kind of awareness I am raising. I want everyone, especially transgender people, to feel comfortable and positive about their own skin. . . .
>
> *Interviewer:* You've previously said that being an LGBTI person in Thailand has an impact on your mental health, can you please elaborate on that?
>
> *Evan:* This goes back to when I was in secondary school. Asking myself who I was, it was pure confusion. I still remember the feeling of alienation and isolation very well. Depression grows out of the environment you are in. For me, at school, I was surrounded by people who were insensitive and showed no respect and effort to understand me. Bullying and harassment became my phobia, to the point where if my friends called me by my given name, my mood would fall off the cliff for days.
>
> Parental rejection was another source of my unbearable anxiety. I knew that not everyone in my family would come to terms with my gender identity and sexual orientation. . . .
>
> Fortunately, I am now getting the counselling that I need. . . . I am not only supported by the LGBTI community, but also my friends and

family members are making efforts. Of course, it takes time but one day it will all pay off.

Source: Wongprasert, T. (2018). Paravee Argasnoum—Being a young trans queer activist in Thailand. *Medium.* https://medium.com/being-lgbti-in-asia/paravee -argasnoum-being-a-young-trans-queer-activist-in-thailand-697fa11fdbe *Being LGBTI in Asia, United Nations Development Programme (UNDP)*

Comprehension Check:

1. What are some of the difficulties that Evan has faced as a trans man?
2. What issues would Evan like to work on as a trans activist, and why?

Activities:

1. Create a Venn diagram showing the similarities and differences between issues that trans people face in Thailand, according to Evan, and in your country or community?
2. As a class, brainstorm questions you have about LGBTQIA+ people around the world. Then work in small groups using the resources below (or others) to seek answers you can present back to the class.

Reflection: What do you think about the WHO's decision to declare that being transgender is not a mental disorder? Why?

Resources:

American Psychological Association. (2019). What does transgender mean? https://www.apa .org/topics/lgbt/transgender

Haynes, S. (2019). The World Health Organization will stop classifying transgender people as having a "mental disorder." https://time.com/5596845/world-health-organization -transgender-identity/

UC Davis. (n.d.). LGBTQIA Resource Center glossary. https://lgbtqia.ucdavis.edu/educated /glossary

---

LESSON 7.2

WHY DID ROMAN WOMEN PROTEST BEING TAXED?

Historical Figure: Hortensia

Event: Second Roman Triumvirate, 43–33 BCE

Introduction: How does the financial status of women in your society today compare to that of men? Give examples.

Mini-Lecture:

- Women in the Roman Republic (510–27 BCE) could not vote, could not address the Senate in the Forum (where senators met), and usually did not have much property of their own.

- In the 2nd century BCE, the Romans had fought against the Carthaginians in the Punic Wars (see Lesson 4.4); some women inherited property when their husbands were killed in the war.
- At that time, women were required to support the war effort by contributing money to the government and going without luxuries.
- In the 1st century BCE, during the rule of the Second Triumvirate (ruled by Caesar Augustus, Marc Antony, and Marcus Lepidus), there was a civil war in Rome, and again, the wealthiest women were required to contribute to the war effort.
- However, some of these wealthy women's husbands opposed the government, and so their contributions would go toward fighting against their own families.
- These women asked Hortensia, a well-educated orator (speaker), to address the Roman senate at the Forum; she was the first woman to do so in Rome's history.
- Our document comes from the speech she made, which was recorded by the historian Appian.

Vocabulary:

pretext: reason given that is not believable
reduce: lower the status of
birth: noble status

public enemies: enemies of the people
offices: positions
dowries: valuable items brought by a woman into a marriage

Document: Speech to the Forum, Hortensia, 42 BCE

You have already deprived us of our fathers, our sons, our husbands, and our brothers on the pretext that they wronged you. But if, in addition, you take away our property, you will reduce us to a condition unsuitable to our birth, our way of life, and our female nature.

If we have done you any wrong, as you claimed our husbands have, punish us as you do them. But if we women have not voted any of you public enemies, nor torn down your house, nor destroyed your army, nor led another against you, nor prevented you from obtaining offices and honors, why do we share in the punishments when we did not participate in the crimes?

Why should we pay taxes when we do not share in the offices, honors, military commands, nor, in short, the government, for which you fight between yourselves with such harmful results? You say "because it is wartime." When has there not been war? . . .

Our mothers did once rise superior to their sex and made contributions when you faced the loss of the empire and the city itself through the conflict with the Carthaginians. But they funded their contributions voluntarily from their jewelry not from their landed property, their fields, their dowries, or their houses, without which it is impossible for free women to live. . . .

Let war with the Celts or Parthians come, we will not be inferior to our mothers when it is a question of common safety. But for civil wars, may we never contribute nor aid you against each other.

Source: Women in World History Curriculum. (2019). Female fury in the Forum. http://www.womeninworldhistory.com/lesson10.html

Comprehension Check:

1. Why does Hortensia object to Roman women being required to contribute to the war effort?
2. Name two ways that, according to Hortensia, the situation in the war against Carthage was different from the civil war.

Activities:

1. Create a T-chart showing the rights/powers versus responsibilities that women in Hortensia's position had during the Roman Republic. Circle the rights/powers and responsibilities that women in your society have today, and X out those they don't have.
2. Write a note back to Hortensia from a Roman woman without wealth or property.

Reflection: In what ways do women in your society contribute to war efforts?

Resources:

Aldrete, G. S. (2018). The role of women in ancient Rome—Piecing together a historical picture. https://www.thegreatcoursesdaily.com/role-of-women-in-ancient-rome/

Encyclopedia Britannica. (2007). Hortensia. https://www.britannica.com/biography /Hortensia

---

LESSON 7.3

WHAT ROLE DID IBN RUSHD THINK WOMEN SHOULD PLAY IN ISLAMIC SOCIETY?

Historical Figure: Ibn Rushd

Event: Ibn Rushd produces commentaries on Aristotle and Plato, 1169–1195

Introduction: What do you know about the role of women in Islamic societies? Where did you learn it?

Mini-Lecture:

- Ibn Rushd (also known as Averroës, 1126–1198) was a Muslim philosopher who lived in Cordoba (now in Spain).
- He lived under the reign of the Almohad Caliphate, which was founded by Berber Muslims from what is now Morocco, and which ruled Northern Africa and what is now southern Spain in the 12th century.

- The Almohad Caliph, or ruler, Abu Ya'qub Yusuf, asked Ibn Rushd to summarize and write commentaries on books by ancient Greek philosophers Plato and Aristotle (see Lesson 5.2).
- Our document is from Ibn Rushd's commentary on Plato's *Republic*, a book that describes an ideal city-state ruled by philosopher-kings called guardians, and also populated by warriors and producers (e.g., merchants, doctors, artists).
- Plato believed men and women were basically equal and that women could serve as guardians, warriors, and all other social roles.
- Ibn Rushd refers to the "City of Women," a city in the Moroccan desert that travelers in his time described in which female warriors ruled society.
- Ibn Rushd uses the pronoun "we" to explain his views on Plato's ideas, and the extent to which he agrees with him.

Vocabulary:

upbringing: raising children
procreation: having children
end: goals
arts: skills
eminence: fame
disposition: character

competence: abilities
suckling: nursing children
nullifies: makes worthless
undertake: do
gymnastic: exercise

Document: Commentary on Plato's *Republic*, Ibn Rushd, 1169–1195

It is fit for investigation whether there exist among women natures resembling the natures of each and every class of citizens—and in particular the guardians— or *whether* women's natures are distinguished from men's natures. If the former is the case, then as regards the activities of the city, women would have the very same standing as men in those classes, so that there would be among them warriors, philosophers, rulers, and the rest. But if this is not the case, then women are only fit in the city for activities that men in general are unfit for, as you were to say upbringing, procreation, and the like.

And we say that women, in so far as they are of one kind with men, necessarily share in the end of man. . . . We see women sharing arts with men except that they are weaker at it, although most of the women in [some] art may be more diligent than the men, as in the art of weaving, sewing, or other such arts. As for their sharing in the art of war and the rest, why this is made clear from the inhabitants of deserts and the "City of Women." Similarly, too, since some women are formed with eminence and a praiseworthy disposition, it is not impossible that there be philosophers and rulers among them. . . .

The competence of women is unknown, however, in these cities since they are only taken in them for procreation and hence are placed at the service of their husband and confined to procreation, upbringing, and suckling. This nullifies their [other] activities. Since women in these cities are not prepared with respect to any of the human virtues, they frequently resemble plants in these cities. Their being a burden upon the men in these cities is one of the causes of the poverty of these cities. This is because they are to be found there in double the number of men, while not understanding through [their] upbringing any of the necessary actions except for the few actions—like the art of spinning and weaving—that they undertake mostly at a time when they have need of them to make up for their lack of spending [power]. This is all self-evident. This being so—and it is clear from the case of the females that they are to share with the males in war and the rest—it is fitting that, in choosing them, we seek for those very natures that we sought for in men and that they should be trained in the same way through music and gymnastic.

Source: Academia Analitica. (n.d.). Averroes on Plato's *Republic.* https://academiaanalitica
.files.wordpress.com/2019/07/averroes_-ralph-lerner-trans.ed_.-averroes-on
-platoe28099s-republic-cornell-university-press-1974.pdf

Comprehension Check:

1. What evidence does Ibn Rushd present that women can become warriors?
2. According to Ibn Rushd, why are societies in which there is inequality between the sexes poor?

Activities:

1. Create a T-chart contrasting Aristotle's views on women (Lesson 5.2) from those of Plato and Ibn Rushd.
2. Look back at other historical figures who lived in the 11th and 12th centuries and compare them to Ibn Rushd. Break into groups and discover whatever you can from the documents or other resources about what the following historical figures believed about the roles of men and women, and then present your findings to the class: Benjamin of Tudela (Lesson 6.5); Chingghis Khan (Lesson 5.4); Bernard of Clairvaux (Lesson 4.6); William the Conqueror (Lesson 4.5); Suryavarman II (Lesson 1.7).

Reflection: Do you think men and women in your society are seen as capable of the same roles and duties? What evidence can you present to support your argument?

Resources:

Oxford Islamic Studies Online. (2019). Women and Islam. http://www.oxfordislamicstudies
.com/article/opr/t125/e2510
Rosenthal, E. I. J. (2019). Averroës. https://www.britannica.com/biography/Averroes

---

LESSON 7.4

How Did Queen Elizabeth I Defend Her Leadership?

Historical Figure: Queen Elizabeth I

Event: Reign of Queen Elizabeth I, 1558–1603

Introduction: Do you think men or women are better leaders in battle, or are they equally good? On what evidence would you base your argument?

Mini-Lecture:

- In the 16th century, after the Reformation (see Lesson 8.4), the Protestant Church broke away from the Roman Catholic Church; King Henry the VIII converted to Protestantism, but his daughter Queen Mary made England Catholic again during her reign (1552–1558).
- Queen Elizabeth I, also the daughter of Henry VIII but a Protestant, took the throne in 1558; the Spanish King, Philip II, who was Catholic, proposed that she marry him.
- Meanwhile, England and Spain were competing for control of the seas and of the Americas; the Spanish Armada, or fleet of military ships, was considered impossible to defeat.
- When it appeared that Elizabeth would not accept Philip's proposal, he sent the armada to England under the command of the Duke of Parma to depose her and make England Catholic again.
- Our document comes from a speech Elizabeth made to her troops before they went into battle against Spain; in the end, the English defeated the Spanish, the country remained Protestant, and Elizabeth ruled until 1603, known as the "Warrior Queen."

Vocabulary:

take heed: pay attention to
commit ourselves: stand in front of
armed multitudes: large groups of people with weapons
treachery: attacks by people who are not loyal
tyrants: rulers who oppress their people
chiefest: most important

disport: entertainment
stomach: guts
foul scorn: it is terrible
grow by me: happen under my rule
forwardness: courage
crowns: coins
stead: place
concord: good behavior

Document: Speech to the troops at Tilbury, Queen Elizabeth I, 1588

My loving people, we have been persuaded by some that are careful of our safety to take heed how we commit ourselves to armed multitudes, for fear of treachery. But I assure you, I do not desire to live to distrust my faithful and loving people.

Let tyrants fear. I have always so behaved myself that, under God, I have placed my chiefest strength and safeguard in the loyal hearts and good-will of my subjects; and therefore I am come amongst you, as you see, at this time, not for my recreation and disport, but being resolved, in the midst and heat of the battle, to live and die amongst you all; to lay down for my God, and for my kingdom, and my people, my honor and my blood, even in the dust.

I know I have the body of a weak and feeble woman; but I have the heart and stomach of a king, and of a king of England too, and think foul scorn that Parma or Spain, or any prince of Europe, should dare to invade the borders of my realm: to which rather than any dishonor shall grow by me, I myself will take up arms, I myself will be your general, judge, and rewarder of every one of your virtues in the field.

I know already, for your forwardness you have deserved rewards and crowns; and We do assure you on a word of a prince, they shall be duly paid. In the meantime, my lieutenant general shall be in my stead, than whom never prince commanded a more noble or worthy subject; not doubting but by your obedience to my general, by your concord in the camp, and your valor in the field, we shall shortly have a famous victory over these enemies of my God, of my kingdom, and of my people.

Source: Royal Museums Greenwich. (n.d.). Queen Elizabeth I's speech to the troops at Tilbury. https://www.rmg.co.uk/discover/explore /queen-elizabeth-i-speech-troops-tilbury

Comprehension Check:

1. According to Elizabeth, why isn't she afraid to stand in front of her troops?
2. In what ways does Elizabeth say she is like a man?

Activities:

1. Work with a partner to brainstorm other strategies Queen Elizabeth I could have used to defend her leadership to her troops; then explain why she may have rejected them.
2. Elizabeth I never married, even though this meant she could not have children to succeed her on the throne. Create a mind map showing the factors that may have influenced her decision.

Reflection: When women defend their leadership by claiming they are similar to men, are they strengthening women's power or undermining it?

Resources:

Johnson, B. (n.d.). The Spanish Armada. https://www.historic-uk.com/HistoryUK /HistoryofEngland/Spanish-Armada/

Paranque, E. (2019). Elizabeth I's Tilbury speech: The birth of a warrior queen. https://artuk .org/discover/stories/elizabeth-is-tilbury-speech-the-birth-of-a-warrior-queen

---

LESSON 7.5

How Did Queen Nzinga Resist Portuguese Colonizers?

Historical Figure: Queen Nzinga

Event: Portuguese colonize Angola, 1575

Introduction: What would you do if you were a ruler, and a strong and wealthy country took over some of your territory?

Mini-Lecture:

- In the 16th century, Portugal colonized what is now Luanda, Angola, and tried to take over other kingdoms in Central Africa, including Ndongo, which was inhabited mostly by the Mbundu people.
- By 1622, Indigenous and Portuguese slave raiders were kidnapping and attacking people in the region; the King of Ndongo sent his sister, Nzinga (also spelled Njinga), to negotiate with the Portuguese.
- In order to stop the slave raiding, protect their own slave trade, and defend against neighboring kingdoms, Nzinga made an alliance with the Portuguese, even converting to Christianity (and taking the name Ana de Souza) to strengthen relations.
- Nzinga became queen of Ndongo in 1624, but the Portuguese broke their treaty and installed a king called Aquiloange Aire in her place; she eventually moved west and founded a new kingdom, Matamba.
- Our document comes from a letter Queen Nzinga wrote to a Portuguese military commander in 1626, after Aire had been put in power.
- Queen Nzinga built up Matamba into a regional power and eventually reopened trade with the Portuguese.

Vocabulary:

war party: attacking force
dispatched: sent
vassal: someone under a ruler's control
obeisance: respect and obedience

ell: a unit of length equal to about 18 inches
arroba: a unit of weight equal to about 32 pounds

Document: Letter from Queen Njinga [Nzinga] of Ndongo to Bento Banha Cardoso, 1626

It gladdens my soul that Your Honor has come to the Fortress of Ambaca [a trading center] so that I may recount to you, as to my father, how a war party led by [Aire] attacked the men I sent [to escort] some slaves to the market of Bumba a Kissanzo, and stole about thirty slaves from me. When I dispatched a party to seek redress, as I would against any vassal of mine, it happened that my army encountered about nine of the men who were stationed inland with [Portuguese commander] Tigre. Having decided to face my army outside the fortress, these nine men, by God's will, were defeated by my men, six of whom were brought to me alive. It caused me great grief that at [Aire's] fortress there were Portuguese forces that I have received with great kindness because they are vassals of the king of Spain, to whom I recognize obeisance as a Christian. On Saturday, one of my . . . servants arrived here and told me that in Ambaca a large force had gathered, waiting for Your Honor to move against me to free the Portuguese held in captivity. Nothing is accomplished by force and to do so would bring both me and them to harm because everything can be done peacefully and without force. And if some of the lords who have settled here have incurred heavy debts and have put it in the minds of Your Honor and the governor that you should wage war in order to get out of debt, they are welcome to do so, but I do not want to make war with the captain. . . .

I ask that Your Honor send me a hammock, and four ells of red wool for a cover, a horse blanket, and good wine, and an arroba of wax for candles, and half a dozen lengths of muslin, and two or three lace tablecloths, and some purple, wine-colored, and blue garnets, and a large broad-brim hat made of blue velvet, or the one Your Honor wears, and four measures of paper.

Source: McKnight, K. J., & Garofalo, L. (2009). *Afro-Latino voices: Narratives from the early modern Ibero-Atlantic world, 1550–1812.* Hackett.

Comprehension Check:

1. What does Queen Nzinga imply might happen if Cardoso attacks her to try to free his men?
2. What does Queen Nzinga ask for in exchange for returning the Portuguese soldiers her men have captured?

Activities:

1. Highlight parts of the speech where Queen Nzinga uses words intended to keep a good relationship with the Portuguese. Then "read between the lines" and state what she meant in a more blunt manner.
2. Create a T-chart comparing the strategies for building power used by Queen Nzinga and Queen Elizabeth I (Lesson 7.4).

Reflection: Do you think female rulers tend to use different strategies than men would when negotiating conflicts? Think of examples from history or the present day.

Resources:

Ademola, A. (2018). How Queen Nzinga of Angola fought and held off Portuguese control for over 30 years. https://face2faceafrica.com/article/how-queen-nzinga-of-angola -fought-and-held-off-portuguese-control-for-over-30-years

Bortolot, A. I. (2003). Women leaders in African history: Ana Nzinga of Ndongo. https:// www.metmuseum.org/toah/hd/pwmn_2/hd_pwmn_2.htm

---

LESSON 7.6

How Did Catherine the Great Present Herself as a Leader?

Historical Figure: Catherine the Great

Event: Catherine the Great rules Russia, 1762–1798

Introduction: Do you think women are likely to be more just, peaceful, and gentle rulers than men? Why or why not?

Mini-Lecture:

- Catherine II, also known as Catherine the Great, ruled Russia from 1762 to 1798; she was born in Prussia, in what is now Germany, and married the heir to the Russian throne, Peter III.
- Catherine and Peter did not get along; he threatened to divorce her, she staged a coup against him in order to become queen, and she had him arrested.
- Catherine was influenced by the ideas of the Enlightenment (see Lesson 3.9) and wanted to be known as an "enlightened despot," who had absolute power but based it on reason and used it for the benefit of her people.
- Catherine initially tried to reform Russia's law code in order to guarantee equal rights to all people; however, when she met with resistance, she gave up this effort.
- In Catherine's time, wealthy landowners had serfs (peasants with very limited rights) to farm their land; at first, Catherine indicated that she was sympathetic to them, but when they rebelled, she crushed their rebellion and decreed that they must obey the landowners.
- Catherine waged wars against the Ottoman and Persian Empires in order to expand Russia's territory and gain access to trading posts on the Black Sea, and she also forged stronger connections with Europe.
- Catherine supported the arts and acquired an art collection that eventually became the Hermitage Museum; she had many portraits made of her, including our document, which shows her as a legislatress (lawmaker) in the temple of the Greek goddess of justice, Themis.
- On the altar, she is burning poppy flowers, which represent peace and restfulness, indicating that she is willing to sacrifice her own leisure time to bring justice for her people, and which also symbolize a move away from strict Christianity toward secularism; the eagle is the symbol of the Russian power.

Document: Catherine II Legislatress in the Temple of the Goddess of Justice, Dmitry Levitsky, 1783 (see Figure 7.1)

Comprehension Check:

1. What could be the meaning of the ship in the background?
2. What might be the contents of the books under the eagle's talons, and what could it symbolize for the eagle to be standing on the books?
3. What are the similarities between the appearances of Catherine II and Themis?

Activities:

1. Write a letter from Catherine II at the end of her reign to the person she was when she married Peter III. What advice might she have for her younger self?

Figure 7.1. Catherine II Legislatress in the Temple of the Goddess of Justice, Dmitry Levitsky, 1783

Source: The State Russian Museum. (n.d.). Catherine II Legislatress in the temple of the goddess of justice. http://en.rusmuseum.ru/collections/painting-of-xviii-first-half-xix-centuries/artworks/ekaterina-ii-zakonodatelnitsa-v-khrame-bogini-pravosudiya/
incamerastock/Alamy Stock Photo

2. Create a new portrait of Catherine that shows what she actually did, as opposed to how she wanted people to perceive her.

Reflection: Do you think Catherine II's actions would have been seen differently by historians or by her own people if she had been a man? Why or why not?

Resources:

Encyclopedia.com. (2019). Catherine the Great. https://www.encyclopedia.com/people/history/russian-soviet-and-cis-history-biographies/catherine-great

State Tretyakov Gallery. (n.d.). Catherine II, Russia's empress of style. https://artsandculture
.google.com/exhibit/catherine-ii-russia-s-empress-of-style-the-state-tretyakov-gallery
/ZQJC5_qBeMhQIg?hl=en

LESSON 7.7

WHAT WERE MARY WOLLSTONECRAFT'S ARGUMENTS FOR WOMEN'S RIGHTS?

Historical Figure: Mary Wollstonecraft

Event: Wollstonecraft publishes *A Vindication of the Rights of Woman*, 1792

Introduction: Do you think women in your society are valued more for their appearance than for their ideas? Give evidence to support your position.

Mini-Lecture:

- Mary Wollstonecraft (1759–1797) was a British philosopher who is often described as the first modern feminist because she believed that women should have equal rights with men.
- Wollstonecraft contributed to the Enlightenment (see Lesson 3.9), when philosophers were trying to rethink social and political issues according to reason.
- In her book *A Vindication of the Rights of Man*, she defended the French Revolution (see Lesson 8.5), in which poor people had rebelled against the royal family, by explaining her view that government that represented the people was better than a monarchy.
- Another philosopher, Jean-Jacques Rousseau, wrote a book about education in which he argued that women were "weak and passive" and should be educated so that they were "pleasing" to men.
- Wollstonecraft then wrote *A Vindication of the Rights of Woman*, from which our document is taken, in which she argued against Rousseau's position.

Vocabulary:

sweep: length
melancholy: sad
indignation: anger
deplore: hate
wretched: unhappy
co-operating: working together
hasty: made too quickly
flamboyant: colorful
barren: useless
alluring mistresses: appealing romantic
   partners

homage: praise
anxious: eager
pre-eminence: superiority
intoxicated: delighted
perpetual: never-ending
susceptibility: sensitivity
sentiment: feelings
refinement: elegance
synonymous: having the same
   meaning
contempt: hatred

Document: *A Vindication of the Rights of Woman*, Mary Wollstonecraft, 1792

After thinking about the sweep of history and viewing the present world with anxious care, I find my spirits depressed by the most melancholy emotions of sorrowful indignation. I have had to admit, sadly, that either nature has made a great difference between man and man, or that the world is not yet anywhere near to being fully civilized. I have looked into various books on education, and patiently observed the conduct of parents and the management of schools; but all this has given me is a deep conviction that the neglected education of my fellow creatures is the main source of the misery I deplore, and that women in particular are made weak and wretched by a number of co-operating causes, originating from one hasty conclusion. The conduct and manners of women, in fact, show clearly that their minds are not in a healthy state; as with flowers planted in soil that is too rich, strength and usefulness are sacrificed to beauty; and the flamboyant leaves, after giving pleasure to viewers, fade on the stalk, disregarded, long before it was the time for them to reach maturity. This barren blooming is caused partly by a false system of education, gathered from the books on the subject by men. These writers, regarding females as women rather than as human creatures, have been more concerned to make them alluring mistresses than affectionate wives and rational mothers; and this homage to women's attractions has distorted their understanding to such an extent that almost all the civilized women of the present century are anxious only to inspire love, when they ought to have the nobler aim of getting respect for their abilities and virtues. . . .

In the government of the physical world—as distinct from the governments of the social or political world—it is observable that the female is, so far as strength is concerned, inferior to the male. This is the law of nature; and it doesn't seem to be suspended or repealed in favor of woman. This physical superiority can't be denied—and it is a noble privilege! But men, not content with this natural pre-eminence, try to sink us lower still, so as to make us merely alluring objects for a moment; and women, intoxicated by the adoration that men (under the influence of their senses) pay them, don't try to achieve a permanently important place in men's feelings, or to become the friends of the fellow creatures who find amusement in their society. . . .

I hope my own sex will excuse me if I treat them like rational creatures, instead of flattering their fascinating graces and viewing them as if they were in a state of perpetual childhood and unable to stand alone. I earnestly wish to point out what true dignity and human happiness consist in; I want to persuade women to aim at strength of mind and body, and to convince them that the soft phrases "susceptibility of heart" "delicacy of sentiment," and "refinement of taste" are almost synonymous with expressions indicating weakness, and that creatures who are the objects only of pity and the kind of love that has been called "pity's sister" will soon become objects of contempt.

Source: Early Modern Texts. (n.d.). A vindication of the rights of woman with strictures on political and moral subjects. https://www.earlymoderntexts.com/assets/pdfs/wollstonecraft1792.pdf

Comprehension Check:

1. Explain Wollstonecraft's comparison of women to plants.
2. According to Wollstonecraft, what mistakes have male writers made about women?

Activities:

1. Would Immanuel Kant (Lesson 3.9) agree or disagree with Wollstonecraft's argument? Find evidence from his text to support your answer.
2. Work with a small group to determine whose leadership would Wollstonecraft support most and least: Queen Elizabeth I's (7.4), Queen Nzinga's (7.5), or Catherine the Great's (7.6). Present your argument to the class.

Reflection: Do you think Wollstonecraft would approve of the opportunities that women have in your society today? Why or why not?

Resources:

BBC Teach. (2019). Mary Wollstonecraft: "Britain's first feminist." https://www.bbc.co.uk /teach/mary-wollstonecraft-britains-first-feminist/zkpk382

Lewis, J. J. (2019). Rousseau's take on women and education. https://www.thoughtco.com /rousseau-on-women-and-education-3528799

LESSON 7.8

WHY DID QIU JIN ARGUE FOR CHINESE WOMEN'S FREEDOMS?

Historical Figure: Qiu Jin

Event: Qiu Jin is executed by the Qing Dynasty, 1907

Introduction: In your society, are women expected or pressured to do anything that harms their health or well-being in order to make themselves attractive to men?

Mini-Lecture:

- Qiu Jin was an activist for political change and women's rights who was born under the Qing Dynasty in what is now China in 1875.
- Like many other Chinese women of her time, she endured foot-binding: when she was a child, her family broke and tightly bound her feet with cloth to force her to walk in a way perceived as more delicate.
- Her parents arranged a marriage for her, but in 1904, she left her husband and children and went to Japan, where she studied and joined with others planning to overthrow the Qing government, which she believed was vulnerable to threats from other countries.
- Qiu Jin returned to China in 1906, where she started the *Chinese Women's Journal*, studied martial arts and bomb-making, and spoke out against sexism and the Qing government; our document comes from her writings at that time.
- In 1907, the Qing government executed her for plotting against them.

Vocabulary:

contemptuous: hateful   *sedan chair:* small carriage lifted and
temperament: personality   carried by several people

Document: An Address to Two Hundred Million Fellow Countrywomen, Qiu Jin, 1907

Alas, the most unfairly treated things on this earth are the two hundred million who are born as Chinese women. We consider ourselves lucky to be born to a kind father. If we are unlucky, our father will be an ill-tempered and unreasonable person who repeatedly says, "How unlucky I am, yet another useless one," as if at any instant he could pick us up and throw us to our death. He will resent us and say things like "she's eventually going to someone else's family" and give us cold and contemptuous looks. When we grow a few years older, without bothering to ask us our thoughts, they will bind our tender, white and natural feet with a strip of cloth, never loosening them even while we sleep. In the end, the flesh is mangled and the bones broken, all so that relatives, friends and neighbors can say, "the girl from so and so's family has tiny feet." When the time comes (for the parents) to select a husband, everything is based on the promises of two shameless matchmakers. The daughter's parents will go along with any proposal as long as his family is rich and powerful. Her parents do not bother to ask if the man's family is respectable, or inquire about the groom's temperament and level of education. On the wedding day, one will sit in the brightly decorated bridal sedan chair barely able to breathe. . . .

In the beginning, Heaven created all people with no differences between men and women. Ask yourselves this, how could these people have been born without women? Why are things so unjust? Everyday these men say, "We ought to be equal and treat people kindly." Then why do they treat women so unfairly and unequally as if they were African slaves? A woman has to learn not to depend on others, but to rely on herself instead. . . . Why can't we reject footbinding? Are they afraid of women being educated, knowledgeable, and perhaps surpassing them? Men do not allow us to study. We must not simply go along with their decision without even challenging them. . . .

If you have a son, send him to school. Do the same for your daughter and never bind her feet. If you have a young girl, the best choice would be for her to attend school, but even if she is unable to attend schools, you should teach her to read and write at home. If you come from a family of officials that has money, you should persuade your husband to establish schools and factories and do good deeds that will help common people. If your family is poor, you should work hard to help your husband. Do not be lazy and do nothing. These are my hopes. All of you are aware that we are about to lose our country. Men can scarcely protect themselves. How can we rely on them? We must revitalize ourselves. Otherwise all will be too late when the country is lost. Everybody! Everybody! Please keep my hopes alive!

Source: HistoryProfessorJoe.com. (n.d.). World History since 1750—Primary source 4. http://historyprofessorjoe.com/wp-content/uploads/2018/01/World -History-Primary-Source-4.pdf

Comprehension Check

1. According to Qiu Jin, what is the purpose of foot-binding?
2. According to Qiu Jin, why is foot-binding wrong?

Activities:

1. Read the first section of the article on foot-binding from the Resources section. Then review the beliefs of Confucianism (Lesson 2.3). Underline the parts of Qiu Jin's text that you can connect with a Confucian perspective.
2. Use Mahommah Baquaqua's autobiography (Lesson 6.10) to corroborate or contradict Qiu Jin's claim that Chinese women are treated like African slaves. Highlight portions of his text that corroborate, and X out parts that contradict her claim.

Reflection: Qiu Jin went against the expectations of her society despite facing serious consequences. Can you think of women around the world from the 21st century who have made similar choices?

Resources:

Foreman, A. (2015). Why footbinding persisted in China for a millennium. https://www .smithsonianmag.com/history/why-footbinding-persisted-china-millennium-180953971/
Qin, A. (2018). Qiu Jin. https://www.nytimes.com/interactive/2018/obituaries/overlooked -qiu-jin.html

---

LESSON 7.9

WHY DID SOME WOMEN OPPOSE GETTING THE RIGHT TO VOTE?

Historical Figure: Violet (Markham) Carruthers

Event: Anti-Suffrage League formed in Great Britain, 1908

Introduction: In the 20th century, many men and women argued against allowing women to vote. What do you think their arguments might have been?

Mini-Lecture:

- In the early 19th century, only property owners in Great Britain (now known as the United Kingdom) could vote, and this included only a small percentage of women; single women who paid taxes, and then some married women, gained the right to vote in local but not national elections later in the century.

- In the 19th century, the suffragists, who believed in expanding voting rights for women, used peaceful and legal means in support of their cause; in the early 20th century, women known as suffragettes began using direct action and civil disobedience to gain the right to vote, trying to break into government buildings, damaging property, and chaining themselves to railings to draw attention to their cause.
- In particular, suffragists were eager to vote for representatives in the Imperial Parliament, which made decisions for all of Great Britain's colonial territories.
- Some men and women opposed granting suffrage, or voting rights, to women, and in 1908 they formed the Anti-Suffrage League.
- Violet Markham (1872–1959), also known by her married name, Carruthers, was a writer and social reformer from England who was active in the Anti-Suffrage League as well as other causes, opening a school and providing assistance to people affected by World Wars I and II; she also served as the first female mayor of the town of Chesterfield.
- Our document comes from a speech that Carruthers gave in 1912 to supporters of the Anti-Suffrage League in London.
- Women over 30 who met educational and wealth qualifications gained the right to vote in 1918, and in 1928 there was "universal suffrage"—all people over 21 gained the right to vote.

Vocabulary:

affirm: confirm
fly in the face of: contradict
shares: parts
severally: both
balance: majority
enfranchise: give the vote to
anomalies: differences

coachman: someone who drives a horse-drawn coach
tropical administration: running Britain's colonies
humbug: nonsense
destitute: poor
erring: people who have made mistakes
part and parcel: included in

Document: Woman's Sphere, Violet (Markham) Carruthers, 1912

In the first place, we are here to affirm that a woman's citizenship is as great and as real as that of any man, that her service is as vitally necessary to the State. But unlike our Suffragist friends, we do not fly in the face of hard facts and natural law. We believe that men and women are different—not similar—beings, with talents that are complementary, not identical, and that, therefore, they ought to have different shares in the management of the State, that they severally compose. . . .

I do not waste your time or mine in combating the statement, that we Anti-Suffragists regard our sex as inferior beings. I treat that suggestion, and you will treat it too, with the contempt it deserves. . . .

And secondly, we stand here tonight for the principle, that you can only judge great national issues by the standard, not of what is good for this or that section or class, but by what promotes the highest interest of the nation as a whole. We are told that women want votes and therefore they must have them. In the first place, the majority of women do not want votes.

But even so, it is not a question of what women want, or what men want for the matter of that. It is a question of what is best for the State. We do not think it will increase the efficiency of the State to put the balance of political power in this country into the hands of women. Obviously if you are going to enfranchise women at all, adult suffrage is the only way out of the injustices and anomalies of any limited Bill. . . . But obviously, you must not take the picked women of every class; and then hold up your hands in surprise that they prove more capable than the gardener and the coachman. . . .

The average political experience of the average woman is bound to be less than that of the average man. Man is and man will continue to remain the business spirit of the world, and the work of Imperial Parliament, work such as defense, commerce, finance, tropical administration, is, in the main, work of a nature which lies outside woman's practical experience, and with which man is best fitted to deal. . . .

If the work of Imperial Parliament belongs more naturally to men, the work of Local Government, with its splendid opportunities for civic betterment and the uplifting of the race, belongs more naturally to women. . . . Is it not humbug to talk about women having no share of the national life when, a small minority excepted, they have shown so little practical interest or sympathy in causes which concern the aged, the sick, the destitute, the erring, and the welfare of little children? . . . The ugly scramble for place and power— . . . —that is all part and parcel of these political fights of men some women are anxious to assume. . . .

In opposing the demand for the vote we claim to stand for the true view of woman's place in the state.

Source: LSE Library. (2018). Violet Markham's speech at the Royal Albert Hall.
https://www.flickr.com/photos/lselibrary/40293290600

Comprehension Check:

1. What does Carruthers think will happen if women from every social class are given the vote?
2. Why does Carruthers believe women should be involved in local but not national government?

Activities:

1. Create a visual Venn diagram using drawings or collage to compare Carruthers's idea of "woman's sphere" compare to Qiu Jin's (Lesson 7.8).
2. Divide the class into three groups representing the anti-suffragists, the suffragists, and the suffragettes, and debate women's suffrage.

Reflection: How did Carruthers's argument confirm or contradict the reasons you gave in the introduction?

Resources:

British Library. (2018). What is the difference between suffragists and suffragettes? https://www.bl.uk/votes-for-women/articles/suffragists-and-suffragettes

Bush, J. (2018). The anti-suffrage movement. https://www.bl.uk/votes-for-women/articles/the-anti-suffrage-movement

Clan Carruthers. (2019). Violet Carruthers, CH. https://clancarrutherssociety.org/2019/02/02/clan-carruthers-violet-carruthers-ch/

LESSON 7.10

HOW DID KÄTHE KOLLWITZ WORK FOR PEACE THROUGH ART?

Historical Figure: Käthe Kollwitz

Event: World War I, 1914–1919

Introduction: Most women did not fight in World War I, but what challenges might they have faced during this time?

Mini-Lecture:

- Käthe Kollwitz (1867–1940) was a German artist who represented the struggles of women, children, and poor people in her prints, drawings, and sculptures.
- In 1914, Germany became involved in World War I (see Lesson 4.9); Kollwitz's son Peter joined the army and died in combat.
- WWI had dire humanitarian consequences for German civilians; about 700,000 died from starvation, malnutrition, or related illnesses due to the Allied blockade on trade with Germany.
- Two million German soldiers died in World War I, leaving 600,000 widows and 1 million orphans.
- After the Axis powers lost the war, the Treaty of Versailles required Germany to pay reparations (money) to Allied countries because of the damage its military actions had caused; the German economy weakened, unemployment was high, children faced starvation and malnutrition, and wounded veterans begged in the streets.
- Our document is an image of Kollwitz's lithograph *The Survivors*, which she created in 1923, and which was made into a poster.

Document: The Survivors, Käthe Kollwitz, 1923 (see Figure 7.2)

Comprehension Check:

1. Describe the people you see in the picture.
2. What is the role of the woman in the picture?

Figure 7.2. Käthe Kollwitz, *The Survivors*, 1923

Source: Culture Matters UK. (n.d.). *The survivors.* https://www.culturematters.org.uk
/media/k2/items/cache/6be84fda5cf0dc80a7c6b782ad45be3c_XL.jpg
Image courtesy of Käthe Kollwitz Museum Berlin

Activities:

1. What message is Kollwitz trying to send with *The Survivors*? To whom? Write the message in the form of a letter; then switch letters with a classmate and discuss the similarities and differences in the message you took from the print.
2. How do you think female leaders who led or advocated for armed conflict would have responded to Kollwitz's messages? Choose Queen Elizabeth I (Lesson 7.4), Queen Nzinga (Lesson 7.5), Catherine the Great (Lesson 7.6), or Qiu Jin (Lesson 7.8), and write a response to Kollwitz.

Reflection: Compared to making speeches, writing books, or protesting, do you think that making art is an effective way to draw attention to women's issue and struggles? Why or why not?

Resources:

Schumann, D. (2014). Post-war societies (Germany). https://encyclopedia.1914-1918-online
.net/article/post-war_societies_germany
The Art Story. (2019). Käthe Kollwitz: Biography and legacy. https://www.theartstory.org
/artist/kollwitz-kathe/life-and-legacy/

LESSON 7.11

HOW DID HUDA SHA'ARAWI ARGUE FOR FEMINIST NATIONALISM IN EGYPT?

Historical Figure: Huda Sha'arawi

Event: Sha'arawi founds Egyptian Feminist Union, 1923

Introduction: What do you know about Sharia (Islam's legal framework)? Where did you learn it?

Mini-Lecture:

- Huda Sha'arawi was an Egyptian nationalist and activist for women's rights who lived from 1879 to 1947.
- Sha'arawi was born into the "harem" system practiced by upper-class families, in which women lived separately from men and had to wear a niqab (veil covering all of the face except the eyes) when they went out.
- Unlike most girls in her situation, Sha'arawi received an education, although it was not as comprehensive as what boys received; at 13, she was forced to marry an older man.
- During a temporary separation from her husband, she pursued further education and became an activist for women's rights to vote and be educated, and for Egypt's independence from British colonization.
- In 1945, she helped to found the Arab Feminist Union; her idea was for Arab women in many countries to join together in demanding their rights; our document comes from a speech in which she described her idea of "pan-Arab" (uniting all Arabs) feminism.
- Sha'arawi believed that Sharia, or Islamic moral principles, supported her argument for women's rights.
- Sha'arawi did not believe that the Quran required women to wear the niqab, and she famously removed her face veil in public in 1923, inspiring many Egyptian women to do the same; today, some Muslim women choose to wear a niqab and/ or hijab (scarf covering the hair and shoulders), while in Sha'arawi's context the niqab and hijab were required for upper-class women.

Vocabulary:

legislate: make laws
sanctions: restrictions

usurped: taken away
avaricious: cruel

Document: Pan-Arab Feminism, Huda Sha'arawi, 1944

> Ladies and Gentlemen, the Arab woman who is equal to the man in duties and obligations will not accept, in the twentieth century, the distinctions between the sexes that the advanced countries have done away with. The Arab woman will not agree to be chained in slavery and to pay for the consequences

of men's mistakes with respect to her country's rights and the future of her children. The woman also demands with her loudest voice to be restored her political rights, rights granted to her by the Sharia and dictated to her by the demands of the present. The advanced nations have recognized that the man and the woman are to each other like the brain and heart are to the body; if the balance between these two organs is upset the system of the whole body will be upset. Likewise, if the balance between the two sexes in the nation is upset it will disintegrate and collapse. The advanced nations . . . have come to believe in the equality of sexes in all rights even though their religious and secular laws have not reached the level Islam has reached in terms of justice towards the woman. . . . The woman, given by the Creator the right to vote for the successor of the Prophet, is deprived of the right to vote for a deputy in a circuit or district election by a (male) being created by God. At the same time, this right is enjoyed by a man who might have less education and experience than the woman. And she is the mother who has given birth to the man and has raised him and guided him. The Sharia . . . has made her equal to the man in all rights and responsibilities, even in the crimes that either sex can commit. However, the man who alone distributes rights, has kept for himself the right to legislate and rule, generously turning over to his partner his own share of responsibilities and sanctions without seeking her opinion about the division. The woman today demands to regain her share of rights that have been taken from her and gives back to the man the responsibilities and sanctions he has given to her. Gentlemen, this is justice, and I do not believe that the Arab man who demands that the others give him back his usurped rights would be avaricious and not give the woman back her own lawful rights, all the more so since he himself has tasted the bitterness of deprivation and usurped rights.

Source: Moynagh, M. (2012). Documenting first wave feminisms: Volume I.
https://books.google.de/books?id=r5_47lZOMHQC&pg=PT295&dq=Huda+Shaarawi+and
+Arab+Feminist+Conference&hl=en&sa=X&ei=AnbvVOTFN8a6ggT2zYCQBg&
redir_esc=y#v=onepage&q=Huda%20Shaarawi%20and%20Arab
%20Feminist%20Conference&f=false

Comprehension Check:

1. On what authority does Sha'arawi base her claims to women's rights?
2. Why does Sha'arawi think that Arab men will give back women their rights at this point in time?

Activities:

1. Imagine a conversation about voting rights and British colonialism between Violet Carruthers (Lesson 7.9) and Huda Sha'arawi, and write it in the form of a comic strip.

2. Sha'arawi compared women's oppression by men to Egyptians' oppression by British colonizers. Write a response to Sha'arawi's address from the perspective of an Egyptian man who agreed that British colonization was wrong, but did not want women to have increased rights.

Reflection: What are the advantages and disadvantages of basing an argument for women's rights on religion?

Resources:

Quraishi-Landes, A. (2016). Five myths about sharia. https://www.washingtonpost.com /opinions/five-myths-about-sharia/2016/06/24/7e3efb7a-31ef-11e6-8758-d58e76e11b12 _story.html
Rachidi, S. (2019). Huda Sharawi: A remarkable Egyptian feminist pioneer. https:// insidearabia.com/huda-sharawi-a-remarkable-egyptian-feminist-pioneer/

LESSON 7.12

HOW DID UNA MARSON PARTICIPATE IN WORLDWIDE STRUGGLES AGAINST SEXISM AND RACISM?

Historical Figure: Una Marson

Event: International Alliance of Women meets in Istanbul, 1935

Introduction: If women from all over the world met today to discuss women's rights, on what issues might they agree and disagree? Why?

Mini-Lecture:

- Jamaica was a British colony from 1707 to 1962, and the British brought enslaved African people there to work on sugar plantations.
- In 1834, due to changing economic needs and fear of slave uprisings, the British abolished slavery in Jamaica and many of their other colonies.
- In 1919, the British granted voting rights to Jamaican women over 25 who met economic qualifications, but universal suffrage was not granted until 1944.
- Una Marson (1905–1965) was a Jamaican poet, playwright, journalist, and activist; she was the first Black broadcaster for the British Broadcasting Corporation (BBC).
- Marson was active both in international feminist movements and in the Pan-Africanist movement, which brought together Black people worldwide in opposition to racism and colonialism.
- In 1902, the International Alliance for Suffrage and Women's Citizenship, now known as the International Alliance of Women (IAW), was founded in the United States by women from 12 countries.
- Some White women involved in the suffragist movement had racist and classist views, and did not support full rights for women of all races and social classes— for instance, Carrie Chapman Catt, a U.S. suffragist who helped found the IAW,

argued for granting educated White women the vote on the basis that it would strengthen White supremacy, or power over other races.

- In 1935, the IAW held a Congress (meeting) of International Women in Istanbul, Turkey; Marson was the only Black woman in attendance, along with representatives from Europe, Asia, and the Americas.
- Our document comes from a speech Marson made to the Congress.

Vocabulary:

lynching: when a group of people kills someone accused of a crime without a trial; White supremacists lynched more than 4,000 Black and other minority people in the United States in the late 19th and 20th centuries.

Document: Speech to the Congress of International Women, Una Marson, 1935

Our country is a British colony. We speak English. We are subject to English laws. We were given the right to vote automatically without asking for it. Since the abolition of slavery 100 years ago, women have progressed. We have women doctors and lawyers. But the situation in rural areas is not so good. However, our organization is doing its best to overcome this and provide help for progress. Some of our women are unpaid laborers who work for low wages and live under unhygienic conditions. . . .

I talk on behalf of all Negroes of the world not only Jamaicans. Although I don't know much about Africa, I consider it part of my being because my forefathers came from there. There is a lot we have to do for Africa. Whatever the color, human beings have the same heart. . . . It is necessary that the great powers who have taken in their hands the destinies of Africa should think also of assuring the status of women of that vast continent. And they must do this in all spheres, social, religious and educational. . . .

You know the situation of American Negroes. I am pleased that in recent years articles in the press have appeared defending their rights. Negroes are asking for things common to all humans. They want justice. How can you accuse people who are being lynched of being "barbarian"? There is no worse barbarism than the act of lynching. In America the National Association for the Advancement of Colored People demands a law which shall put an end to the barbarous habit of lynching. Our alliance ought to be able to collaborate in this work.

Even in London one sometimes sees discrimination against black people, even those who are British subjects. Negroes are suffering under enormous difficulties in most countries in the world. We must count up on all countries where there are Negroes—for women always possess a better developed sense of justice—to obtain for them a life more pleasant and less severe. Apart from this, however sad the Negroes may be, they smile and hope always when they see the Negro women side by side with the women of the universe that will reinforce their hopes and make them feel that for them too happiness is not far off. . . . I get the impression that representatives gathered here are big-hearted and will defend and help my race.

> *Source:* Jarrett-McCauley, D. (1988). The life of Una Marson, 1905–1965.
> https://books.google.de/books?id=WTOBypHXZLgC&pg=PA96&lpg=PA96&dq
> =%22una+marson%22+speech&source=bl&ots=8ilP5N_gx1&sig
> =ACfU3U0CcrAfEodwJ24xwSlxRNhE-pPyPA&hl=en&sa=X&ved=2ahUKEwiA2J
> -otK7mAhVzolwKHczNA_gQ6AEwBXoECAoQAQ#v=snippet&q=speech&f=false
> *Reprinted courtesy of Delia Jarrett-McCauley*

Comprehension Check:

1. What issues that affect women is Marson concerned about?
2. Why does Marson believe that her audience will be open to her ideas?

Activities:

1. Name Marson's strategy for addressing the racism that existed in the IAW. Then brainstorm other strategies she could have chosen. List reasons why she may have chosen the strategy she did, and why she may have rejected the others.
2. Consult the "Our Work" section of the IAW website in the Resources section to learn what issues the IAW currently focuses on. Divide into teams to research these issues and present them to the class.

Reflection: Which issues do you consider "women's issues"? Why? Or do you believe women's issues are the same as men's?

Resources:

International Alliance of Women. (2019). Homepage. https://womenalliance.org/
Iyer, A. (2018). Remembering Una Marson: Black feminist pioneer. https://newint.org
/features/2018/10/30/remembering-una-marson-black-feminist-pioneer

Resistance, Revolution, and Reform

Unit Question: How Should People Bring About Political and Social Change?

In previous units, students have looked at why things are the way they are—how societies came to be. In this unit, they examine how and why people have taken action to change the status quo. The 21st-Century Issue—which could be replaced by a more recent example of revolutionary activism—shows how Asmaa Mahfouz used social media to help spark the Egyptian Revolution in 2011. Julius Caesar's fateful decision to cross the Rubicon and install himself as dictator for life provides a classical example of how to force political change, while an account of Shah Abbas's court illustrates how the Safavid Empire allied with Europe to combat their rivals. Martin Luther's 95 Theses presents a medieval prototype for a protest "going viral." Documents from the French and Haitian Revolutions that put forth arguments for using violence to change the social order contrast with documents that show Gandhi's satyagraha and Southeast Asian hill peoples' methods of passive resistance. Zapata's Plan de Ayala and Joseph Stalin's "modernize or perish" speech introduce students to the range of effects that revolutionary change can have on ordinary people's lives. Frantz Fanon's explanation of decolonization contrasts with Gandhi's while echoing Jean-Jacques Dessalines'. Finally, Rigoberta Menchú's *testimonio* and Václav Havel's explanation of resistance to totalitarian governments show how ordinary people can work for justice.

This unit is a culmination of the book in the sense that it brings up issues of gender, economic and social inequality, conflict, identity, belief, and governance—all with the highest possible stakes. By this point, students may have developed a worldview informed by their studies that allows them to argue more confidently for their positions. The stark contrasts between violent and nonviolent resistance, and between successful and unsuccessful attempts to improve people's lives, are likely to make this summit a rich discussion. Teachers might show students a video from their first summit to show them how far they have come in their skills of portraying historical figures' views.

LESSON 8.1

How Did Egyptians Use Social Media and Protest to Bring About Political Change?

Historical Figure: Asmaa Mahfouz

Event: Egyptian Revolution, 2011

Introduction: Do you think social media is a force for positive or negative change in the world? Why?

Mini-Lecture:

- In 2010, demonstrations against dictatorships occurred in several Arab countries, including Tunisia, Libya, Egypt, Yemen, Syria, and Bahrain; collectively, these events became known as the "Arab Spring" or the "Jasmine Revolution."
- In December 2010, a Tunisian man frustrated with poverty, police brutality, and government corruption self-immolated (set himself on fire and burned to death) in front of a government office; news of this event was spread on social media and led to protests that toppled the Tunisian dictator.
- Activists in Egypt, who had already been protesting the human rights abuses by Hosni Mubarak's regime, took inspiration from the Tunisians' success; one was a 26-year-old woman named Asmaa Mahfouz.
- Mahfouz created a video blog (vlog) encouraging Egyptians to protest against the government in Tahrir Square, in downtown Cairo, on January 25, 2011.
- This vlog, a transcript of which makes up our document, went viral on Facebook and Twitter; it contributed to organizing a demonstration that grew to about 250,000 people, during which security forces killed hundreds of people.
- Less than three weeks later, the Egyptian military removed Mubarak from office and took power, and democratic elections were held in 2012.
- Mahfouz was detained by the military following the demonstrations, but she continues to advocate for human rights; along with four other activists from the Arab Spring, she won the Sakharov Prize for Freedom of Thought in 2011.
- In 2013, the military staged a coup, and as of 2019, Egypt has been led by a ruler whom many activists consider much like Mubarak.

Vocabulary:

degradation: poor treatment   *'net:* internet
SMS: text message

Document: Vlog, Asmaa Mahfouz, 2011

> Four Egyptians have set themselves on fire, to protest humiliation and
> hunger and poverty and degradation they had to live with for 30 years.
> Four Egyptians set themselves on fire, thinking maybe we can have a

revolution like Tunisia. Maybe we can have freedom, justice, honor, and human dignity. . . .

I'm making this video to give you one simple message: We want to go down to Tahrir Square on January 25. If we still have honor, and to live in dignity on this land, we have to go down on 25th January. We'll go down and demand our rights, our fundamental human rights. . . . This entire government is corrupt—a corrupt president and a corrupt security force. These self-immolators were not afraid of death but were afraid of security forces! . . . I'm going down on January 25th, and from now till then, I'm going to distribute fliers in the street everyday. I will not set myself on fire! If the security forces want to set me on fire, let them come and do it!

If you think yourself a man, come with me on January 25th. Whoever says women shouldn't go to protests because they will get beaten, let him have some honor and manhood and come with me on January 25th. Whoever says it's not worth it [because] there will only be a handful of people, I want to tell you, you are the reason behind this, and you are a traitor, just like the president and the security cop who beats us in the streets. . . . Sitting at home and just following us on news or Facebook leads to our humiliation, leads to my own humiliation! If you have honor and dignity as a man, come. Come and protect me, and other girls in the protest. If you stay at home, then you deserve all that's being done to you, and you will be guilty, before your nation and before your people, and you'll be responsible for what happens to us on the street while you sit at home. Go down to the street, send SMS's, post it on the 'net, make people aware. You know your own social circle, your building, your family, your friends, tell them to come with us. Bring 5 people, bring 10 people: if each of us manages to bring 5 or 10 to Tahrir Square and talk to them and tell them, this is enough!

Instead of setting ourselves on fire, let's do something positive. It will make a difference, a big difference. Never say there's no hope, hope only disappears when you say there's no hope. So long as you come down with us, there will be hope. Don't be afraid of the government, fear none but God! God says that He "will not change the condition of a people until they change what is in themselves" (Qu'ran 13:1). Do not think you can be safe anymore! None of us are! Come down with us, and demand your rights, my rights, your family's rights. I am going down on January 25th, and I will say "No" to corruption, "No" to this regime.

Source: Iyad El-Bahgdadi. (Trans.). (2011). Meet Asmaa Mahfouz and the vlog that helped spark the revolution. https://www.youtube.com/watch?v=eBg7O48vhLY

Comprehension Check:

1. According to Mahfouz, why is sitting at home and following the protesters on Facebook the same as being a traitor?
2. What message did Mahfouz give to Egyptian men?

Activities:

1. What tactics does Mahfouz use to convince people to join the demonstration? Underline them in her vlog and make marginal notes to explain to the class.
2. Research the current political situation in Egypt. What do you think Mahfouz's comments on it would be?

Reflection: There were also large demonstrations in Egypt in 1954, when the monarchy was overthrown. Before social media, how do you think people organized them?

Resources:

Encyclopedia Britannica. (2019). Egypt uprising of 2011. https://www.britannica.com/event /Egypt-Uprising-of-2011
Kouddous, S. A. (2011). Egyptians defend activist charged in military court. https:// pulitzercenter.org/reporting/egyptians-defend-activist-charged-military-court

---

LESSON 8.2

HOW DID JULIUS CAESAR GAIN CONTROL OF ROME?

Historical Figure: Julius Caesar

Event: Caesar starts Roman Civil War, 49 BCE

Introduction: Have you ever made a bold decision, not knowing what the results would be? How did it work out?

Mini-Lecture:

- The Roman Republic in the 1st century BCE was ruled by consuls who supervised the Senate.
- In the 50s BCE, Julius Caesar led a military campaign for the Roman Empire to conquer Cisalpine Gaul (today northern Italy and France) and other areas; his soldiers were very loyal to him, and he also had influence in Rome.
- Caesar's rival, Pompey, a politician and general, was afraid of Caesar's growing power, and convinced the Senate to order him to give up his military position.
- Caesar chose not to obey the Senate, and instead led his troops across the Rubicon River and into Italy; the result was a civil war that Caesar eventually won.
- Caesar had himself appointed dictator for life, and ruled until he was assassinated in 44 BCE by political rivals.
- Plutarch was a Greek philosopher and historian who wrote a book about Julius Caesar's life, from which our document is taken.

Vocabulary:

legionary: describing a division of 3,000 to 6,000 soldiers in the Roman army

centurion: commander of a group of 100 soldiers

irresolute: undecided

perplexities: confusions

posterity: history

calculations: thinking

cast: thrown

Document: Caesar crosses the Rubicon, Plutarch, 75 CE

Caesar had with him at the time no more than 300 cavalry and 5,000 legionary soldiers. The rest of his army had been left on the other side of the Alps and was to be brought up to him by officers who had been sent back to do so. He saw, however, that the very beginning and the first stages of his enterprise did not require the use of large forces for the time being. Better results could be obtained by surprise, daring, and taking the quickest advantage of the moment; it would be easier, he thought, to strike panic into his enemies by acting in a way which they never expected than it would be to force them back after having first made all the preparations for a regular invasion. So he ordered his centurions and other officers to take just their swords, leaving their other arms behind, and to occupy the large Gallic city of Rimini; they were to avoid all disturbance and bloodshed as far as they possibly could. . . .

He himself got into one of the hired carriages and, setting out at first on a different road, finally turned and took the road to Rimini. When he came to the river (it is called the [Rubicon]) which forms the frontier between Cisalpine Gaul and the rest of Italy he became full of thought; for now he was drawing nearer and nearer to the dreadful step, and his mind wavered as he considered what a tremendous venture it was upon which he was engaged. He began to go more slowly and then ordered a halt. For a long time he weighed matters up silently in own mind, irresolute between the two alternatives. In these moments his purpose was constantly changing. For some time too he discussed his perplexities with his friends who were there, among whom was [the future historian] Asinius Pollio. He thought of the sufferings which his crossing the river would bring upon mankind and he imagined the fame of the story of it which they would leave to posterity. Finally, in a sort of passion, as though he were casting calculation aside and abandoning himself to whatever lay in store for him, making use too of the expression which is frequently used by those who are on the point of committing themselves to desperate and unpredictable chances, 'Let the die be cast,' he said, and with these words hurried to cross the river.

Source: Livius.org. (2015). Caesar's Rubico crossing.
https://www.livius.org/sources/content/plutarch/plutarchs-caesar
/plutarch-on-caesars-rubico-crossing/

Comprehension Check:

1. Why did Caesar hesitate before crossing the Rubicon?
2. What did Caesar mean by "Let the die be cast?"

Activities:

1. Caesar is one of many rulers who secured power for themselves through military means. Work with a partner to research another dictator who took power by force, and present their similarities and differences with Caesar to the class.
2. Consider the dictators you learned about. Whose support did they need to take power? How did their reigns end? Describe the patterns you notice.

Reflection: Do you think most dictators who take power by force believe they are acting for themselves, or doing what is best for their country, empire, or nation? Why?

Resources:

Marks, J. J. (2011). Julius Caesar. https://www.ancient.eu/Julius_Caesar/
Redonet, F. L. (2017). How Julius Caesar started a big war by crossing a small stream.
    https://www.nationalgeographic.com/history/magazine/2017/03-04/julius-caesar
    -crossing-rubicon-rome/

LESSON 8.3

HOW DID THE SAFAVID EMPIRE USE DIPLOMACY TO ACCOMPLISH ITS GOALS?

Historical Figure: Shah Abbas

Event: Safavid Dynasty, 1501–1736

Introduction: As a leader, what would you do if you had wars on two separate fronts and not enough resources to fight both?

Mini-Lecture:

- From the 16th to the 18th centuries, the Safavid Dynasty ruled Persia (now Iran), and built an empire that stretched into what is now Turkey, Saudi Arabia, and South Asia.
- Shah Abbas I, also known as Abbas the Great, ruled this empire from 1587 to 1629; when he took power, there were conflicts with the Ottoman Empire to the east (based in what is now Turkey), as well as with the Uzbek people to the north.
- Shah Abbas I made a peace treaty with the Ottoman Empire, giving up territory to them, and then focused on building up his army and fighting the Uzbeks.
- Shah Abbas I knew that the British and other Europeans feared the growing power of the Ottoman Empire.
- To secure European help in recapturing the territory he had ceded earlier, Shah Abbas I invited two brothers from England to help him achieve his diplomatic and military goals: Sir Robert Sherley helped him reform and train his army, while Sir Anthony Sherley led a diplomatic mission to the British.

- Shah Abbas I cultivated commercial relationships with Europeans, and his capital at Isfahan became a center of trade in Persian rugs and other goods.
- Shah Abbas I was a Shi'a Muslim who suppressed Sunni Islam (another branch of the religion practiced by Ottoman Turks, among others), but he was tolerant of Christians.
- Uruch Beg was a Safavid official who accompanied Sir Anthony Sherley on the diplomatic mission to Europe; he settled in Spain, took the name Don Juan of Persia, and wrote a book about his travels, from which our document is taken.

Vocabulary:

low countries: The Netherlands, Belgium, and Luxembourg

Sassanian Empire: Persian Empire that ruled what is now Iran and other parts of the Middle East from the 3rd to the 7th centuries

peculiar: unique

doctrine: religious teachings

imams: Muslim religious leaders

orthodox: true

heretical: describing a religious belief considered false

infidel: someone who practices a religion other than one's own, which is believed to be false

flank attack: attack parts of an army from an unexpected direction

mortally: to the death

propitious: fortunate

credentials: qualifications

in her confidence: with her trust

forthwith: immediately

accredited: officially recognized

Document: Don Juan of Persia, Uruch Beg, 1604

[Don Juan of Persia] had left Persia in the year 1599, being one of the four secretaries to the Persian ambassador whom Shah Abbas was sending to the princes of Europe under the guidance and personal conduct of Sir Anthony Sherley, and Don Juan of Persia at this period was a Shi'a Muslim, and bore the name of Uruch Beg.

As regards the Englishman who was to conduct this Persian embassy, Sir Anthony Sherley was already of European fame for his services in the Low Countries under the Earl of Essex, and in France, where King Henry IV had knighted him, a rank, however, never officially confirmed by Queen Elizabeth I. Also he had led a celebrated expedition to the West Indies and the Spanish Main, and then had left England late in 1598 on what proved a fruitless political mission to bring help and intervene in the affairs of the Duke of Ferrara. His services in North Italy, however, not being accepted or required, he and his brother Robert, with twenty-five other Englishmen, took ship at Venice in May 1599, proceeding to the East, where, landing at the mouth of the river Orontes, the party went up to Antioch. Thence they passed on to Aleppo, and then crossing the desert to the Euphrates, floated down in boats, reaching the neighborhood of the ruins of Babylon, which lay at no great distance from Baghdad, at that time in the occupation of the Turks. From here they made their way into Persia to Qazvin, and thence on to Isfahan, where the Englishmen found favor with [His Majesty] Abbas the Great. . . .

Persia, then a great power, was enjoying . . . prosperity that had been unknown since the Arab conquest in the 7th century. Its frontiers were once more very nearly those that had been held under the Sassanian kings. A century before this, the founder of the Safavid monarchy, Shah Ismail, great grandfather of [His Majesty] Abbas, had made the Persians a nation by the vigor of his rule, further by proclaiming that the Shi'a faith, with the peculiar doctrine of the Imams (from whom he traced his descent), was to be the one and only orthodox belief; thus branding the Turks of the Sunni sect as heretical and infidel. For a hundred years he and his successors down to Shah Abbas had continually waged war against the Turkish Sultans, but with such varying success that Shah Abbas had now made up his mind to seek alliances with the Christian powers or Europe, who, he trusted, would be willing to combine with him against the Sultan and by making a flank attack on [the Ottoman capital] Constantinople mortally harass the Turk.

Sherley therefore had come at a propitious hour; he had no credentials to show from Queen Elizabeth I, but he represented himself as a noble in her confidence, and offered to introduce the Shah's ambassador to her Majesty and to the sovereigns of the various courts of Europe. The Persians of that age were well accustomed to embassies from Christian potentates, and of Englishmen in particular in the reign of Shah Tahmasp, the grandfather of Shah Abbas, Anthony Jenkinson, coming from Queen Elizabeth I, had been received very honorably at Qazvin in the year 1562. The embassy therefore was forthwith organized and set out, Sherley and one Persian ambassador being jointly accredited to eight of the European courts. . . .

Source: Internet Archive. (n.d.). Full text of Don Juan of Persia. https://archive.org /stream/donjuanofpersiaa010345mbp/donjuanofpersiaa010345mbp_djvu.txt

Comprehension Check:

1. Why was Shah Abbas I seeking help from the Europeans against the Ottoman Turks?
2. What was Anthony Sherley's role in the diplomatic mission?

Activities:

1. If Shah Abbas had been with Julius Caesar (Lesson 8.2) on the banks of the Rubicon, what advice might he have given the Roman leader? Write it out in the form of a short letter.
2. Research your country's current situation. Who are its strongest allies and opponents? Would those allies be likely to help your country against its opponents? Why or why not?

Reflection: Do you think it shows weakness or strength to seek alliances in order to achieve political change? Why?

Resources:

New World Encyclopedia. (2019). Safavid Empire. https://www.newworldencyclopedia.org
    /entry/Safavid_Empire

Savory, R. M. (2019). 'Abbas I. https://www.britannica.com/biography/Abbas-I-Safavid-shah
    -of-Persia

LESSON 8.4

How Did Martin Luther Bring About the Protestant Reformation?

Historical Figure: Martin Luther

Event: Martin Luther starts the Protestant Reformation, 1517

Introduction: If you had a message to share and you wanted as many people as possible to read it, what would you do?

Mini-Lecture:

- In medieval Europe, it was common for priests to sell "indulgences" on behalf of the Roman Catholic Church and its leader, the Pope; these supposedly granted believers forgiveness from sin, and thus a better chance of getting into heaven, in exchange for paying money and doing a good deed or saying a prayer.
- The Church used the proceeds from the sale of indulgences to raise funds for buildings and projects.
- Around 1515, Pope Leo X announced that he would sell indulgences to finance the reconstruction of St. Peter's Basilica, a church in Rome.
- A reverend named Martin Luther, who lived in Wittenberg, in what is now Germany, saw the sale of indulgences as a form of corruption; he believed that only God could grant forgiveness for sins.
- In 1517, Martin Luther wrote 95 Theses, or arguments, on his concerns about the sale of indulgences and sent them to his superiors in the church; according to legend, he also nailed them to the door of the church in Wittenberg.
- Catholics believe in the Pope's infallibility (inability to be wrong), so they saw Martin Luther's act as blasphemous, or going against their religion; Luther was excommunicated from (forced out of) the Catholic Church and faced penalties including death.
- Many people shared Luther's concerns about indulgences, and they read and shared his 95 Theses; these Theses, from which our document is taken, sparked the Reformation, in which the Protestant Church broke off from the Catholic Church and came to dominate Northern Europe.

Vocabulary:

elucidate: explain
dispute: debate

papal: relating to the pope
erroneously: wrongly

wrath: anger   *hawkers:* sellers
squander: waste   *cajole:* beg
exactions: payment   *tribulations:* difficult experiences
sheep: metaphor for followers of
    Jesus Christ

Document: 95 Theses, Martin Luther, 1517

Out of love for the truth and from desire to elucidate it, the Reverend Father
Martin Luther, Master of Arts and Sacred Theology, and ordinary lecturer
therein at Wittenberg, intends to defend the following statements and to dispute
on them in that place. Therefore he asks that those who cannot be present and
dispute with him orally shall do so in their absence by letter. In the name of our
Lord Jesus Christ, Amen. . . .

Papal indulgences must be preached with caution, lest people erroneously
think that they are preferable to other good works of love.

Christians are to be taught that the pope does not intend that the buying of
indulgences should in any way be compared with works of mercy.

Christians are to be taught that he who gives to the poor or lends to the
needy does a better deed than he who buys indulgences.

Because love grows by works of love, man thereby becomes better. Man
does not, however, become better by means of indulgences but is merely freed
from penalties.

Christians are to be taught that he who sees a needy man and passes him by,
yet gives his money for indulgences, does not buy papal indulgences but God's
wrath.

Christians are to be taught that, unless they have more than they need, they
must reserve enough for their family needs and by no means squander it on
indulgences.

Christians are to be taught that the buying of indulgences is a matter of free
choice, not commanded.

Christians are to be taught that the pope, in granting indulgences, needs and
thus desires their devout prayer more than their money.

Christians are to be taught that papal indulgences are useful only if they do
not put their trust in them, but very harmful if they lose their fear of God
because of them.

Christians are to be taught that if the pope knew the exactions of the
indulgence preachers, he would rather that the basilica of St. Peter were burned
to ashes than built up with the skin, flesh, and bones of his sheep.

Christians are to be taught that the pope would and should wish to give of
his own money, even though he had to sell the basilica of St. Peter, to many of
those from whom certain hawkers of indulgences cajole money. . . .

Christians should be exhorted to be diligent in following Christ, their Head,
through penalties, death and hell.

And thus be confident of entering into heaven through many tribulations rather than through the false security of peace (Acts 14:22).

Source: MartinLuther.de. (n.d). The 95 Theses. https://www.luther.de/en/95thesen.html

Comprehension Check:

1. According to Luther, why is he posting these Theses?
2. What problems does Luther see with the sale of indulgences?

Activities:

1. Draw a Venn diagram showing the similarities and differences between Martin Luther's and Asmaa Mahfouz's (Lesson 8.1) approaches to creating change.
2. A philosophy blogger has opened a Twitter account sharing quotes from Martin Luther (@Lutherquots). Choose one of his quotes (or one he retweeted from another philosopher) and explain to the class how you connect it to his ideas on the sale of indulgences.

Reflection: If you have concerns about an organization you belong to, do you think it is better to try to change it from within or to create a new organization? Give examples.

Resources:

Orta, J. P. (2017). How Martin Luther started a religious revolution. https://www .nationalgeographic.com/history/magazine/2017/09-10/history-martin-luther-religious -revolution/

Protestantism.co.uk. (2019). Introduction to Protestantism. http://protestantism.co.uk/

LESSON 8.5

WHY DID MAXIMILIEN ROBESPIERRE BELIEVE VIOLENCE WAS NECESSARY TO ACHIEVE THE GOALS OF THE FRENCH REVOLUTION?

Historical Figure: Maximilien Robespierre

Event: French Revolution begins, 1789

Introduction: Do you think it is wise and/or necessary to use violence to overthrow violent regimes? Why or why not?

Mini-Lecture:

- In the 18th century, what is now France was ruled by an absolute monarchy led by King Louis XVI, who believed he had "divine right"—that he had been chosen by God.
- French society was divided into three social classes, or "Estates"; King Louis XVI lived in luxury and gave special privileges to the First and Second Estates

(Catholic clergy and nobles), whereas the Third Estate (craftspeople and peasants, making up 98% of the population) had few rights and had to pay taxes to the other Estates.
- In 1789, members of the Third Estate, frustrated with this situation, stormed (took over) the Bastille, a prison that symbolized the king's power to punish anyone for whatever he chose.
- Many nobles fled the country, and in 1791, King Louis XVI tried to join them; revolutionaries captured and executed him and his family, along with many other nobles.
- A group of revolutionaries took control, published the "Declaration of the Rights of Man and the Citizen," and established the French Republic, using the slogan "Liberty, Equality, and Fraternity."
- Different factions competed for power, and one was the Jacobins, led by Maximilien Robespierre, who believed it was necessary to use violence against anyone who did not support his strict interpretation of the revolution; they launched the "Reign of Terror," and killed about 20,000 people.
- Our document comes from a speech that Robespierre gave in 1794, shortly before political rivals executed him; after that, Napoleon Bonaparte (see Lesson 4.7) established a dictatorship.

Vocabulary:

deduce: figure out

popular government: government by the people

severity: harshness

vessel: ship

tempest: storm

smother: get rid of

perish: die

maxim: rule

terror: violence

spring: source

emanation: something that comes from a source

despotism: government by one person with absolute power

henchmen: people assisting an unjust cause

royalists: supporters of the monarchy

conspirators: people working on a secret plot

intriguers: people creating drama

mandate: rule

mercenary: working for pay on behalf of someone else's cause

pamphleteers: people distributing pamphlets or information

civil discord: fighting among the people

counterrevolution: backlash against a revolution

Document: Justification of the use of terror, Maximilien Robespierre, 1794

From all this let us deduce a great truth: the characteristic of popular government is confidence in the people and severity towards itself.

The whole development of our theory would end here if you had only to pilot the vessel of the Republic through calm waters; but the tempest roars, and the revolution imposes on you another task. . . .

We must smother the internal and external enemies of the Republic or perish with it; now in this situation, the first maxim of your policy ought to be to lead the people by reason and the people's enemies by terror.

If the spring of popular government in time of peace is virtue, the springs of popular government in revolution are at once virtue and terror: virtue, without which terror is fatal; terror, without which virtue is powerless. Terror is nothing other than justice, prompt, severe, inflexible; it is therefore an emanation of virtue; it is not so much a special principle as it is a consequence of the general principle of democracy applied to our country's most urgent needs.

It has been said that terror is the principle of despotic government. Does your government therefore resemble despotism? Yes, as the sword that gleams in the hands of the heroes of liberty resembles that with which the henchmen of tyranny are armed. Let the despot govern by terror his brutalized subjects; he is right, as a despot. Subdue by terror the enemies of liberty, and you will be right, as founders of the Republic. The government of the revolution is liberty's despotism against tyranny. Is force made only to protect crime? And is the thunderbolt not destined to strike the heads of the proud? . . .

Indulgence for the royalists, cry certain men, mercy for the villains! No! mercy for the innocent, mercy for the weak, mercy for the unfortunate, mercy for humanity. Society owes protection only to peaceable citizens; the only citizens in the Republic are the republicans. For it, the royalists, the conspirators are only strangers or, rather, enemies. This terrible war waged by liberty against tyranny—is it not indivisible? Are the enemies within not the allies of the enemies without? The assassins who tear our country apart, the intriguers who buy the consciences that hold the people's mandate; the traitors who sell them; the mercenary pamphleteers hired to dishonor the people's cause, to kill public virtue, to stir up the fire of civil discord, and to prepare political counterrevolution by moral counterrevolution—are all those men less guilty or less dangerous than the tyrants whom they serve?

Source: Halsall, P. (2019). Maximilien Robespierre: Justification of the use of terror.
https://sourcebooks.fordham.edu/mod/robespierre-terror.asp

Comprehension Check:

1. According to Robespierre, why is violence okay when revolutionaries like him use it, but not okay when despotic governments use it?
2. In your own words, who is on the list of people that Robespierre wants to use violence against?

Activities:

1. Divide the class in half and debate the following proposition: A revolution that begins with violence will establish a government that continues to be violent.

2. Like the revolution in Egypt (Lesson 8.1), the revolution in France succeeded in getting rid of the existing government but did not succeed in sustaining the democratic government that the revolutionaries were seeking. Brainstorm a list of reasons for this outcome in each case.

Reflection: If you had been a member of the Third Estate at the time of the French Revolution, would you have supported it? If so, at what point would you have stopped supporting it, if any, and why?

Resources:

Bouloiseau, M. (2019). Maximilien Robespierre. https://www.britannica.com/biography /Maximilien-Robespierre

TEDEd. (2016). What caused the French Revolution? https://www.youtube.com/watch?v =PBn7iWzrKoI

LESSON 8.6

HOW DID HAITIANS END SLAVERY AND GAIN INDEPENDENCE FROM FRANCE?

Historical Figure: Jean-Jacques Dessalines

Event: Haitian Revolution, 1791–1804

Introduction: In the late 18th century, France had colonies around the world. How do you think people living in France's colonies, including enslaved people, reacted to the French Revolution? Why?

Mini-Lecture:

- In the 15th century, Spain had colonized the island they called Hispaniola (now Haiti and the Dominican Republic), killed many of the Indigenous inhabitants, and brought enslaved Africans to work on sugar plantations and in gold mines.
- In the 17th century, the French established a colony called Saint Domingue on the western part of the island; by the late 18th century, there were about 35,000 White people (both wealthy plantation owners and middle-class people); 500,000 enslaved Africans; 25,000 free Black people, some of whom were of mixed heritage; and an unknown number of maroons (enslaved people who had run away and lived together in rural areas).
- Some Black people living in San Domingue learned of the French Revolution and became inspired by the Enlightenment ideas of freedom and equality; those included two former slaves, Toussaint L'Ouverture and Jean-Jacques Dessalines.
- L'Ouverture, assisted by Dessalines, led a slave revolt against plantation owners in 1791, and then expanded his control across the island, defeating French, British, and Spanish forces; abolishing slavery; and declaring himself governor-general for life.
- In 1802, France, under the rule of Napoleon Bonaparte (see Lesson 4.7), captured L'Ouverture, recolonized Saint Domingue, and tried to reinstitute slavery.

- Dessalines defeated the French in 1804, 14 years after the revolution began, and wrote a declaration of independence for the country he called by its Indigenous name, Haiti (from which our document is taken); Haiti was the first independent republic led by Black people.
- Dessalines declared himself emperor, instituted a system of forced labor, took the White people's land, and killed many of them; conflicts among Haitians continued, and Dessalines was killed trying to put down a rebellion in 1806.

Vocabulary:

factions: competing groups supporting one political cause
specter: promise
torpor: inability to act
credulity: being easily fooled

indulgence: patience
eloquence: skill in speaking
avenging: harsh
exterminated: killed

Document: Haitian Declaration of Independence, 1804

The Commander in Chief to the People of Haiti

Citizens: It is not enough to have expelled the barbarians who have bloodied our land for two centuries; it is not enough to have restrained those ever-evolving factions that one after another mocked the specter of liberty that France dangled before you. We must, with one last act of national authority, forever assure the empire of liberty in the country of our birth; we must take any hope of re-enslaving us away from the inhuman government that for so long kept us in the most humiliating torpor. In the end we must live independent or die.

Independence or death . . . let these sacred words unite us and be the signal of battle and of our reunion. Citizens, my countrymen, on this solemn day I have brought together those courageous soldiers who, as liberty lay dying, spilled their blood to save it; these generals who have guided your efforts against tyranny have not yet done enough for your happiness; the French name still haunts our land.

Everything revives the memories of the cruelties of this barbarous people: our laws, our habits, our towns, everything still carries the stamp of the French. Indeed! There are still French in our island, and you believe yourself free and independent of that Republic which, it is true, has fought all the nations, but which has never defeated those who wanted to be free.

What! Victims of our [own] credulity and indulgence for 14 years; defeated not by French armies, but by the pathetic eloquence of their agents' proclamations; when will we tire of breathing the air that they breathe? What do we have in common with this nation of executioners? The difference between its cruelty and our patient moderation, its color and ours the great seas that separate us, our avenging climate, all tell us plainly that they are not our brothers, that they never will be, and that if they find refuge among us, they will plot again to trouble and divide us. . . .

We have dared to be free, let us be thus by ourselves and for ourselves. Let us imitate the grown child: his own weight breaks the boundary that has become an obstacle to him. What people fought for us? What people wanted to gather the fruits of our labor? And what dishonorable absurdity to conquer in order to be enslaved. Enslaved? . . . Let us leave this description for the French; they have conquered but are no longer free.

Let us walk down another path; let us imitate those people who, extending their concern into the future, and dreading to leave an example of cowardice for posterity, preferred to be exterminated rather than lose their place as one of the world's free peoples.

Source: Duke Office of News and Communications. (n.d.).
The Haitian Declaration of Independence. https://today.duke.edu
/showcase/haitideclaration/declarationstext.html

Comprehension Check:

1. According to Dessalines, what did the French promise to the residents of San Domingue that they did not deliver?
2. List the differences between the French and the Haitians, as described by Dessalines.

Activities:

1. Line up on an "opinion cline" based on how much you agree with the following statement: Violence was necessary to bring about the end of slavery in Haiti. Talk with someone near you, and then someone with a different opinion.
2. Create a Venn diagram comparing and contrasting the actions of Robespierre (Lesson 8.5) and Dessalines.

Reflection: Do you feel differently about Robespierre's killings of "counterrevolutionaries" and Dessalines's killings of White residents of Haiti? Why or why not?

Resources:

Encyclopedia Britannica. (2019). Jean-Jacques Dessalines. https://www.britannica.com
    /biography/Jean-Jacques-Dessalines
Sutherland, C. (2007). Haitian revolution (1791–1804). https://www.blackpast.org/global
    -african-history/haitian-revolution-1791-1804/

LESSON 8.7

HOW DID SOUTHEAST ASIANS AVOID RULERS WHO WANTED TO CONTROL THEM?

Historical Figure: James G. Scott

Event: British colonize but fail to completely control Burma, 1885

Introduction: Are there people in your country, society, or school who manage to escape being totally controlled by the authorities? If so, how do they do it?

Mini-Lecture:

- Some historians (see Asia Society video in Resources section) have argued that for the past several thousand years, people throughout Southeast Asia who did not want to be controlled or enslaved by governments fled to mountainous regions and became nomadic, thus avoiding incorporation in any state until the 20th century.
- In what is now known as Myanmar or Burma, culturally and linguistically diverse peoples have lived for thousands of years; the lowlands have often been dominated by Buddhist kingdoms, but in the thickly forested mountainous regions, nomadic groups were able to live independently in "stateless societies" (see Lesson 1.10).
- Great Britain began to colonize this region in the 19th century; in 1885, they captured Mandalay, the capital of the Konbaung Dynasty, which had claimed control over much of the area the British had conquered.
- The British then tried to "pacify" the area they had decreed that they ruled; many people living in this area did not recognize their authority and fought back against them—the British called these people "dacoits," meaning bands of armed robbers.
- James G. Scott (1851–1935) was a colonial administrator in British Burma who helped to "pacify" the mountainous regions and wrote a book about this effort, from which our document is taken.

Vocabulary:

trifle: easy task
object lesson: simple example
gallantry: bravery
stockades: place where weapons are stored
ambuscade: ambush
terai: swampy lowland

tortuous: twisting
malaria: a mosquito-borne illness causing fever
recommence: start again
impassable: impossible to cross
position: military action
slightly clad: not wearing many clothes

Document: *Gazetteer of Upper Burma and the Shan States*, James G. Scott, 1893

[The pacification of Upper Burma] was not effected without very great toil and considerable loss of life. The advance on and the taking of Mandalay were the merest trifle, little more than an object lesson in military movements compared with the work of the pacification. That was a perpetual record of acts of gallantry which passed unnoticed because they were so constant; of endless marches by night and by day, through dense jungle, where paths could hardly be traced, over paths which were so deep in mud that men could hardly march over them and animals stuck fast, over stretches where no water was to be found and nothing grew but thorn-bushes, over hills where there were no paths at all; and with all this but rarely the chance of an engagement to cheer the men, stockades found empty, villages deserted, camps evacuated, endless disappointments, and yet everywhere the probability of an ambuscade in every clump of trees, every turn of the road, from each stream bed, line of rocks, or ravine. . . .

The hill and jungly tracts were those in which the dacoits held out longest. Such [was] the country between Minbu and Thayetmyo and the terai at the foot of the Shan Hills and the Arakan and Chin Hills. Here pursuit was impossible. The tracts are narrow and tortuous and admirably suited for ambuscades. Except by the regular paths there were hardly any means of approach; the jungle malaria was fatal to our troops; a column could only penetrate the jungle and move on. The villages are small and far between; they are generally surrounded by dense, impenetrable jungle. The paths were either just broad enough for a cart, or very narrow, and, where they led through the jungle were overhung with brambles and thorny creepers. A good deal of the dry grass is burned in March, but as soon as the rains recommence the whole once more becomes impassable. . . .

As the dacoits so rarely stood and when attacked disappeared so quickly, columns composed entirely of infantry operated at a great disadvantage. They would have to march for five or six hours, pushing on as fast as they could and making a circuit over unfrequented paths and in the end had to go in straight for the position, for if they halted for a moment the dacoits would have vanished. To follow them up for long was impossible, for the gang spread in every direction; they were slightly clad, fresh, knew the country, and could keep out of sight in patches of jungle and villages. . . .

Source: Northern Illinois University. *Gazetteer of Upper Burma and the Shan States,*
part I, vol. I, pp. 148, 154–155.
https://www.niu.edu/burma/Two%20Journeys/Histories/gazeteerI.pdf

Comprehension Check:

1. List the difficulties the British soldiers had in controlling the area due to geography and climate.
2. According to Scott, what did the "dacoits" do when they saw the British?

Activities:

1. Imagine a conversation between one of the nomadic people living in mountainous regions of Burma and James G. Scott. What would they say to each other? Role-play their conversation with a classmate.
2. The title of this unit is resistance, revolution, and reform. Work with a partner to classify each of the topics you have studied so far, including this one, into one of these categories, and be ready to justify your decisions to the class.

Reflection: In what situations might passive, nonconfrontational resistance be more effective than active, confrontational resistance?

Resources:

Asia Society. (2010). The art of not being governed. https://www.youtube.com/watch?v
=RsTunrXFXcw

Frederick, W. H. (2018). History of Southeast Asia. https://www.britannica.com/topic/history
-of-Southeast-Asia-556509

Lesson 8.8

How Did Gandhi Use Nonviolent Resistance Against British Colonization?

Historical Figure: Mohandas Karamchand Gandhi

Event: Quit India movement, 1942

Introduction: What are the pros and cons of using nonviolent methods to create social or political change?

Mini-Lecture:

- Great Britain colonized what is now India in the 19th century, after hundreds of years of ruling indirectly through the British East India Company; this rule was part of British imperialism, or the expansion of their empire, which included a quarter of the earth's land area and population by the early 20th century.
- Mohandas Gandhi (1869–1948) was an Indian political and spiritual leader who led movements for Indian independence from Britain; he is also known by his admirers as "Mahatma," which means "Great Soul."
- Gandhi believed in the Hindu principle of ahimsa (nonviolence); however, he also supported working together with Muslims and other religious groups.
- Gandhi was a leader in the Indian National Congress, a political party that advocated for independence; he also mentored "Pandit" Jawaharlal Nehru, who would later become India's first prime minister.
- In 1942, the British involved India in World War I, using Indian soldiers and resources to further its own goals; this move sparked Gandhi's "Quit India" (leave India) campaign of satyagraha (civil disobedience), in which he urged Indians to passively resist by refusing to follow British laws.
- Our document comes from a speech Gandhi made in Mumbai (Bombay) when launching the Quit India movement.
- Although Gandhi encouraged people to be nonviolent, some did destroy property, and the British blamed and imprisoned Gandhi.
- Nonetheless, India gained independence from Britain in 1947; the following year, Gandhi was assassinated by a Hindu nationalist who saw him as a traitor to his religion.

Vocabulary:

military coup: when someone in the army   *inasmuch as:* because
seizes power by force   *envisaged:* envisioned

critical juncture: important time   *abyss:* deep hole that you will never get
willy-nilly: without compensation   out of
purge: get rid of

Document: Quit India, Mahatma Gandhi, 1930

Ours is not a drive for power, but purely a non-violent fight for India's independence. In a violent struggle, a successful general has been often known to effect a military coup and to set up a dictatorship. But under the Congress scheme of things, essentially non-violent as it is, there can be no room for dictatorship. A non-violent soldier of freedom will covet nothing for himself, he fights only for the freedom of his country. The Congress is unconcerned as to who will rule, when freedom is attained. The power, when it comes, will belong to the people of India, and it will be for them to decide to whom it should be entrusted. . . .

I believe that in the history of the world, there has not been a more genuinely democratic struggle for freedom than ours. I read Carlyle's French Revolution while I was in prison, and Pandit Jawaharlal has told me something about the Russian revolution. But it is my conviction that inasmuch as these struggles were fought with the weapon of violence they failed to realize the democratic ideal. In the democracy which I have envisaged, a democracy established by non-violence, there will be equal freedom for all. Everybody will be his own master. It is to join a struggle for such democracy that I invite you today. Once you realize this you will forget the differences between the Hindus and Muslims, and think of yourselves as Indians only, engaged in the common struggle for independence.

Then, there is the question of your attitude towards the British. I have noticed that there is hatred towards the British among the people. The people say they are disgusted with their behavior. The people make no distinction between British imperialism and the British people. To them, the two are one. . . . Our quarrel is not with the British people, we fight their imperialism. The proposal for the withdrawal of British power did not come out of anger. It came to enable India to play its due part at the present critical juncture. It is not a happy position for a big country like India to be merely helping with money and material obtained willy-nilly from her while the [Allies] are conducting the war. We cannot evoke the true spirit of sacrifice and valor, so long as we are not free. I know the British Government will not be able to withhold freedom from us, when we have made enough self-sacrifice. We must, therefore, purge ourselves of hatred. Speaking for myself, I can say that I have never felt any hatred. As a matter of fact, I feel myself to be a greater friend of the British now than ever before. One reason is that they are today in distress. My very friendship, therefore, demands that I should try to save them from their mistakes. As I view the situation, they are on the brink of an abyss. It, therefore, becomes my duty to warn them of their danger even though it may, for the time being, anger them to the point of cutting off the friendly hand that is stretched out to help them. People may laugh, nevertheless that is my claim. At a time when I may have to launch the biggest struggle of my life, I may not harbor hatred against anybody.

Source: The Economic Times. (2017). Full text of Mahatma Gandhi's inspiring speech when he launched Quit India movement. https://economictimes.indiatimes.com/news/politics-and-nation/full-text -of-mahatma-gandhis-inspiring-speech-when-he-launched-quit-india -movement/a-friend-of-the-british/slideshow/59988997.cms

Comprehension Check:

1. According to Gandhi, how is his movement different from previous revolutions?
2. According to Gandhi, why is he doing the British a favor by advocating for Indian independence?

Activities:

1. What advice would Gandhi and Jean-Jacques Dessalines (Lesson 8.6) give each other about ending colonization? Write their conversation in the form of a comic strip.
2. Gandhi advised people around the world to use nonviolent civil disobedience to bring about change—including Jews facing Hitler's genocide. Brainstorm the kind of situations where Gandhi's tactics are more—and less—likely to succeed.

Reflection: Violent conflicts among Hindus, Muslims, and other religious groups continue in India even today. Why do you think the principle of ahimsa, which Gandhi tried to spread, has not ended these conflicts?

Resources:

AETN. (2019). Mahatma Gandhi. https://www.history.co.uk/biographies/mahatma-gandhi
New World Encyclopedia. (2019). Quit India movement. https://www.newworldencyclopedia .org/entry/Quit_India_Movement

---

LESSON 8.9

Why Did Emiliano Zapata Think Land Reform Was Necessary for Mexico?

Historical Figure: Emiliano Zapata

Event: Mexican Revolution, 1910–1920

Introduction: How long do you think it takes to replace a repressive government with a democratic one? Use examples from history.

Mini-Lecture:

- Spain had colonized the area now known as Mexico in the 16th century, and Mexico fought a war for its independence in the 19th century; however, Spanish-speaking landowners with European heritage still dominated the much more numerous Indigenous people and people of mixed Indigenous and European descent (mestizos).

- In the encomienda system, landowners forced Indigenous people to work on their haciendas (plantations) with little compensation and few rights.
- By 1910, dictator Porfirio Díaz had been in power for 34 years, violating Mexico's constitution; both intellectuals and campesinos (landless peasants) started fighting against his rule.
- Emiliano Zapata was a mestizo whose parents worked on a hacienda; in 1910, he took up arms against the government and helped Díaz's political rival Francisco Madero come to power.
- However, when Madero did not fulfill his promises to respect the campesinos' rights, Zapata and his supporters (called Zapatistas) in the Revolutionary Junta of the State of Morelos drafted the Plan de Ayala (a town in Morelos), from which our document is taken.
- Zapata united with another military leader, Pancho Villa, to implement the Plan de Ayala, the principles of which were included in the Mexican Constitution.
- When the new government of Mexico did not follow these principles, Zapata continued to rebel, and government forces murdered him in 1919; in 1920, the revolution ended when Mexican people democratically elected President Álvaro Obregón.

Vocabulary:

undersign: signed the document below
junta: group of military leaders
transactions: deals
científicos: scientific advisers to Porfirio Díaz
usurped: taken illegally
pueblos: peasants
despoiled: robbed
deduced: figured out
tribunals: courts
in virtue of: because
monopolized: had total economic control over

expropriated: taken away by the government
the third part: one-third
proprietors: owners
indemnization: compensation
ejidos: plot of land that is shared and farmed by a group of people
convoke: organize
bayonet: sword fitted onto the end of a gun
personalist: someone who favors one political leader
partisan: someone who favors one political party

Document: Plan de Ayala, 1911

We who undersign, constituted in a revolutionary junta to sustain and carry out the promises which the revolution of November 20, 1910, just past, made to the country, declare solemnly before the face of the civilized world which judges us and before the nation to which we belong and which we [love], propositions which we have formulated to end the tyranny which oppresses us and redeem the fatherland from the dictatorships which are imposed on us, which are determined in the following plan: . . .

5. The Revolutionary Junta of the State of Morelos will admit no transactions or compromises until it achieves the overthrow of the dictatorial elements of Porfirio Díaz and Francisco I. Madero, for the nation is tired of false men and traitors who make promises like liberators and who on arriving in power forget them and constitute themselves tyrants.

6. As an additional part of the plan, we invoke, we give notice: that [regarding] the fields, timber, and water which the landlords, científicos, or bosses have usurped, the pueblos or citizens who have the titles corresponding to those properties will immediately enter into possession of that real estate of which they have been despoiled by the bad faith of our oppressors, maintain at any cost with arms in hand the mentioned possession; and the usurpers who consider themselves with a right to them [those properties] will deduce it before the special tribunals which will be established on the triumph of the revolution.

7. In virtue of the fact that the immense majority of Mexican pueblos and citizens are owners of no more than the land they walk on, suffering the horrors of poverty without being able to improve their social condition in any way or to dedicate themselves to Industry or Agriculture, because lands, timber, and water are monopolized in a few hands, for this cause there will be expropriated the third part of those monopolies from the powerful proprietors of them, with prior indemnization, in order that the pueblos and citizens of Mexico may obtain ejidos, colonies, and foundations for pueblos, or fields for sowing or laboring, and the Mexicans' lack of prosperity and well-being may improve in all and for all. . . .

12. Once triumphant the revolution which we carry into the path of reality, a Junta of the principal revolutionary chiefs from the different States will name or designate an interim President of the Republic, who will convoke elections for the organization of the federal powers. . . .

15. Mexicans: consider that the cunning and bad faith of one man is shedding blood in a scandalous manner, because he is incapable of governing; consider that his system of government is choking the fatherland and trampling with the brute force of bayonets on our institutions; and thus, as we raised up our weapons to elevate him to power, we again raise them up against him for defaulting on his promises to the Mexican people and for having betrayed the revolution initiated by him, we are not personalists, we are partisans of principles and not of men!

Source: Brown University Library. (n.d.). Document #6: "Plan de Ayala," Emiliano Zapata (1911). https://library.brown.edu/create/modernlatinamerica/chapters/chapter-3 -mexico/primary-documents-with-accompanying-discussion-questions /document-6-plan-de-ayala-emilio-zapata-1911/

Comprehension Check:

1. Under this plan, what will happen to the land that peasants have been farming but landowners have controlled?
2. Who is the "one man" that the Plan refers to in section 15?

Activities:

1. Create a timeline and sketch out the continuities and changes in the lives of Indigenous peasants in the Maya Empire (Lesson 5.3), the Aztec Empire (Lesson 6.9), under Spanish rule, under Díaz's dictatorship, and after the Mexican Revolution.
2. Research the Mexican government today. Do you think Zapata would believe it is carrying out the Plan de Ayala? Why or why not?

Reflection: Zapata wanted to redistribute land to the peasants, but he did not call for the landowners to be killed as long as they followed the Plan de Ayala. How do you view his attitude in comparison to that of Maximilien Robespierre's (Lesson 8.5) and Jean-Jacques Dessalines (Lesson 8.6) in the French and Haitian Revolutions?

Resources:

Alba, V. (2019). Emiliano Zapata. https://www.britannica.com/biography/Emiliano-Zapata
EDSITEment! (2012). The Mexican Revolution, November 20th, 1910. https://edsitement
    .neh.gov/closer-readings/mexican-revolution-november-20th-1910

LESSON 8.10

How Did Joseph Stalin Try to Revolutionize Soviet Society?

Historical Figure: Joseph Stalin

Event: Famine in the Ukraine, 1931–1932

Introduction: Is it better that societies change quickly, or slowly? Why? Give some examples from history or your own experience.

Mini-Lecture:

*   In 1917, a group of Russian communists called the Bolsheviks, who included Vladimir Lenin and Joseph Stalin, staged a revolution in which they overthrew and killed members of the Romanov Dynasty, a monarchy that had ruled Russia for the previous 300 years.
*   The Bolsheviks, led by Lenin, tried to implement the ideas of Karl Marx (see Lesson 5.7) by establishing the Union of Soviet Socialist Republics (USSR), redistributing land from wealthy landowners to the peasants who farmed it, and taking away the property of businesspeople.
*   The formation of the USSR involved taking over countries including Armenia, Azerbaijan, Belarus, and the Ukraine.

- In 1924, when Lenin died, Joseph Stalin became the head of the Communist Party and the dictator of the Soviet Union.
- Stalin's totalitarian style of government involved surveillance and brutal punishment of anyone who disagreed with his ideas or methods; he is considered responsible for the deaths of hundreds of thousands of people who he had deported to remote prison camps.
- Stalin oversaw the creation of a command economy, in which the government controlled production and distribution of goods; through a series of Five Year Plans, he tried to quickly industrialize the country and collectivize agriculture (see Lesson 6.12).
- Our document comes from a speech Stalin made to officials in charge of the command economy in 1931.
- Stalin set quotas of grain to be produced by each region; when Ukraine could not meet its quota, Stalin ordered all their remaining grain to be confiscated, resulting in the Holodomor, a famine that killed between 3 and 4 million people.

Vocabulary:

tempo: pace
dictated to us: required
backwardness: being old-fashioned rather than modern
khan: leader of Mongolian Empire
bey: Turkish leader

gentry: nobles
impunity: without consequences
impotent: powerless
wary: afraid
make good: make up

Document: Modernize or Perish, Joseph Stalin, 1931

It is sometimes asked whether it is not possible to slow down the tempo a bit, to put a check on the movement. No, comrades, it is not possible! The tempo must not be reduced! On the contrary, we must increase it as much as is within our powers and possibilities. This is dictated to us by our obligations to the workers and peasants of the USSR. This is dictated to us by our obligations to the working class of the whole world.

To slacken the tempo would mean falling behind. And those who fall behind get beaten. But we do not want to be beaten. No, we refuse to be beaten! One feature of the history of old Russia was the continual beatings she suffered because of her backwardness. She was beaten by the Mongol khans. She was beaten by the Turkish beys. She was beaten by the Swedish feudal lords. She was beaten by the Polish and Lithuanian gentry. She was beaten by the British and French capitalists. She was beaten by the Japanese barons. All beat her because of her backwardness, military backwardness, cultural backwardness, political backwardness, industrial backwardness, agricultural backwardness. They beat her because to do so was profitable and could be done with impunity. Do you remember the words of the prerevolutionary poet: "You are poor and abundant, mighty and impotent, Mother Russia." Those gentlemen were quite familiar with the verses of the old poet. They beat her, saying: "You are abundant; so one can enrich oneself at your expense. They beat her, saying: "You are poor and impotent" so you can be beaten and plundered with impunity. Such is the law of the exploiters—to beat the backward and the weak. It is the jungle law of capitalism. You are backward, you are weak—therefore you are wrong; hence, you can be beaten and enslaved. You are mighty— therefore you are right; hence, we must be wary of you. That is why we must no longer lag behind.

In the past we had no fatherland, nor could we have one. But now that we have overthrown capitalism and power is in our hands, in the hands of the people, we have a fatherland, and we will defend its independence. Do you want our socialist fatherland to be beaten and to lose its independence? If you do not want this you must put an end to its backwardness in the shortest possible time and develop genuine Bolshevik tempo in building up its socialist system of economy. There is no other way. That is why Lenin said on the eve of the October Revolution: "Either perish, or overtake and outstrip the advanced capitalist countries."

We are fifty or a hundred years behind the advanced countries. We must make good this distance in ten years. Either we do it, or we shall be crushed.

Source: Lockport Schools. (n.d.). Modernize or perish.
https://www.lockportschools.org/cms/lib/NY19000563/Centricity
/Domain/256/Reading%20Modernize%20or%20Perish.pdf

Comprehension Check:

1. According to Stalin, how have other countries viewed Russia in the past, and why?
2. According to Stalin, why must the USSR modernize as quickly as possible?

Activities:

1. Do you think Stalin succeeded in carrying out Marx's vision for society (Lesson 5.7)? Why or why not? Write a letter from Marx to Stalin praising or criticizing his policies.
2. Work with a partner to create a Venn diagram comparing Mao's (Lesson 6.12) and Stalin's command economies.

Reflection: Do you think Stalin's plans would have been more successful if he had not insisted that they be carried out so quickly? Why or why not?

Resources:

British Library. (n.d.). Russian Revolution. https://www.bl.uk/russian-revolution
Kiger, P. J. (2019). How Stalin starved millions in the Ukrainian famine. https://www.history
    .com/news/ukrainian-famine-stalin

LESSON 8.11

Why Did Algerians Believe That Violence Was Necessary to Decolonize Their Country?

Historical Figure: Frantz Fanon

Event: Algeria wins independence from French colonization, 1962

Introduction: Do violent revolutionaries usually start with violence, or do they try other tactics first? Give some examples from history to support your argument.

Mini-Lecture:

- France began colonizing what is now Algeria in 1830; facing resistance from the local population, France used violence to subdue them.
- Algerians tried to use legal means to reform the colonial system, gain political rights, and achieve better conditions.
- During World War II, France promised that if Algerians fought on their side, they would get the rights they were seeking; however, after the war, France did not follow through.
- After attempts at political reform were unsuccessful, the Front de Líberation Nationale (FLN, or the National Liberation Front) formed in 1954; it engaged in violent struggle against the French authorities and succeeded in ending colonization in 1962.
- Guy Mollet was the prime minister of France from 1956 to 1957; he first tried to negotiate with the FLN, then led a counterterrorism campaign in which FLN members were killed and tortured.
- Frantz Fanon, a Black man born in the French colony of Martinique, was a writer and psychiatrist who worked with the National Liberation Front to end the colonization of Algeria.
- Our document comes from his book *The Wretched of the Earth*, in which he describes the rationale behind the FLN's violent resistance to colonialism.

Vocabulary:

By dint of: through

Document: *The Wretched of the Earth*, Frantz Fanon, 1961

Decolonization, which sets out to change the order of the world, is, obviously, a program of complete disorder. But it cannot come as a result of magical practices, nor of a natural shock, nor of a friendly understanding. . . . Decolonization is the meeting of two forces, opposed to each other by their very nature. . . . Their first encounter was marked by violence and their existence together—that is to say the exploitation of the native by the settler—was carried on by dint of a great array of bayonets and cannons. The settler and the native are old acquaintances. In fact, the settler is right when he speaks of knowing "them" well. For it is the settler who has brought the native into existence and who perpetuates his existence. The settler owes the fact of his very existence, that is to say, his property, to the colonial system. . . .

And it is clear that in the colonial countries the peasants alone are revolutionary, for they have nothing to lose and everything to gain. The starving peasant, outside the class system, is the first among the exploited to discover that only violence pays. For him there is no compromise, no possible coming to terms; colonization and decolonization are simply a question of relative strength. The exploited man sees that his liberation implies the use of all means, and that of force first and foremost. When in 1956, after the capitulation of Monsieur Guy Mollet to the settlers in Algeria, the Front de Libération Nationale, in a famous leaflet, stated that colonialism only loosens its hold when the knife is at its throat, no Algerian really found these terms too violent. The leaflet only expressed what every Algerian felt at heart: colonialism is not a thinking machine, nor a body endowed with reasoning faculties. It is violence in its natural state, and it will only yield when confronted with greater violence.

Source: Abahlali.org. (n.d.). *The wretched of the earth.*
http://abahlali.org/wp-content/uploads/2011/04/Frantz-Fanon
-The-Wretched-of-the-Earth-1965.pdf

Comprehension Check:

1. According to Fanon, why is violence necessary to end colonization?
2. Which group does Fanon think is most likely to revolt against the colonizers, and why?

Activities:

1. Create a chart comparing the goals, tactics, and results of the FLN and the Palestinian Liberation Organization (Lesson 4.12).
2. Divide the class in half, and debate Fanon's proposition, "colonialism only loosens its hold when the knife is at its throat."

Reflection: Fanon says that the colonizer "brought the native into existence," and that the settler "owes the fact of his existence" to the native. What does he mean?

Resources:

Peterson, C. (2019). Frantz Fanon. https://www.britannica.com/biography/Frantz-Fanon
The Choices Program, Brown University. (2017). Why did France colonize Algeria? https://www.choices.edu/video/france-colonize-algeria/

LESSON 8.12

How Did Rigoberta Menchú Resist the Human Rights Abuses of the Guatemalan Government?

Historical Figure: Rigoberta Menchú

Event: Guatemalan Civil War, 1960–1996

Introduction: If you had no weapons, what would you use to fight if your life was being threatened?

Mini-Lecture:

- Rigoberta Menchú Tum, usually known by her first two names, is a human rights activist born in Guatemala in 1959; she belongs to the k'iche' (or Quiché) Maya Indigenous group.
- The Guatemalan Civil War occurred between the government of Guatemala and rebel groups fighting for the rights of poor and Indigenous people, who had been impoverished by land ownership policies that favored large companies over local people.
- The Guatemalan government "disappeared" (kidnapped and murdered) at least 40,000 people they accused of collaborating with armed rebel groups; they targeted Maya Indigenous people in particular.
- Alongside her family, Menchú worked to document and end these human rights abuses; the Guatemalan army murdered two of Menchú's brothers and both her parents because of their activism.
- In 1982, Menchú narrated her autobiography to an anthropologist; our document is taken from this book.
- Menchú won the Nobel Peace Prize in 1992, and she helped to broker peace in Guatemala in 1996; since then, she has focused on holding the military leaders responsible for human rights abuses and continuing to advocate for the rights of women, poor people, and Indigenous people.

Vocabulary:

testimony: statement about things one has personally witnessed

ladino: Spanish-speaking Indigenous person

fincas: plantations

péones: someone who is forced to work for very little pay

Document: I, Rigoberta Menchú, Rigoberta Menchú and Elisabeth Burgos, 1983

> My name is Rigoberta Menchú. I am twenty-three years old. This is my testimony. I didn't learn it from a book and I didn't learn it alone. I'd like

to stress that it's not only my life, it's also the testimony of my people. . . . my story is the story of all poor Guatemalans. . . .

My parents moved [to El Quiché] in 1960 and began cultivating the land. No-one had lived up there before because it's so mountainous. But they settled there and were determined not to leave no matter how hard the life was. . . . They'd been forced to leave the town because some ladino families came to settle there. . . .

The land up there belonged to the government and you had to get permission to settle there. When you'd got permission, you had to pay a fee so that you could clear the land and then build your house. Through all my parents' efforts in the fincas, they managed to get enough money together to pay the fee, and they cleared the land. . . .

The government says the land belongs to the nation. It owns the land and gives it to us to cultivate. But when we've cleared and cultivated the land, that's when the landowners appear. However, the landowners don't just appear on their own—they have connections with the different authorities that allow them to maneuver like that. . . . This meant we could either stay and work as peónes or leave our land. . . . So my father travelled all over the place seeking advice. We didn't realize then that going to the government authorities was the same as going to the landowners. . . . My father was tireless in his efforts to seek help. He went to other sectors, like the workers' unions. He asked them to help because we were already being thrown off our land. . . .

We began to understand that the root of all our problems was exploitation. That there were rich and poor and that the rich exploited the poor—our sweat, our labor. . . . So was the cultural oppression which tries to divide us by taking away our traditions and prevents unity among our people. The situation got worse when the murderous generals came to power. . . .

And one day a troop of soldiers arrived. . . . We couldn't resist but we did nothing to provoke them either. The community knew more or less what to do if any one of us was taken. The idea from the beginning was that they either left us alone or they'd have to kill all of us. . . .

That's when we started preparing things we had to do secretly, like the traps. . . . They were usually large ditches with invisible nets so that neither animals nor soldiers could see them. They might also be something metal to stop the army. . . .

We thought of what would happen if at any time, we couldn't use our traps, or rather that they didn't work. If we couldn't use our escape route or any other of our security measures, we should at least have our weapons ready—the weapons of the people: machetes, stones, hot water, chili, salt. We found a use for all these things.

Source: Minerva at KGI. (n.d.). *I, Rigoberta Menchú*. https://course-resources.minerva.kgi .edu/uploaded_files/mke/nAXkZr/i-rigoberta-menchu-excerpts.pdf

Comprehension Check:

1. How did Menchú's parents come to settle in El Quiché?
2. According to Menchú, why didn't the government help her family when the landowners kicked them out?

Activities:

1. Imagine a conversation between Mohandas Gandhi (Lesson 8.8) and Rigoberta Menchú, and sketch it out in the form of a comic strip.
2. Create a visual Venn diagram showing a comparison of the survival tactics of Indigenous people in Southeast Asia (Lesson 8.7) and Guatemala.

Reflection: What do you think gave Menchú the confidence to persist in her activism despite the opposition and violence she encountered?

Resources:

Nobel Women's Initiative. Rigoberta Menchú Tum. https://nobelwomensinitiative.org /laureate/rigoberta-menchu-tum/
PBS News Hour. (2011). Timeline: Guatemala's brutal civil war. https://www.pbs.org /newshour/health/latin_america-jan-june11-timeline_03-07

LESSON 8.13

How Did Václav Havel Spread Dissent Against the Totalitarian Regime in Czechoslovakia?

Historical Figure: Václav Havel

Event: Velvet Revolution, 1989

Introduction: If you disagreed with your government, but saying so out loud would cause you to lose your job and endanger your family, would you still do it? Why or why not?

Mini-Lecture:

- Czechoslovakia (today the Czech Republic and Slovakia) was ruled by a totalitarian communist regime from 1948 until 1989; this government tried to control all aspects of people's lives.
- Czechoslovakia was part of the Eastern Bloc, a group of countries heavily influenced by the USSR during the Cold War, a struggle that occurred in various parts of the world between capitalist countries led by the United States and communist countries led by the USSR beginning after World War II.
- Václav Havel was a Czech writer and dissident (someone who expresses disagreement with the government).
- Our document comes from an essay Havel wrote in 1978, "The Power of the Powerless," in which he suggested that people living under repressive

governments "always have the power within themselves to remedy their own powerlessness" by "living in truth," or refusing to go along with the lies of their government; he uses a fictional example of a shop owner to make his point.
- The essay was illegally photocopied and distributed throughout communist countries in Eastern Europe, where the government censored all official publications, through a network called samizdat, which means "self-publishing" in Russian.
- In the essay, Havel mentions the slogan "Workers of the world, unite!" a line from Karl Marx's *The Communist Manifesto* (see Lesson 5.7), which was used to try to inspire people in many communist countries.
- Shortly after this essay was distributed, the government imprisoned Havel, but he continued his dissident activities, and in 1989 he was one of the leaders of the Velvet Revolution, which earned its name because peaceful protesters were able to bring down the communist dictatorship without violence.
- Havel became president after this revolution and served until 2003, by which point Slovakia had peacefully become independent of the Czech Republic.

Vocabulary:

irrepressible: impossible to ignore
impulse: desire
acquaint: introduce
enterprise headquarters: the central authority in charge of businesses
ingratiate himself: win favor from powerful people

farce: a joke; a fake
solidarity: sympathy and unity among people who face similar problems
suppressed: hidden
bill: price one has to pay
relieved of his post: fired
evaporate: disappear

Document: The Power of the Powerless, Václav Havel, 1978

The manager of a fruit-and-vegetable shop places in his window, among the onions and carrots, the slogan: "Workers of the world, unite!" Why does he do it? What is he trying to communicate to the world? Is he genuinely enthusiastic about the idea of unity among the workers of the world? Is his enthusiasm so great that he feels an irrepressible impulse to acquaint the public with his ideals? Has he really given more than a moment's thought to how such a unification might occur and what it would mean? I think it can safely be assumed that the overwhelming majority of shopkeepers never think about the slogans they put in their windows, nor do they use them to express their real opinions. That poster was delivered to our greengrocer from the enterprise headquarters along with the onions and carrots. He put them all into the window simply because it has been done that way for years, because everyone does it, and because that is the way it has to be. If he were to refuse, there could be trouble. He could be reproached for not having the proper decoration in his window; someone might even accuse him of disloyalty. He does it because these things must be done if one is to get along in life. . . .

Let us now imagine that one day something in our greengrocer snaps and he stops putting up the slogans merely to ingratiate himself. He stops voting in elections he knows are a farce. He begins to say what he really thinks at political meetings. And he even finds the strength in himself to express solidarity with those whom his conscience commands him to support. In this revolt the greengrocer steps out of living within the lie. He rejects the ritual and breaks the rules of the game. He discovers once more his suppressed identity and dignity. He gives his freedom a concrete significance. His revolt is an attempt to live within the truth. The bill is not long in coming. He will be relieved of his post as manager of the shop and transferred to the warehouse. His pay will be reduced. His hopes for a holiday in Bulgaria will evaporate. His children's access to higher education will be threatened. His superiors will harass him and his fellow workers will wonder about him.

Source: Nonviolent-conflict.org. (n.d.). Power of the powerless. https://www.nonviolent
-conflict.org/wp-content/uploads/1979/01/the-power-of-the-powerless.pdf
Copyright 1985 From Power of the Powerless *by Václav Havel. Reproduced by permission of Taylor and Francis Group, LLC, a division of Informa plc*

Comprehension Check:

1. According to Havel, why does the greengrocer put the sign in his window?
2. According to Havel, what are the pros and cons for the greengrocer of taking the sign down?

Activities:

1. Work with a partner to create and illustrate a "spectrum of dissent" ranging from following all official and unspoken rules to openly defying the system. In what other small and large ways might people show their resistance?
2. Make a Venn diagram comparing and contrasting Gandhi's (Lesson 8.8) and Havel's approach to creating political change.

Reflection: What percentage of people in totalitarian societies do you think choose to, as Havel describes it, "live within the truth"? On what do you base your estimate?

Resources:

Aleeva, E. (2017). Samizdat: How did people in the Soviet Union circumvent state censorship? https://www.rbth.com/arts/literature/2017/07/10/samizdat_797635
Encyclopedia Britannica. (2018). Václav Havel. https://www.britannica.com/biography/Vaclav-Havel

Continuity and Change

Unit Question: What Are the Long-Term Changes and Recurring Patterns in World History?

This unit is meant to conclude the course by helping students think about how the themes they have studied map onto chronology. Using a unit question and a set of eras taken from the National World History Content Standards (UCLA, 2019), students reexamine several documents from each period in order to understand global trends.

There is no need for a summit in this unit, but students could work in groups to create a presentation about one of the eras as a year-end project.

LESSON 9.1
How Did Human Societies Begin?

Era: Early human societies emerge, c. 45,000 BCE–4,000 BCE

Documents:

a. Grinding stone and fish hooks, Australian Aboriginal people, c. 30,000–1000 BCE (Lesson 6.2)
b. Agricultural tools, c. 5000 BCE (Lesson 6.3)

LESSON 9.2
How Did Early Civilizations and Pastoral Peoples Emerge
in the Fifth to the First Millennia BCE?

Era: Early civilizations and the emergence of pastoral peoples, 4000–1000 BCE

Documents:

a. Cuneiform tax receipt, c. 3000 BCE (Lesson 3.2)
b. Hymn to the Nile, 2100 BCE (Lesson 6.4)
c. Code of Hammurabi, 1750 BCE (Lesson 1.2)

LESSON 9.3

How Did Classical Traditions, Major Religions, and Giant Empires Emerge in the First Millennium BCE?

Era: Classical traditions, major religions, and giant empires, 1000 BCE–300 CE

Documents:

a. *Pericles' Funeral Oration*, 431 BCE (Lesson 1.3)
b. Luxuriant Gems of the Spring and Autumn Annals, Dong Zhongshu, 2nd century BCE (Lesson 1.5)
c. Rock Edicts, Aśoka, 2nd century BCE (Lesson 4.3)

LESSON 9.4

How Did Zones of Exchange and Encounter Expand in the First Millennium CE?

Era: Expanding zones of exchange and encounter, 300–1000 CE

Documents:

a. Alaric's Sack of Rome, Procopius, c. 550 (Lesson 3.4)
b. Presentation of captives to a Maya ruler, c. 785 (Lesson 5.3)
c. *The Book of the Maghrib*, Ibn Said, 13th century (Lesson 1.8)

LESSON 9.5

How Did Hemispheric Interactions Intensify in the Second Millennium CE?

Era: Intensified hemispheric interactions, 1000–1500 CE

Documents:

a. Letter on the Second Crusade, Bernard of Clairvaux, 1147 (Lesson 4.6)
b. Commentary on Plato's *Republic*, Ibn Rushd, 1169–1195 (Lesson 7.3)
c. *Travels in Asia and Africa*, Ibn Battuta, 1354 (Lesson 6.6)

LESSON 9.6

Why Did the First Global Age Emerge in the 15th to 18th Centuries?

Era: The emergence of the first global age, 1450–1770

Documents:

a. Requerimiento, Council of Castille, 1510 (Lesson 3.7)
b. *The Turkish Letters*, Ogier Ghiselin de Busbecq, c. 1555 (Lesson 3.6)
c Letter from Queen Njinga [Nzinga] of Ndongo to Bento Banha Cardoso, 1626 (Lesson 7.5)

LESSON 9.7

What Were the Causes and Effects of Revolutions in the 18th to 20th Centuries?

Era: The age of revolutions, 1750–1914

Documents:

a. *The Wealth of Nations*, Adam Smith, 1776 (Lesson 6.11)
b. Haitian Declaration of Independence, Jean-Jacques Dessalines, 1804 (Lesson 8.6)
c. *The Communist Manifesto*, Karl Marx and Friedrich Engels, 1848 (Lesson 5.7)

LESSON 9.8

What Were the Crises and Achievements of the First Half of the 20th Century?

Era: A half-century of crisis and achievement, 1900–1945

Documents:

a. Constitution of the Black Hand, 1911 (Lesson 4.9)
b. *The Survivors*, Käthe Kollwitz, 1923 (Lesson 7.10)
c. Obersalzberg Speech, Adolf Hitler, 1939 (Lesson 3.12)

LESSON 9.9

What Have Been the Promises and Paradoxes of the Second Half of the 20th Century?

Era: Promises and paradoxes, the 20th century since 1945

Documents:

a. Universal Declaration of Human Rights, 1948 (Lesson 3.13)
b. Speech to the UN General Assembly, Yasser Arafat, 1974 (Lesson 4.12)
c. Constitution of the Democratic Republic of Kampuchea, 1978 (Lesson 5.10)

Appendixes

Key:
- ⏱ Event
- † Historical Figure
- 🖺 Document

APPENDIX A: QUICK REFERENCE GUIDE

Unit 1: Forms of Government

Unit Question: What should be the relationship between the rulers and the ruled?

1.1 21st-Century Issue: What are activists asking the United Nations to do about the murder of journalist Jamal Khashoggi?
- ⏱ 2018: Jamal Khashoggi killed in Saudi embassy
- † Jamal Khashoggi
- 🖺 Open letter to Secretary General Guterres, PEN America, 2018

1.2 What kind of laws did King Hammurabi make for his subjects?
- ⏱ 1750 BCE: Hammurabi publishes code of law
- † Hammurabi
- 🖺 Code of Hammurabi, 1750 BCE

1.3 How did Pericles describe direct democracy in Athens?
- ⏱ 431–404 BCE: Peloponnesian War
- † Pericles
- 🖺 *Pericles' Funeral Oration*, 431 BCE

1.4 How did Sparta's oligarchy work?
- ⏱ 9th century BCE: Lycurgus rules Sparta
- † Lycurgus
- 🖺 Spartan Constitution, Xenophon, c. 378 BCE

1.5 What was the role of the imperial monarch in Han Dynasty China?
- ⏱ 202 BCE–9 CE: Han Dynasty rules in China
- † Emperor Wu of Han
- 🖺 Luxuriant Gems of the Spring and Autumn Annals, Dong Zhongshu, 2nd century BCE

1.6 How did the Roman Republic resemble a monarchy, an aristocracy, and a democracy?
- ⏱ 509 BCE–27 BCE: Roman Republic
- † Polybius
- 🖺 *The Histories*, Polybius, 2nd century BCE

1.7   How did Suryavarman II rule as a *devaraja*?
      🕑 12th century: Angkor Wat built
      🜚 Suryavarman II
      🖹 Bas-Relief of Suryavarman II, 12th century

1.8   How did Muawiyah I govern his caliphate?
      🕑 661–750: Umayyad Caliphate
      🜚 Muawiyah I
      🖹 *The Book of the Maghrib*, Ibn Said, 13th century

1.9   How did Louis XIV create an absolute monarchy in France?
      🕑 1643–1715: Reign of Louis XIV
      🜚 Louis XIV
      🖹 Revocation of the Edict of Nantes, Louis XIV, 1685

1.10 How did Igbo women command respect in a stateless society?
      🕑 late 19th century: Eze Nwanyi mask created, Nigeria
      🜚 (legendary) Eze Nwanyi, Queen of Women
      🖹 Queen of Women mask, 19th century

1.11 How is India's democracy structured?
      🕑 1949: India becomes a democracy
      🜚 Indira Gandhi
      🖹 Democracy in India, Indira Gandhi, 1971

1.12 How does Finland guarantee social welfare to its citizens?
      🕑 2000: Finnish Constitution ratified
      🜚 Sanna Marin
      🖹 Constitution of Finland, 2000

1.13 How have Inuit people practiced egalitarianism?
      🕑 1999: Nunavut territory created
      🜚 Sheila Watt-Cloutier
      🖹 Turaaqtavut, 2018

Unit 2: Religion and Society

Unit Question: How should belief systems influence our lives?

2.1   What were Albert Einstein's arguments for agnosticism?
      🕑 1908: Albert Einstein develops his theory of special relativity
      🜚 Albert Einstein
      🖹 Quotations on religion, Albert Einstein, 20th century

2.2   How is Brahman described in the Hindu Upanishads?
      🕑 1500–500 BCE: Vedic period
      🜚 Maitreyi
      🖹 Mundaka Upanishad, 800 BCE–500 BCE

2.3   How did Confucius envision the ideal society?
      🕑 551–479 BCE: Life of Confucius
      🜚 Confucius
      🖹 Analects, Confucius, c. 200 BCE

2.4   What did the Dao De Jing advise people to do?
      🕐 C. 500 BCE: Laozi writes the Dao De Jing
      ⸸ Laozi
      🗎 Dao De Jing, Laozi, c. 500 BCE
2.5   What did the Buddha teach was the path to enlightenment?
      🕐 5th century BCE: The Buddha reaches enlightenment
      ⸸ Siddhartha Gautama
      🗎 Setting in Motion the Wheel of Dharma, 5th century BCE
2.6   What did God command Jewish people to do in the Torah?
      🕐 c. 1200 BCE: Torah says God gave Ten Commandments to Moses
      ⸸ Moses
      🗎 Exodus 20, c. 1200 BCE
2.7   What did Jesus command Christians to do in the Holy Bible?
      🕐 1st century CE: Jesus's Sermon on the Mount
      ⸸ Jesus Christ
      🗎 Sermon on the Mount, 1st century CE
2.8   What did Allah command Muslims to do in the Holy Quran?
      🕐 610: Quran says Allah revealed the Quran to Muhammad
      ⸸ The Prophet Muhammad
      🗎 The Holy Quran, 610

Unit 3: Us vs. Them

Unit Question: Who is civilized, and who is a barbarian?

3.1   21st-Century Issue: How did François Hollande react to ISIS's attack on France?
      🕐 2015: ISIS attacks in Paris
      ⸸ François Hollande
      🗎 Speech by the President of the Republic to a joint session of Parliament, François Hollande, 2015
3.2   How was Sumerian civilization different from what came before it?
      🕐 c. 4300–1500 BCE: Sumerian civilization
      ⸸ Gilgamesh
      🗎 Cuneiform tax receipt, c. 3000 BCE
3.3   How did Alexander the Great try to civilize the world?
      🕐 336–323 BCE: Alexander the Great's reign
      ⸸ Alexander the Great
      🗎 On Alexander, Plutarch, 90 CE
3.4   Why did ancient Romans blame the collapse of their empire on barbarians?
      🕐 5th–6th centuries: Decline of Western Roman Empire
      ⸸ Alaric I
      🗎 Procopius, Alaric's Sack of Rome, c. 550 CE

3.5 Why did Portuguese colonists portray Africans as uncivilized?
- 🕐 1444: Portuguese colonize Guinea
- ⚲ Prince Henry the Navigator
- 📄 Chronicle of the Discovery of Conquest of Guinea, Gomes de Zurara, 1450

3.6 How did ideas of civilization differ in the Ottoman and Austrian empires?
- 🕐 1299–1922: Ottoman Empire
- ⚲ Suleiman the Magnificent
- 📄 The Turkish Letter, Ogier Ghiselin de Busbecq, c. 1555

3.7 Did Spanish colonization of the Americas bring civilization or barbarism?
- 🕐 1492: Spanish colonization of the Americas begins
- ⚲ King Ferdinand of Spain
- 📄 Requerimiento, Council of Castille, 1510

3.8 Why did Qing Dynasty Chinese see the people from Europe as barbarians?
- 🕐 1644–1912: Qing Dynasty
- ⚲ Qianlong Emperor
- 📄 Edict from the Qianlong Emperor, 1793

3.9 How did Enlightenment Philosophers redefine civilization?
- 🕐 18th century: the Enlightenment
- ⚲ Immanuel Kant
- 📄 *What Is Enlightenment?*, Immanuel Kant, 1784

3.10 Why did French people think they needed to civilize "inferior races"?
- 🕐 1887–1945: French colonization of Indochina
- ⚲ Jules Ferry
- 📄 Speech before the French Chamber of Deputies, Jules Ferry, 1884

3.11 How did Meiji Japanese leaders define civilization?
- 🕐 1868–1912: Meiji Restoration
- ⚲ Emperor Meiji
- 📄 Meiji Constitution, 1889

3.12 What kind of civilization did Hitler envision for the world?
- 🕐 1933–1945: Third Reich in Germany
- ⚲ Adolf Hitler
- 📄 Obersalzberg speech, Adolf Hitler, 1939

3.13 How does the Universal Declaration of Human Rights describe a civilized society?
- 🕐 1948: UDHR
- ⚲ Charles Malik
- 📄 Universal Declaration of Human Rights, 1948

Unit 4: Conflict

Unit Question: What is worth fighting for?

4.1 21st-Century Issue: What are the effects of the war in Yemen on civilians?
- 🕐 2015: Civil war in Yemen begins
- ⚲ Tawakkol Karman
- 📄 Eleven Facts about the Yemen Crisis, UN Humanitarian, 2019

4.2   How did the Greeks try to convince the Ionians to join their fight against the Persians?
       🕐 480 BCE: Battle of Thermopylae
       👤 Themistocles
       📋 Themistocles' appeal to the Ionians, Herodotus, 440 BCE
4.3   Why did King Aśoka want to stop wars?
       🕐 322 BCE–180 BCE: Mauryan Empire
       👤 Aśoka
       📋 Rock Edicts, Aśoka, 2nd century BCE
4.4   Why did Hannibal attack the Roman Empire?
       🕐 2nd century BCE: Hannibal attacks Roman empire
       👤 Hannibal
       📋 *The Histories*, Polybius, 2nd century BCE
4.5   Why did the Normans Attack the Anglo-Saxons in the Battle of Hastings?
       🕐 1066: Battle of Hastings
       👤 William the Conqueror
       📋 Bayeux Tapestry, 11th century, female needleworkers
4.6   How did Christians justify the Crusades?
       🕐 1147–1149: Second Crusade
       👤 Bernard of Clairvaux
       📋 Letter on the Second Crusade, Bernard of Clairvaux, 1147
4.7   How did Napoleon motivate soldiers to fight for him?
       🕐 1803–1815: Napoleonic Wars
       👤 Napoleon
       📋 Speeches at the Battle of Austerlitz, Napoleon, 1805
4.8   Why did King Leopold II fight for control of the Congo?
       🕐 1885: King Leopold announces creation of the Congo Free State
       👤 King Leopold II
       📋 Report on the Congo Commission of Enquiry, 1905
4.9   Why did Serbian nationalists ignite World War I?
       🕐 1914: Assassination of Archduke Franz Ferdinand
       👤 Gavrilo Princip
       📋 Constitution of the Black Hand, 1911
4.10   Why did Costa Rica abolish its military?
       🕐 1948: Costa Rica abolishes its military
       👤 José Figueres Ferrer
       📋 Costa Rican Constitution, 1948
4.11   Why were Jewish people willing to fight for a country of their own?
       🕐 1948: State of Israel created
       👤 Theodor Herzl
       📋 *The Jewish State*, Theodor Herzl, 1895
4.12   Why have Palestinians fought against Israel?
       🕐 1964: Creation of the Palestinian Liberation Organization
       👤 Yasser Arafat
       📋 Speech to the UN General Assembly, Yasser Arafat, 1974

4.13 Why were Hutus willing to kill Tutsis in Rwanda?
     🕐 1994: Rwandan Genocide
     👤 Hassan Ngeze
     📄 Hutu Ten Commandments, 1990

Unit 5: Hierarchy vs. Equality

Unit Question: What should be the balance between social equality and social hierarchy?

5.1 21st-Century Issue: How are ordinary people in South Sudan working together for justice?
     🕐 2011: South Sudan becomes an independent country
     👤 Lilian Riziq
     📄 Voices of South Sudan, anonymous Sudanese people, 2011
5.2 How did Athenian democrats justify slavery?
     🕐 5th–4th century BCE: Athenian democracy
     👤 Aristotle
     📄 On Politics, Aristotle, c. 330 BCE
5.3 What social classes existed in the Maya Empire?
     🕐 c. 250–900: Maya Empire
     👤 Bird Jaguar IV
     📄 Presentation of captives to a Maya ruler, c. 785
5.4 How did Mongol pastoralists organize their nomadic society?
     🕐 1206: Chinggis Khan proclaims the Mongol empire
     👤 Chinggis Khan
     📄 *The Mongol Mission*, Giovanni da Pian del Carpini, 1247
5.5 How did the Incan *allyu* system work?
     🕐 14th–16th century: Incan empire
     👤 Pachacuti Inca Yupanqui
     📄 *Chronicles of the Incas*, Pedro de Cieze de Leon, 1540
5.6 How did the Tokugawa Shogunate practice feudalism?
     🕐 1603–1868: Tokugawa Shogunate
     👤 Tokugawa Ieyasu
     📄 Military Government and Social Order, Tokugawa Ieyasu, c. 1610
5.7 Why did Karl Marx envision a classless society?
     🕐 1848: *Communist Manifesto* published
     👤 Karl Marx
     📄 *The Communist Manifesto*, Karl Marx and Friedrich Engels, 1848
5.8 How did white South Africans justify apartheid rule?
     🕐 1948–1994: Apartheid rule in South Africa
     👤 Nelson Mandela
     📄 The Policy of Apartheid, H. F. Verwoerd, 1948

5.9 How did Dalit people seek equality in India?
- 🕑 1950s: Mass conversion of Dalits to Buddhism
- 🕯 B. R. Ambedkar
- 🖹 Why Go for Conversion?, B. R. Ambedkar, 1935

5.10 How did the Khmer Rouge justify violence in the name of equality?
- 🕑 1975–1978: Khmer Rouge regime
- 🕯 Pol Pot
- 🖹 Constitution of the Democratic Republic of Kampuchea, 1978

Unit 6: Economics, Technology, and the Environment

Unit Question: How should people get the resources they need?

6.1 21st-Century Issue: What did Greta Thunberg ask world leaders to do about climate change?
- 🕑 2019: UN Climate Action Summit
- 🕯 Greta Thunberg
- 🖹 Speech to the UN Climate Action Summit, Greta Thunberg, 2019

6.2 How have Australian Aboriginal people interacted with their environment?
- 🕑 c. 125,000 BCE–c. 10,000 BCE: Late Pleistocene era
- 🕯 Essie Coffey
- 🖹 Grinding stone and fish hooks, c. 30,000–1000 BCE

6.3 What were the causes and effects of the Neolithic Revolution?
- 🕑 c. 10,000 BCE: Neolithic Revolution
- 🕯 James Suzman
- 🖹 Agricultural tools, c. 5000 BCE

6.4 How did ancient Egyptians use the Nile River to gain resources?
- 🕑 2705–2213 BCE: Egypt's Old Kingdom
- 🕯 Djoser
- 🖹 Hymn to the Nile, 2100 BCE

6.5 How did trade promote cultural diffusion along the Silk Road?
- 🕑 2nd century BCE–15th century CE: Silk Road trade
- 🕯 Benjamin of Tudela
- 🖹 Itinerary of Benjamin of Tudela, 12th century

6.6 How did the Mali Empire profit from trade in gold and salt?
- 🕑 c. 1230–1670: Mali Empire
- 🕯 Mansa Musa
- 🖹 Travels in Africa and Asia, Ibn Battuta, 1354

6.7 How did Leonardo da Vinci envision the ideal city during the Renaissance?
- 🕑 c. 1300–1600: Renaissance
- 🕯 Leonardo da Vinci
- 🖹 Ideal City drawings, Leonardo da Vinci, 1487

6.8   How did the Netherlands profit from colonization?
       🕒 1602: Dutch East India Company founded
       🧍 Jan Pieterszoon Coen
       📄 Charter of the Dutch East India Company, 1602
6.9   How did Aztec technology aid agriculture?
       🕒 1428–1521: Aztec Empire
       🧍 Moctezuma II
       📄 Sun Stone, c. 1520
6.10   How did enslaved Africans experience the transatlantic slave trade?
       🕒 16th–19th centuries: Transatlantic slave trade
       🧍 Mahommah G. Baquaqua
       📄 *Biography of Mahommah G. Baquaqua*, Baquaqua and Samuel Moore, 1854
6.11   How was free-market capitalism supposed to work?
       🕒 c. 1760–c. 1840: Industrial Revolution
       🧍 Adam Smith
       📄 *The Wealth of Nations*, Adam Smith, 1776
6.12   What were the goals and results of Mao Zedong's command economy?
       🕒 1959: Mao's "Great Leap Forward"
       🧍 Mao Zedong
       📄 The Question of Agricultural Cooperation, Mao Zedong, 1955
6.13   What were the effects of the Chernobyl nuclear disaster?
       🕒 1986: Chernobyl nuclear power plant explosion
       🧍 Mikhail Gorbachev
       📄 Untitled notice on levels of radiation at Chernobyl NPP, 1986

Unit 7: Gender

Unit Question: What should be the roles of women and men in society?

7.1   21st-Century Issue: How are transgender people challenging assumptions about
       women and men?
       🕒 2019: World Health Organization states that being transgender is not a mental
       illness
       🧍 Paravee Argasnoum
       📄 Interview with Paravee Argasnoum, 2018
7.2   Why did ancient Roman women protest being taxed?
       🕒 42 BCE: Civil war in Rome
       🧍 Hortensia
       📄 Speech to the Forum, Hortensia, 42 BCE
7.3   What role did Ibn Rushd think women should play in Islamic society?
       🕒 1169–1195: Ibn Rushd produces commentaries on Aristotle and Plato
       🧍 Ibn Rushd
       📄 Commentary on Plato's *Republic*, 1169–1195

7.4   How did Queen Elizabeth I defend her leadership?
  🕐 1588–1603: Reign of Queen Elizabeth I
  🧍 Queen Elizabeth I
  📄 Speech to the Troops at Tilbury, Queen Elizabeth I, 1588
7.5   How did Queen Nzinga resist Portuguese colonizers?
  🕐 1575: Portuguese colonize Angola
  🧍 Queen Nzinga
  📄 Letter from Queen Njinga [Nzinga] of Ndongo to Bento Banha Cardoso,
     1626
7.6   How did Catherine the Great present herself as a leader?
  🕐 1762–1798: Catherine the Great rules Russia
  🧍 Catherine the Great
  📄 Catherine II, Legislatress in the Temple of the Goddess of Justice, Dmitry
     Levitsky, 1780s
7.7   What were Mary Wollstonecraft's arguments for women's rights?
  🕐 1792: Wollstonecraft publishes *A Vindication of the Rights of Woman*
  🧍 Mary Wollstonecraft
  📄 *A Vindication of the Rights of Woman*, Mary Wollstonecraft, 1792
7.8   Why did Qiu Jin argue for Chinese women's freedoms?
  🕐 1907: Qiu Jin is executed by the Qing Dynasty
  🧍 Qiu Jin
  📄 An Address to Two Hundred Million Fellow Countrywomen, Qiu Jin, 1907
7.9   Why did some women oppose getting the right to vote?
  🕐 1908: Anti-Suffrage League formed in Great Britain
  🧍 Violet (Markham) Carruthers
  📄 Woman's Sphere, Violet (Markham) Carruthers, 1912
7.10 How did Käthe Kollwitz work for peace through art?
  🕐 1914–1919: World War I
  🧍 Käthe Kollwitz
  📄 *The Survivors*, Käthe Kollwitz, 1923
7.11 How did Huda Sha'arawi argue for feminist nationalism in Egypt?
  🕐 1923: Sha'arawi founds Egyptian Feminist Union
  🧍 Huda Sha'arawi
  📄 Pan-Arab Feminism, Huda Sha'arawi, 1944
7.12 How did Una Marson participate in worldwide struggles against sexism
     and racism?
  🕐 1935: International Congress of Women meet in Istanbul
  🧍 Una Marson
  📄 Speech to the International Congress of Women, Una Marson, 1935

Unit 8: Resistance, Revolution, and Reform

Unit Question: How should people bring about political and social change?

8.1   21st-Century Issue: How did Egyptians use social media and protest to bring about political change?
      🕐 2011: Egyptian Revolution
      ⚲ Asmaa Mahfouz
      📄 Vlog by Asmaa Mahfouz, 2011

8.2   How did Julius Caesar gain control of Rome?
      🕐 49 BCE: Caesar starts Roman Civil War
      ⚲ Julius Caesar
      📄 Caesar Crosses the Rubicon, Plutarch, 75 CE

8.3   How did the Safavid Empire use diplomacy to accomplish its goals?
      🕐 1501–1736: Safavid Empire
      ⚲ Shah Abbas
      📄 Don Juan of Persia, Uruch Beg, 1604

8.4   How did Martin Luther bring about the Protestant Reformation?
      🕐 1517: Martin Luther starts the Protestant Reformation
      ⚲ Martin Luther
      📄 95 Theses, Martin Luther, 1517

8.5   Why did Maximilien Robespierre believe violence was necessary to achieve the goals of the French Revolution?
      🕐 1789: French Revolution begins
      ⚲ Maximilien Robespierre
      📄 Justification of the use of terror, Maximilien Robespierre, 1794

8.6   How did Haitians end slavery and gain independence from France?
      🕐 1791–1804: Haitian Revolution
      ⚲ Jean-Jacques Dessalines
      📄 Haitian Declaration of Independence, 1804

8.7   How did Southeast Asians avoid rulers who wanted to control them?
      🕐 1885: British colonize but fail to completely control Burma
      ⚲ James G. Scott
      📄 *Gazetteer of Upper Burma and the Shan States*, James G. Scott, 1893

8.8   How did Gandhi use nonviolent resistance against British colonization?
      🕐 1942: Quit India movement
      ⚲ Mohandas Gandhi
      📄 Quit India, Mohandas Gandhi, 1942

8.9   Why did Emiliano Zapata think land reform was necessary for Mexico?
      🕐 1910–1917: Mexican Revolution
      ⚲ Emiliano Zapata
      📄 Plan de Ayala, 1911

8.10 How did Joseph Stalin try to revolutionize Soviet society?
     🕐 1931–1932: Famine in the Ukraine
     ⫰ Joseph Stalin
     🕐 Modernize or Perish, Joseph Stalin, 1931

8.11 Why did Algerians believe that violence was necessary to decolonize their country?
     🕐 1962: Algeria wins independence from French colonization
     ⫰ Frantz Fanon
     🖺 *The Wretched of the Earth*, Frantz Fanon, 1961

8.12 How did Rigoberta Menchú resist the human rights abuses of the Guatemalan government?
     🕐 1960–1996: Guatemalan Civil War
     ⫰ Rigoberta Menchú
     🖺 *I, Rigoberta Menchú*, Rigoberta Menchú and Elisabeth Burgos, 1983

8.13 How did Václav Havel spread dissent against the totalitarian regime in Czechoslovakia?
     🕐 1989: Velvet Revolution
     ⫰ Václav Havel
     🖺 *Power of the Powerless*, Václav Havel, 1978

Unit 9: Continuity and Change

Unit Question: What are the long-term changes and recurring patterns in world history?

9.1 How did human societies begin?
     🖺 Grinding stone and fish hooks, c. 30,000–1000 BCE
     🖺 Agricultural tools, c. 5000 BCE

9.2 How did early civilizations and pastoral peoples emerge in the fifth to the first millennia BCE?
     🖺 Cuneiform tax receipt, c. 3000 BCE
     🖺 Hymn to the Nile, 2100 BCE
     🖺 Code of Hammurabi, 1750 BCE

9.3 How did classical traditions, major religions, and giant empires emerge in the first millennium BCE?
     🖺 *Pericles' Funeral Oration*, 431 BCE
     🖺 Luxuriant Gems of the Spring and Autumn Annals, Dong Zhongshu, 2nd century BCE
     🖺 Rock Edicts, Aśoka, 2nd century BCE

9.4 How did zones of exchange and encounter expand in the first millennium CE?
     🖺 Procopius, Alaric's Sack of Rome, c. 550 CE
     🖺 Presentation of captives to a Maya ruler, c. 785
     🖺 *The Book of the Maghrib*, Ibn Said, 13th century

9.5   How did hemispheric interactions intensify in the second millennium CE?
- Letter on the Second Crusade, Bernard of Clairvaux, 1147
- Commentary on Plato's *Republic*, Ibn Rushd, 1169–1195
- *Travels in Asia and Africa,* Ibn Battuta, 1354

9.6   Why did the first global age emerge in the 15th to 18th centuries?
- Requerimiento, Council of Castille, 1510
- *The Turkish Letters*, Ogier Ghiselin de Busbecq, c. 1555
- Letter from Queen Njinga [Nzinga] of Ndongo to Bento Banha Cardoso, 1626

9.7   What were the causes and effects of revolutions in the 18th to 20th centuries?
- *The Wealth of Nations*, Adam Smith, 1776
- Haitian Declaration of Independence, 1804
- *The Communist Manifesto*, Karl Marx and Friedrich Engels, 1848

9.8   What were the crises and achievements of the first half of the 20th century?
- Constitution of the Black Hand, 1911
- *The Survivors*, Käthe Kollwitz, 1923
- Obersalzberg Speech, Adolf Hitler, 1939

9.9   What have been the promises and paradoxes of the second half of the 20th century?
- Universal Declaration of Human Rights, 1948
- Speech to the UN General Assembly, Yasser Arafat, 1974
- Constitution of the Democratic Republic of Kampuchea, 1978

Printable, full-page PDFs of the following Appendixes are available online at www .tcpress.com/MetroWorld. These versions may be printed out for use with students without permission. Space is included on those versions of Appendixes B, C, D, F, and G for students to write their answers.

APPENDIX B: COURSE ENTRY SURVEY

1. List the top three most important events in world history.
2. Why did you choose each one?
3. List the top three most important historical figures.
4. Why did you choose each one?

APPENDIX C: COURSE EXIT SURVEY

1. List the top three most important events in world history.
2. Why did you choose each one?
3. List the top three most important historical figures.
4. Why did you choose each one?
5. How were your views of the world changed or reinforced during this course?
6. Which historical figure did you find you agreed most with, and why?

APPENDIX D: UNIT ENTRY SURVEY

1. What do you know about the theme of this unit?
2. What would you like to learn about the theme of this unit?
3. How would you answer the Unit Question?
4. Why would you answer that way?
5. What are your views on the 21st-Century Issue?
6. Why do you hold those views?

APPENDIX E: BIOGRAPHICAL RESEARCH PAPER INSTRUCTIONS

You will write a research paper about the historical figure you will represent in the summit. Your paper should contain six paragraphs:

1. Explain why this person was important in world history.
2. Provide a brief biography.
3. Describe two of the person's character traits, supported by examples from their life.
4. Present the person's answer to the Unit Question and give an example of something the person did or said that proves you would answer that way. Include a quotation from the document we studied in class to support your answer.
5. Predict how the person would respond to the 21st-Century Issue if he or she were alive today. Explain why the person would have been likely to hold that view.
6. Explain what you learned about world history by studying this person's life. Add a References section at the end of your paper, including the document we read in class and at least one other source.

APPENDIX F: SUMMIT RESEARCH WORKSHEET

1. I will portray this historical figure in the summit:
2. What I already know about my historical figure:
3. What I want or need to know about my historical figure:
4. Document we will read in class related to my historical figure:
5. Outside sources of information about my historical figure:
6. My historical figure was important in world history because:
7. Three facts about my historical figure's life that are relevant to how they would answer the Unit Question or respond to the 21st-Century Issue:
8. Two characteristics or qualities my historical figure has:
9. Evidence from the document we read that shows how my historical figure would answer the Unit Question:

10. Evidence from my own research that shows how my historical figure would answer the Unit Question:
11. I think my historical figure would answer the Unit Question by saying:
12. Evidence from the document we read that shows how my historical figure would respond to the 21st-Century Issue:
13. Evidence from my own research that shows how my historical figure would answer the 21st-Century Issue:
14. I think my historical figure would respond to the 21st-Century Issue by saying:
15. Which other historical figures we studied in this unit would my historical figure be most likely to agree with? Why?
16. Which other historical figures we studied in this unit would my historical figure be most likely to disagree with? Why?
17. One question I think my historical figure will be asked:
18. How my historical figure would answer:
19. Another question I think my historical figure will be asked:
20. How my historical figure would answer:
21. One question my historical figure would have for _____:
22. My historical figure would ask _____ this question because:
23. One question my historical figure would have for _____:
24. My historical figure would ask _____ this question because:

APPENDIX G: UNIT EXIT SURVEY

Look back on your answers to the Unit Entry Survey from the beginning of the unit, and review the lessons we have done.

1. Which event, historical figure, or document that we studied changed or reinforced your opinion on the Unit Question? Why?
2. Which event, historical figure, or document that we studied changed or reinforced your opinion on the 21st-Century Issue? Why?
3. Which historical figure that we studied did you agree with most? Why?
4. What did you learn about the theme of this unit?
5. Provide one new question you have about the material we studied in this unit.

APPENDIX H: 21ST-CENTURY ISSUE LETTER INSTRUCTIONS

1. Consider your views on the 21st-Century Issue for this unit.
2. Decide upon a leader or institution that has decisionmaking power over this issue, and think of an action you would like the leader to take on the issue.
3. Write a letter explaining your views to this leader or institution and state why you hold those views. Reference at least one historical event you have studied in this unit that provides a comparison or evidence to support your view.

Explain the action you would like the leader or institution to take on the issue and why. Thank the leader or institution for reading your letter.
4. Send your letter and share any response you receive with the class!

APPENDIX I: DESIGNING YOUR OWN THEMATIC UNITS

1. Identify an essential question that is relevant in multiple eras of world history.
2. Generate a list of about a dozen people who have offered answers to this question and/or a list of about a dozen events in which this question came to the fore.
3. Locate a document that illustrates the perspective of each historical figure or relates to the event.
4. Isolate an excerpt of each document that is most relevant to the essential question.
5. Identify vocabulary in each document that may be unfamiliar to students.
6. For each document, generate several comprehension questions that can help you assess whether students have understood what they've read.
7. For each document, generate several activities students can use to do in which they apply higher-order thinking skills.
8. Create appropriate introduction and reflection questions or activities for each document.

APPENDIX J: ONLINE CONTENT

www.tcpress.com/MetroWorld

1. Links to most of the full documents that are excerpted in the book
2. Downloadable, printable copies of most of the documents excerpted in this book, for classroom use
3. Downloadable, printable copies of instructions and surveys included in these appendixes

www.rosaliemetro.com

1. Blog about my academic work related to this approach to teaching history, and about my professional development work with teachers
2. Ideas for other thematic units related to world and U.S. history

References

Anderson, B. (2016). *Imagined communities: Reflections on the origin and spread of nationalism* (rev. ed.). Verso.

Apple, M. (1990). *Ideology and curriculum*. Routledge.

Armstrong, K. (2011). *The battle for God: A history of fundamentalism*. Ballantine Books.

Boal, A. (1993). *Theatre of the oppressed* (C. A. & M.-O. L. McBride, Trans.). Theatre Communications Group.

Brown, Russell C., & Schnell, Stephen C. (2016). Not your grandfather's U.S. history class: Abandoning chronology and teaching thematically. *The American Historian, 3*(2).

Casale-Giannola, D. P., & Green, L. S. (2013). *41 active learning strategies for the inclusive classroom, Grades 6–12*. Corwin.

Chakrabarty, D. (2007). *Provincializing Europe: Postcolonial thought and historical difference*. Princeton University Press.

Chatterjee, P. (1994). *The nation and its fragments: Colonial and postcolonial histories*. Princeton University Press.

Cohen, E. G., & Lotan, R. A. (2014). *Designing groupwork: Strategies for the heterogeneous classroom* (3rd ed.). Teachers College Press.

Common Core State Standards Initiative. (2016). Frequently asked questions. corestandards .org/about-the-standards/frequently-asked-questions/

Dozono, T. (2020). The passive voice of white supremacy: Tracing epistemic and discursive violence in world history curriculum. *Review of Education, Pedagogy, and Cultural Studies*, 1-26.

Dunbar-Ortiz, R. (2015). *An indigenous peoples' history of the United States*. Penguin Random House.

Fanon, F. (2004). *The wretched of the earth*. (R. Philcox, Trans.). Grove Press.

Foreman, P. G., et al. "Writing about Slavery/Teaching About Slavery: This Might Help" community-sourced document. docs.google.com/document/d/1A4TEdDgYslX -hlKezLodMIM71My3KTN0zxRv0IQTOQs/mobilebasic

Foucault, M. (1982). *The archaeology of knowledge: And the discourse on language*. (A. M. Sheridan Smith, Trans.). Vintage.

Freire, P. (2000). *Pedagogy of the oppressed*. (M. Ramos, Trans.). Bloomsbury.

Gibbons, P. (2009). *English learners, academic literacy, and thinking: Learning in the challenge zone*. Heinemann.

Gopal, P. (2019). *Insurgent empire: Anticolonial resistance and British dissent*. Verso.

Gore, M. C. (2012). *Inclusion strategies for secondary classrooms: Keys for struggling learners*. Corwin.

Hess, D. E., & McAvoy, P. (2015). *The political classroom: Evidence and ethics in democratic education*. Routledge.

Hobsbawm, E. (1996). *The age of extremes: A history of the world, 1914–1991.* Vintage.

Iowa State University of Science and Technology. (2016). Revised Bloom's Taxonomy. celt.iastate.edu/teaching/effective-teaching-practices/revised-blooms-taxonomy

Kendi, I. X. (2016). *Stamped from the beginning: The definitive history of racist ideas in America.* Bold Type Books.

King, L. (2016). Epilogue: Black history is more than skin color. *Social Studies Journal, 36,* 72–79.

Lepore, J. (2018). *These truths: A history of the United States.* W.W. Norton & Co.

Levstik, L. S., & Barton, K. C. (2005). *Doing history: Investigating with children in elementary and middle schools.* Routledge.

Loewen, J. (2008). *Lies my teacher told me: Everything your American history textbook got wrong* (2nd ed.). The New Press.

Mann, C. C. (2006). *1491: New revelations of the Americas before Columbus.* Vintage.

Marzano, R. J. (2009). *Formative assessment and standards-based grading.* Marzano Research.

McTighe, J., & Wiggins, G. (2013). *Essential questions: Opening doors to student understanding.* Association for Supervision and Curriculum Development.

Metro, R. (2019). The white gunman, the anti-Semitic entrepreneur, and other dilemmas of a history textbook author. *Social Education 38*(3), 138–141.

Milner, R. (2010). *Start where you are but don't stay there: Understanding diversity, opportunity gaps, and teaching in today's classrooms.* Harvard Education Press.

Said, E. (1994). *Orientalism.* Random House.

Scott, J. C. (2018). *Against the grain: A deep history of the earliest states.* Yale University Press.

Sewall, G. T. (2004). *World history textbooks: A review.* American Textbook Council.

Shear, S. B., Knowles, R. T., Soden, G. J., & Castro, A. J. (2015). Manifesting destiny: Re/presentations of Indigenous peoples in K-12 U.S. history standards. *Theory and Research in Social Education 43*(1): 68–101.

Spivak, G. C. (2006). *In other worlds: Essays in cultural politics.* Routledge.

Stanford History Education Group (SHEG). (n.d.). Reading like a historian curriculum. sheg.stanford.edu/rlh

Trouillot, M.-R. (2015). *Silencing the past: Power and the production of history.* Beacon Press.

UCLA History. (2019). National world history content standards. phi.history.ucla.edu/nchs /world-history-content-standards/

Visual Thinking Strategies (VTS). (2016). What is VTS? vtshome.org/

Williams, J. D., Woodson, A. N., & Wallace, T. L. (2016). "Can we say the n-word?" Exploring psychological safety during race talk. *Research in Human Development 13*(1), 15–31.

Wineburg, S. (2001). *Historical thinking and other unnatural acts.* Temple University Press.

Winichakul, T. (1997). *Siam mapped: History of the geo-body of a nation.* Hawaii University Press.

Index

About the Author

Rosalie Metro is an assistant teaching professor in the Department of Learning, Teaching and Curriculum in the College of Education at the University of Missouri-Columbia. She has taught U.S. and world history at the middle and high school levels.